Epistemology: *The Classic Readings*

PHILOSOPHY: *The Classic Readings*

This series of collections offers classic readings by philosophers ranging from ancient times to the first part of the twentieth century, and contains seminal writings from both Western and non-Western traditions of philosophy. Combined with valuable editorial guidance, including a substantial Introduction to each volume as well as to individual pieces, they are intended to serve as core texts for historically orientated philosophy courses.

Already published:

Aesthetics: *The Classic Readings*
Ethics: *The Classic Readings*
Epistemology: *The Classic Readings*

Forthcoming:

Philosophy of Religion: *The Classic Readings*
Metaphysics: *The Classic Readings*
Political Philosophy: *The Classic Readings*

Epistemology:

The Classic
Readings

Edited by David E. Cooper
University of Durham

Advisory Editors
J. N. Mohanty
Ernest Sosa

Copyright © Blackwell Publishers Ltd 1999
Introduction and editorial apparatus copyright © David E. Cooper 1999

First published 1999
Reprinted 1999, 2001
Transferred to digital print 2003
Reprinted 2004

Blackwell Publishers Ltd
108 Cowley Road
Oxford OX4 1JF
UK

Blackwell Publishers Inc.
350 Main Street
Malden, Massachusetts 02148
USA

British Library Cataloguing in Publication Data
A CIP catalogue record for this book is available from the British Library.

Library of Congress Cataloging-in-Publication Data
Epistemology: the classic readings / edited by David E. Cooper;
  advisory editors, J.N. Mohanty, Ernest Sosa.
    p. cm. — (Philosophy: the classic readings)
  Includes bibliographical references and index.
  ISBN 0–631–21807–3 (hb : alk. paper). — ISBN 0–631–21088–1 (pbk.
  : alk. paper)
    1. Knowledge, Theory of. I. Cooper, David Edward. II. Mohanty,
  J.N. (Jitendra Nath), 1928– . III. Sosa, Ernest. IV. Series.
  BD161.E633 1999
  121–dc21   98–28675
                                                                       CIP

Typeset in 10 on 12 ½ pt Galliard
By Ace Filmsetting Ltd, Frome, Somerset

Contents

vi   Contents

Series Preface

Philosophers in the English-language world are becoming increasingly aware of the importance of the history of their subject. *Philosophy: The Classic Readings* is a series which provides students and teachers with the central historical texts in the main branches of philosophy. The texts selected range from ancient times to the first part of the twentieth century. In response to a growing and laudable interest in the contributions of non-Western philosophers, the volumes in the series will contain seminal writings from the Indian, Chinese and other traditions as well as the classics of Western philosophical literature.

Each volume in the series begins with a substantial introduction to the relevant area of philosophy and its history, and to the bearing of this history on contemporary discussion. Each selected text is prefaced by a discussion of its importance within the development of that area.

Taken individually, each volume will serve as a core text for courses which adopt a historical orientation towards the relevant branch of philosophy. Taken together, the volumes in the series will constitute the largest treasury of classic philosophical writings available.

The books in the series are edited and introduced by David E. Cooper, Professor of Philosophy at the University of Durham, England, and author of many books, including *World Philosophies: An Historical Introduction*, also published by Blackwell.

Acknowledgements

The source of each reading is given underneath the relevant chapter title. The editor and publishers gratefully acknowledge all copyright holders for permission to reproduce copyright material. The publishers apologize for any errors or omissions in the copyright information, and would be grateful to be notified of any corrections that should be incorporated in the next edition or reprint of this book.

Introduction

I

The Greeks employed several words translatable by our word 'knowledge'. The most familiar of these was *episteme*, a term applicable both to what a person who knows possesses and, in Aristotle for example (chapter 2), to more or less systematic bodies of knowledge. Thus, current scientific knowledge and the knowledge I myself have of science are both *episteme*. That vast area of philosophical enquiry referred to as epistemology is, therefore, an enquiry into knowledge. Indeed, many writers prefer to use the label 'theory of knowledge'. 'Epistemology', however, has the advantage of being a philosopher's term of art, whereas 'theory of knowledge' could also apply to the investigations of sociologists of knowledge and historians of ideas, for example.

As with other philosophical terms of art, such as 'aesthetics', attempts at a precise definition of epistemology are liable to be contentious. These days, for instance, one frequently encounters a definition of epistemology as the endeavour to determine the indubitable foundations of our claims to knowledge. Since this definition is especially favoured by those who reject the viability of that endeavour, the implication is that epistemology is something to abandon, something we should pronounce 'dead'. But this is an invidious definition which does not capture everything which has gone on under the heading of epistemology, and it would surely be preferable to regard 'foundationalism' as just one tendency, however important, within epistemology on a broader and more neutral understanding of that term.

A more neutral characterization of epistemology would be this: it is that branch of philosophy which aims at (1) understanding such concepts as belief, memory, certainty, doubt, justification, evidence and knowledge, and (2) enquiring into the criteria for the application of such terms and so, in particular, the criteria for identifying, in Bertrand Russell's phrase, 'the scope and limits' of human knowledge. This characterization raises the question of why such concepts as belief, memory, etc. constitute a fairly unified field of enquiry. The short answer, indicated by the etymology of the word 'epistemology', is that they all revolve more or less obviously around the notion of knowledge. A justified belief which is true amounts, on a familiar view, to an item of knowledge. If I really remember some event, I know it happened. If the evidence for some hypothesis puts it beyond doubt, then someone who recognizes this and who possesses that evidence, knows the hypothesis to be true. One can, of course, be interested in, say, belief and memory apart from their connections with knowledge – in, for example, their assumed basis in the brain. But the fact that any full discussion of knowledge is bound, at some point, to invoke such concepts makes it readily intelligible why certain examinations of them should belong in the field we call epistemology.

Several of the readings in the two previous volumes in this series, on aesthetics and ethics, directly addressed issues of knowledge: the issue, for example, of whether there exists a special moral sense which reliably informs us about right and wrong. So why were such texts not included in the present volume rather than the previous ones? Part of the answer is that there is a degree of arbitrariness and mere precedent in regarding a given discussion as belonging primarily to epistemology rather than to, say, ethics. The more helpful part of the answer, however, is that a useful, if rough, distinction can be made between 'general' epistemology and 'special' epistemologies, such as moral epistemology. General epistemology will be concerned with questions, such as 'What does it mean to know something?' or 'Are there general reasons to think knowledge of any kind is unobtainable?', which can be raised in relative isolation from the particular areas – ethics, mathematics, or whatever – where knowledge-claims are made. Special epistemological questions, like the one about moral intuition, will tend to be treated within the appropriate branch of philosophy – ethics, for example. In this volume, the concern is general epistemology.[1]

---

[1] A good guide to epistemology is Jonathan Dancy, *An Introduction to Contemporary Epistemology*, Oxford: Blackwell, 1985. Reliable articles on nearly all the thinkers and topics represented in this reader may be found in J. Dancy and E. Sosa (eds), *A Companion to Epistemology*, Oxford: Blackwell, 1992.

II

Many people have the impression that epistemology is the most central area of philosophy, or even that philosophy should really be identified with epistemology. Certainly there is a popular image of philosophers as people obsessively and almost solely concerned with determining whether we *really* know the things we ordinarily think we do.

Even if epistemology does have a peculiarly central place within philosophy, however, some of the reasons for thinking this are unpersuasive. It might be held, inspired perhaps by Aristotle's dictum that 'All men by nature have a desire to know', that knowledge is the ultimate goal of all reflective enquiry – in which case, those reflective enquirers *par excellence*, philosophers, must have knowledge as their primary concern. After all, the claim may continue, whenever people seriously raise questions they are in search of answers, ones in which, ideally, they can have complete confidence. Such answers would then amount to knowledge. Hence all serious questioning has knowledge as its concern.

This line of thought is uncompelling. For one thing, it is implausible to think that the ultimate goal of enquiry and reflection is anything like knowledge 'for its own sake'. Human beings are surely not as 'disinterested' as that would suggest. A more plausible and historically accurate view of philosophical enquiry might be that the overarching goal is to provide accounts of the world, ourselves and our relation to the world which make sense of our condition and suggest how we should 'cope with' and conduct ourselves in the world.[2] For another thing, sleight-of-hand is involved in turning *all* our serious questions into ones *about* knowledge. True, if I ask, say, what the most just form of society is, I may hope to come up with an answer so compelling that I thereby expand my knowledge. But what my question was *about*, what it concerned, was justice, not knowledge.

Still, it is not difficult to see how questions which are not initially about knowledge may give rise to ones which are; and not difficult, therefore, to appreciate how philosophical enquiries into, say, justice or the nature of God may engender ones into knowledge and related epistemic notions. Suppose two people disagree as to which form of society is the more just. It may turn out that the basis of the disagreement is that one does, while the other does not, regard traditional and popularly accepted convictions as good or relevant reasons for thinking that a certain society is justly

---

[2] So I have tried to show in my *World Philosophies: An Historical Introduction*, Oxford: Blackwell, 1996.

organized. And so the debate will shift to one about the cogency or relevance of certain kinds of reasons for an opinion. Or it may be that people from one religious tradition realize that it differs from another by accepting as authoritative the testimony of certain religious texts – so that again the focus of argument will switch to the reliability of a certain kind of alleged evidence.

But there is a more general and disturbing way in which our enquiries can be transmuted into ones about knowledge and its criteria. We shall hardly be confident that we are properly 'coping' or conducting ourselves if the suspicion sets in that even our most natural assumptions and beliefs may be badly out of alignment with how the world actually is. And that is a suspicion which, from the earliest days of philosophical enquiry, many people have had. From Thucydides and Protagoras in Ancient Greece to Montaigne and Pascal in sixteenth- to seventeenth-century France, for example, people have been so impressed by the diversity of beliefs, convictions and modes of reasoning found in different cultures as to have despaired of the possibility of rationally securing *any* of these.

When doubts of this kind, despairing or otherwise, take hold, we are faced with *scepticism*. So important and endemic at certain periods in the history of philosophy has scepticism been that it is unsurprising how much attention has been paid by philosophers to notions like doubt and knowledge, certainty and evidence, in the attempt to estimate, and perhaps dispel, the threat to our confidence which scepticism poses. Although it is not the only concern of epistemology, 'the problem of doubt' has surely been the one which has given epistemology its vitality. Given this, a few further remarks on scepticism are called for.

First, it is useful to distinguish a broader from a narrower sense of 'scepticism'. In the broad sense, a sceptic is someone who denies or casts doubt on the availability, at least to us humans, of objective knowledge. Or rather, this is the position of the sceptic *tout court*, the 'global' sceptic as he might be called. For it is quite possible for someone to be sceptical towards knowledge-claims in certain areas – morality, say, or science – but to think that knowledge is perfectly possible in other areas, mathematics perhaps. In the narrower sense, scepticism (whether 'global' or 'local') is distinguished from other '-isms' – what I'll call 'relativism' and 'nihilism' – which also reject the possibility of objective knowledge. The sceptic, in this narrower sense, does not deny that there is an objective order, knowable perhaps by a creature with superhuman intelligence, but only denies that we humans have the capacity to establish, with any certainty at least, what that order is. *Our* evidence for, say, scientific hypotheses is always too shaky, corrupt or uncompelling to warrant confidence in the truth of such hypotheses.

This sceptic needs distinguishing, first, from the relativist. The latter's position is at once more and less radical than the sceptic's: more, because he denies that there *is* any objective order to have knowledge of; less, because he happily allows that claims can be true, and known to be true, but only *relative to* . . . well, to what? Relativists of different shapes and sizes have offered various answers: truth is relative to cultures, or to conceptual schemes, or to individual perspectives, or to 'forms of life', and so on. The sceptic in the narrower sense should also be distinguished from the nihilist, who denies that we are ever entitled to make any assertions, *including* those which the relativist allows, the sceptical assertions of the sceptic and even his own nihilistic claims. Asserting anything at all presupposes the viability of some notion of truth, and this is what the nihilist (unassertively) rejects.

It is not always easy to decide which label – 'sceptic (narrow sense)', 'relativist' or 'nihilist' – to pin on particular thinkers. Each of the three tends, up to a point, to use similar arguments, such as invoking the great diversity of beliefs found in mankind or the unreliability of the senses. Several thinkers, moreover, tend to oscillate between, or try to combine, two or more of the '-isms'. Pyrrho (see chapter 3) and Nāgārjuna (chapter 6), for example, seem to put forward sceptical claims but also to deny, in nihilistic fashion, that these really are *claims*. Kant (chapter 11) denies that we can have knowledge of 'things in themselves', whilst rejecting scepticism towards our knowledge of 'phenomena', of the world as experienced. Nietzsche (chapter 12), too, is sceptical about the possibility of knowing how the 'real' world is, but allows for knowledge-claims which are true within, or relative to, our 'perspectives'. In Chuang Tzu (chapter 4), arguably, there are hints of all three positions: a sceptical view of our capacity to have knowledge, of any discursive kind at least, of the *tao*, and a willingness to admit the relative truth of our discourses, but one combined with distinct echoes of a nihilistic attitude towards the whole business of assertion.

III

A second important remark to make about scepticism, broadly construed, is that it has a history. As indicated above, scepticism has been more entrenched or virulent at certain periods than at others, with the consequence that attention to epistemology itself has been uneven. For example, in comparison with what came before and after, the attention paid by medieval philosophers to the sceptical challenge and to general issues about knowledge was scant. And in the Chinese philosophical tradition, where issues of a 'practical' or 'humanistic' kind were more generally to the fore, it was only occasionally, as in Chuang Tzu's book, that such issues received sustained attention.

Scepticism is also historical for the more interesting reason that what one might call the *styles* of sceptical thinking which prospered at different periods themselves differed significantly. In the West, there have been at least two great periods of debate about scepticism: one running from the 'golden age' of Greek philosophy through the Hellenistic age of Greek and Roman thought, and a second which began with Descartes' rehearsal of 'hyperbolic doubt' (chapter 7) and continued, with occasional pauses, until well into the twentieth century.

Much of Socrates' and Plato's (chapter 1) thinking was a direct response to sceptical, especially relativistic, assaults on knowledge by Protagoras and other sophists, and various groups of sceptics (such as the Pyrrhonists) were among the schools, including the Stoic and Epicurean ones, whose battles enlivened the Hellenistic era. At the risk of overgeneralizing, three features were characteristic of the style of scepticism which, during this era, was perceived to be the most challenging. First, scepticism was viewed by its proponents not as a 'threat', apt for producing 'despair', but, on the contrary, as a recipe for the good life – for inducing a relaxed 'freedom from [the] disturbance' (*ataraxia*) which results from a febrile search for knowledge. Second, this scepticism was universal in scope, no distinction being made, for example, between dubitable claims about the physical world and indubitable ones about the contents of one's mind. Finally, scepticism in this style was self-referential: not even the claims of the sceptic were to be accorded any certainty, and any attempt to do so would conflict with that abandonment of a craving for certainty which was the main attraction of the sceptical stance. (It is worth noting that this style of scepticism has parallels with the approach of some Buddhist thinkers during the same centuries (see chapter 6).)

Although Descartes' philosophy was partly inspired by the revival of Hellenistic scepticism in Renaissance Europe, the 'hyperbolic doubt' which he rehearses – and later tries to rebut – was scepticism in a different style.[3] Far from inducing 'freedom from disturbance', the hyperbolic sceptic threatens to destroy confidence in religious belief, the immortality of the soul

[3] On the contrasts between ancient and modern scepticism, see M. F. Burnyeat (ed.), *The Skeptical Tradition*, Berkeley: University of California Press, 1983, and John McDowell, 'Singular thought and the extent of "inner space" ', in *Subject, Thought and Context*, ed. P. Pettit and J. McDowell, Oxford: Clarendon Press, 1986. An excellent history of early modern scepticism is Richard H. Popkin, *The History of Scepticism from Erasmus to Spinoza*, Berkeley: University of California Press, 1979.

and the prospects of the recently emerging physical and mathematical sciences. Moreover, he makes a sharp distinction between an 'inner space' – that of our own 'ideas', mental images and so on – and what supposedly lies outside that space, above all a physical world. The sceptic's central contention becomes that any inference from what occurs within the 'inner space' of the mind to the existence or nature of anything outside it is illegitimate, and hence that each of us faces an insoluble 'egocentric predicament'. Finally, the hyperbolic doubter professes to *prove*, by incontrovertible argument, the correctness of his sceptical position, so that all trace of an earlier scepticism's hesitancy towards its own position is erased.

It was attempts to counter hyperbolic doubt – beginning with Descartes' own – which shaped epistemological enquiry in the following centuries. Most of the positions familiar in today's literature – 'foundationalism', 'coherentism', 'pragmatism', 'naturalism' and so on – may be seen as responses to, often as rebuttals of, Cartesian scepticism. Given its historical importance and popularity, so-called foundationalism deserves some remarks at this stage. Foundationalism is the view that there is a class of basic beliefs or propositions which register genuine knowledge, and that all other beliefs or propositions, if they too are to register knowledge, must be suitably supported by or derived from those basic ones. Foundationalism is important, not only as suggesting a strategy for responding to scepticism, but as proposing a seemingly natural architecture of knowledge. Unless there is a sure foundation of beliefs which themselves stand in no need of justification, it seems that no beliefs at all could be finally justified. (Given how natural this suggestion is, it is unsurprising that it is to be found in other philosophical traditions as well. See chapter 5 on the approach of the Indian Nyāya School.)

Foundationalism has taken many different forms, with philosophers disagreeing over both the nature of the basic beliefs and their relationship to non-basic, derived ones. On the latter question, one should compare, for example, the thought that basic beliefs serve to 'generate' non-basic ones with the idea that they serve, rather, to *confirm* the latter, however these might have been generated (see Husserl and Schlick (chapters 14 and 16)). Over the first issue, 'What beliefs, if any, are basic?', there has been prolonged controversy. At least three broad answers should be distinguished.

First, there is the kind of 'rationalist' answer essayed by Descartes himself. The possibility of doubt comes to end with the identification, by 'the light of reason', of a small number of indubitable truths, 'clear and distinct ideas', which enable us to infer the truth of many beliefs, including ones originally subjected to doubt. Second, there is the 'empiricist' view that the basic propositions, requiring no further support, are those which report immediate experience, both sensory and introspective, and which are such as to permit at least reasonable inferences to what lays beyond experience. Finally, there is the claim that there are many familiar 'commonsense' beliefs which enjoy greater certainty than any claims which might be used either to support those beliefs or to call them into question. Those latter two positions are represented in this volume by Russell (chapter 15) and Reid (chapter 10) respectively.

Over the last two centuries, foundationalism has come under attack from various directions. Some philosophers, for example, have challenged the idea that any beliefs are unrevisable through registering, allegedly, what is *given* to us. This idea, they argue, ignores both the way in which beliefs, to be acceptable, must suitably 'cohere' with a wider set of beliefs, and the role that beliefs play in enabling us to act in and cope with the world. Such 'coherentist' and 'pragmatist' thoughts are already apparent in Peirce (chapter 13). Others, sometimes called 'naturalists' or 'contextualists', according to the details of their position, have argued that while certain propositions may be basic, this is not because they are true by 'the light of reason' or directly furnished by experience, but because they constitute the very framework of thought within which questions of evidence, rationality and truth can arise. Different versions of that position have been advanced, perhaps by Hume (chapter 9) and certainly by Wittgenstein (chapter 17).

IV

Coherentism, pragmatism, naturalism and other rivals to foundationalism are often presented as alternative responses to scepticism. So, for example, it has been held that while certainty cannot be achieved by comparing beliefs with how things are, it can be achieved by showing that these beliefs are required if our total body of beliefs is to be fully consistent and coherent. Knowledge is therefore established, not by comparing beliefs with anything outside of them, but with one another. Or it might be held that a given belief is fully justified, not because it rests on something foundational, but because it plays an indispensable role in enabling us to predict, control and otherwise manage our conduct so as to achieve our ends.[4]

Many writers, however, prefer to present these rivals to foundationalism, less as rebuttals of scepticism, than as strategies for side-lining it, for dismissing its importance and relevance. Thus the coherentist may be viewed,

---

[4] Foundationalism, coherentism, contextualism etc. are clearly discussed by Susan Haack, *Evidence and Inquiry: Towards Reconstruction in Epistemology*, Oxford: Blackwell, 1993.

not as proposing a new, non-foundationalist route to knowledge, but as simply describing how, in practice, we do come to accept some beliefs rather than others. And the naturalist will be interpreted, not as defending our knowledge-claims, but as articulating the background conditions and assumptions which make possible activities such as providing evidence, giving reasons and casting doubt.

This helps explain why some recent philosophers prefer not to regard these non-foundationalist approaches as *continuing* the enterprise of epistemology, but as signalling 'the death of epistemology' and so belonging to a very different enterprise. For, according to these writers, epistemology is defined by 'the problem of doubt' and its attempt to resolve that problem. Once we cease to be concerned with that problem and no longer see radical scepticism as something that can be clearly articulated or as having a bearing on our epistemic practices, then we are no longer doing epistemology.[5] Indeed, for some very recent writers, what should replace epistemology is not philosophical enquiry at all, but a blend of evolutionary biology and cognitive psychology. The interesting questions, they argue, are not 'How can any of our claims to knowledge be justified?' or 'How do our beliefs relate to the world?', but ones like 'Why should certain sorts of belief have been naturally selected for?' and 'How do those neural states, described in "folk" psychology as beliefs, connect up with one another and with physical states outside of them?'

It is not only from these 'scientistic' directions that epistemology has come under fire. A characteristic emphasis of many 'continental' philosophers in our century, from Heidegger to his 'postmodernist' admirers, has been that scepticism – and hence epistemology itself – requires an unacceptable picture of an individual subject able, like Descartes' doubter, to isolate its 'inner space' from everything 'outside'. Such writers tend to stress that a person's engagement with the world is so thorough, and his capacity for thought so much a function of communal practices in which he participates, that the kind of 'bracketing' or suspension of belief in an external world and other persons advocated, in Cartesian style, by Husserl is absurd. Hence such traditional epistemological tasks as trying to prove the existence of a physical world and other minds lose all point.

Arguably, these various ways of side-lining scepticism do nothing of the sort: rather, they reinstate it, albeit in new styles. If scepticism is the thought that our beliefs may fail to match what is objectively the case, then insist-

[5] See Michael Williams, 'Death of epistemology', in *A Companion to Epistemology*, ed. Dancy and Sosa.

ence on the shaping of those beliefs by evolutionary pressures, or by the contingent practices of communities, might be thought to give the sceptic what he wants, though for different reasons from those traditionally advanced. Whatever one's judgement on that, it is surely a pity – to revert to a point made much earlier – to impose on 'epistemology' a definition which entails that epistemology is dead simply because 'the problem of doubt' has allegedly been dissolved. For one thing, it seems perfectly reasonable to describe as epistemological the investigation into the claims that the problem has been dissolved and into the consequences, for the nature of belief, knowledge and so on, which follow from those claims. For another thing – a point to which I will return shortly – it is wrong to suppose that traditional epistemology has been myopically concerned with just that one problem.

V

My selection of texts for this volume reflects, to be sure, the central place that scepticism has enjoyed within epistemology. More than half the texts directly or indirectly address issues which surround it. In the selection of these and the remaining texts, other considerations have also operated. Thus I have avoided texts which, while expressing views that are certainly of importance to the theory of knowledge, are even more germane to, say, metaphysics or the philosophy of mind, and hence would have their appropriate places in later volumes in this series. For instance, J. S. Mill's 'phenomenalism' incorporates a robustly empiricist view of knowledge, but is even more significant as a metaphysical conception of what reality consists in. Again, I have omitted some important discussions of belief and memory, by Plato and Russell, for example, where these are treated less in relation to truth and knowledge than as topics for philosophical psychology, ones giving rise to such questions as 'What are the *objects* of belief and memory – facts, propositions, or whatever?' and 'Are there logical relations between belief or memory and behaviour?'

I have exercised a mixture of taste and judgement in selecting texts, not overtly addressed to 'the problem of doubt', which deal with other issues in epistemology. Thus no account of the Western epistemological tradition could be adequate which failed to register the abiding strength of the idea that certainty and knowledge are not to be sought in the realm of empirical, contingent claims, but only in that of necessary, *a priori* truths. Hence I have included what are surely the two most famous, classic statements of that distinction and its relevance to epistemology, Plato's (chapter 1) and Kant's (chapter 11). Another debate which began with Plato and has continued to surface, in various forms, right up to our own times, concerns the origins of knowledge: specifically, the existence (or otherwise) of concepts or truths 'innately' known by us, prior to and independently of experience. I have included the most famous round in that recurrent debate, fought between Locke and Leibniz in the seventeenth century (chapter 8).

I remarked at the beginning that '*episteme*', and indeed our word 'knowledge', can refer to what might be called more or less systematic bodies of knowledge, such as those which the sciences seek, as well as to what it is that a knower possesses. Philosophy of science is something of a twentieth-century speciality, but there have, of course, been earlier important discussions of scientific knowledge, and attempts to articulate the character and rationale of such knowledge. So I have included the first classic discussion in this area, Aristotle's (chapter 2), and Peirce's famous defence of a scientific approach to knowledge (chapter 13).

Another ambiguity in the term 'knowledge' has often been noted. Where we have the one word 'know', many other languages have two. Thus the German speaker *kennt* his mother, but *weiss* that his mother is ill. Some philosophers have taken this distinction very seriously, arguing that 'knowledge by acquaintance' is both different from and perhaps more fundamental than knowledge *that* something is the case. I have included the best-known discussion of this distinction, by Russell (chapter 15), who integrates it with his own brand of foundationalism.

Finally, I wanted to include a discussion, however brief, of an epistemological issue whose importance contrasts with the scant attention it has received in the Western tradition: that of the credentials of *testimony* as a distinct source of knowledge. This issue is one that long vexed Indian philosophers, especially those 'orthodox' ones whose orthodoxy consisted, precisely, in their acceptance of certain testimony as authoritative. This is one reason for selecting passages from the *Nyāya-Sūtras* and the most famous commentary upon them (chapter 5).

So the texts in this volume cover a wide range of issues. But there are some issues which readers may be surprised to find untouched. In comparison with contemporary epistemology, earlier writers displayed remarkably little concern with the question of what, exactly, is *meant* by the word 'know' – with the adequacy or otherwise, for example, of defining knowledge as justified true belief. Thus there are hardly any early discussions of the problems raised for the definition of 'know' by 'Gettier cases' and other brain-teasers (Gettier cases are ones where, arguably, there is justified true belief, but not knowledge, because – roughly – an element of luck is involved in the believer's being correct).[6] Earlier philosophers, it seems, were not intent on precise articulation of the concept of knowledge – either because they thought it was not an entirely determinate notion, or because they thought that the 'big questions' about knowledge could be raised and tackled without such an articulation. If there is truth to the view that some of 'present disillusionment with epistemology is just plain *boredom*' with interminable discussions of Gettier-like conundrums,[7] then perhaps it is no bad thing that the texts in this reader address issues of a different – many would say, more exciting – sort.

---

[6] On Gettier cases and other topics of contemporary epistemology, see Keith Lehrer, *Theory of Knowledge*, Boulder, CO: Westview Press, 1990.

[7] Haack, *Evidence and Inquiry*, p. 7.

Plato, *Republic*, 475e–480a, 506d–518c

From Plato, *Republic*, tr. Robin Waterfield. Oxford: Oxford University Press, 1993, pp. 196–202 and 233–45 [translator's commentary and some short passages omitted]; reprinted by permission of Oxford University Press.

Like other volumes in this series, this one begins with sections from the most famous of all philosophical works, including its best-known pages – inspiration for poets, painters and movie directors, as well as philosophers – the Cave allegory. Plato (*c*.427–347 BCE) was not the first Greek to have raised questions about the nature of knowledge, but he was the first to provide extended and seminal treatment of a range of epistemological issues that have since so occupied philosophers. Thus, in *Meno* he addresses the problem of how, seemingly, we can know things, like geometrical truths, without having to learn them, while in *Theaetetus* he attacks the view that knowledge and truth are necessarily relative to individuals. But, in epistemology as in other areas, it is in *Republic* that his most influential ideas are found.

In Book 5 (475e–480a), Plato's teacher Socrates is represented as distinguishing knowledge from belief and ignorance, while in Books 6–7 (506d–518c), Socrates presents three analogies to illuminate his contention that knowledge presupposes an acquaintance with 'goodness'. In the 'Sun' analogy, the relation between visual perception and the sun is compared to that between knowledge and the source of intellectual 'light', goodness. In the 'Line', the relation between perceiving 'likenesses' and perceiving the things they are likenesses of is compared to that between mathematical understanding of physical things, like diagrams, and pure understanding of the 'Forms' ('types' in the present translation), including that 'Form of Forms', 'the Good'. In the 'Cave' allegory, the prisoners' ascent through and out of the cave into the sunlight is compared to 'the mind's ascent to the intelligible realm' from the everyday world of sense-experience.

Both sections are difficult and have accordingly generated many competing interpretations. It has been said of the three analogies that 'more has probably been written on them than on any other specific part of Plato's work'.[1] It

---

[1] R. C. Cross and A. D. Woozley, *Plato's* Republic: *A Philosophical Commentary*, London: Macmillan, 1964, p. 201.

helps to understand the following pages if they are taken in the wider context of *Republic*. Plato is trying to show that 'communities [should] have philosophers as kings' (473c), or put less royally, as 'guardians'. The main reasons for this are that philosophers possess knowledge that others lack and that they stand in a special relation to goodness. Naturally enough, Socrates' interlocutors request him to spell out what he means by knowledge and how it relates to good.

Bearing this context in mind helps us appreciate, first, that Plato's main interest, unlike that of most recent philosophers, is not in knowledge in the sense of someone's knowing that such-and-such is the case, of knowing that a proposition is true. Philosophers are not distinguished from other people by knowing lots more facts. So much is obvious, indeed, from Plato's contention that knowledge, in the relevant sense, is not 'introduced into a mind' by teaching, but is the result of a certain 'orientation' of the mind. We get closer to what Plato intends if we think of expressions like 'a person of great historical knowledge' or 'knowing a country well', which suggest a notion of knowledge consisting, not of possession of lots of facts, but of a capacity to understand and explain, to fit things together and into the wider picture. The context also helps us to understand the allegedly intimate connection between knowledge and goodness, which would be unintelligible if the former were simply knowledge of the facts. It is not similarly unintelligible to suppose that someone with deep understanding of some field has it in virtue of models or exemplars which guide his or her enquiries and with which the messier actual world can be compared and contrasted.

Ideal models or exemplars are at least part of what Plato means by Forms or 'types', and it is because of the philosopher's acquaintance with these that he possesses knowledge. It is with this latter claim that Plato's main legacy to epistemology is to be found. On what was once the 'orthodox' or 'two worlds' interpretation, Plato is holding that only the realm of abstract, immaterial Forms can be the domain of knowledge, so that the everyday world of material objects, actions and so on is one about which only mere belief is possible. More recently, commentators have challenged this interpretation, pointing out how it conflicts with Plato's whole rationale for philosopher-kings as people who should rule precisely because they *do* know what actions are just, say, or what things are ugly.[2]

Nothing, it seems, in the Book 5 sections, nor in the first two analogies, explicitly rules out the possibility of someone having knowledge of the everyday, empirical world. What is excluded is the possibility of knowledge without acquaintance with the Forms, at any rate with such 'polar' Forms as 'the Just' *versus* 'the Unjust' or 'the Beautiful' *versus* 'the Ugly'. In the 'Cave' allegory, to

[2] See especially Julia Annas, *An Introduction to Plato's* Republic, Oxford: Clarendon Press, 1981.

be sure, Plato leaves us in no doubt as to the superiority of a purely contemplative wisdom whose domain is the Forms alone. But it is a matter of continuing debate whether the philosopher who can be persuaded to descend from this domain back into the cave of everyday life is thereby abandoning the realm of knowledge for that of mere opinion, or whether, equipped with what he has come to understand in that higher realm, he brings with him a capacity to know how things are 'down here' which the rest of us, who never made the ascent, lack.

The Book 5 extract begins with Glaucon ('he'), who has just misunderstood Socrates' ('I') description of the philosopher as one who 'desires the whole of knowledge' to mean that philosophers, like 'sightseers', simply desire to amass information, asking Socrates to clarify matters. The second extract begins with Socrates converting Glaucon's question about the nature of goodness into one about the nature of knowledge or intelligence, 'the child of goodness'.

. . . 'Who are the true philosophers you have in mind?' he asked.

'Sightseers of the truth,' I answered.

475c

'That must be right, but what exactly does it mean?' he asked.

'It wouldn't be easy to explain to anyone else,' I said. 'But you'll grant me this, surely.'

'What?'

'Since beautiful is the opposite of ugly, they are two things.'

'Of course.'

476a

'In so far as they are two, each of them is single?'

'Yes.'

'And the same principle applies to moral and immoral, good and bad, and everything of any type [or Form]; in itself, each of them is single, but each of them has a plurality of manifestations because they appear all over the place, as they become associated with actions and bodies and one another.'

'You're right,' he said.

'Well,' I continued, 'this is what enables me to distinguish the sightseers (to borrow your term) and the ones who want to acquire some expertise or other and the men of action from the people in question, the ones who are philosophers in the true sense of the term.'

b

'What do you mean?' he asked.

'Theatre-goers and sightseers are devoted to beautiful sounds and colours and shapes, and to works of art which consist of these elements, but their minds are constitutionally incapable of seeing and devoting themselves to beauty itself.'

'Yes, that's certainly right,' he said.

'However, people with the ability to approach beauty itself and see beauty as it actually is are bound to be few and far between, aren't they?'

c   'Definitely.'

'So does someone whose horizon is limited to beautiful things, with no conception of beauty itself, and who is incapable of following guidance as to how to gain knowledge of beauty itself, strike you as living in a dream-world or in the real world? Look at it this way. Isn't dreaming precisely the state, whether one is asleep or awake, of taking something to be the real thing, when it is actually only a likeness?'

'Yes, that's what I'd say dreaming is,' he said.

'And what about someone who does the opposite – who does think that
d   there is such a thing as beauty itself, and has the ability to see it as well as the things which partake in it, and never gets them muddled up? Do you think he's living in the real world or in a dream-world?'

'Definitely in the real world,' he said.

'So wouldn't we be right to describe the difference between their mental states by saying that while this person has knowledge, the other one has beliefs?'

'Yes.'

'Now, suppose this other person – the one we're saying has beliefs, not knowledge – were to get cross with us and query the truth of our assertions. Will we be able to calm him down and gently convince him of our
e   point of view, while keeping him in the dark about the poor state of his health?'

'We really ought to,' he said.

'All right, but what shall we say to him, do you think? Perhaps this is what we should ask him. We'll tell him that we don't resent any knowledge he might have – indeed, we'd be delighted to see that he does know something – and then we'll say, "But can you tell us, please, whether someone with knowledge knows something or nothing?" You'd better answer my questions for him.'

'My answer will be that he knows something,' he said.

'Something real or something unreal?'

477a   'Real. How could something unreal be known?'

'We could look at the matter from more angles, but we're happy enough with the idea that something completely real is completely accessible to knowledge, and something utterly unreal is entirely inaccessible to knowledge. Yes?'

'Perfectly happy.'

'All right. But if something is in a state of both reality and unreality, then it falls between that which is perfectly real and that which is utterly unreal, doesn't it?'[1]

'Yes.'

'So since the field of knowledge is reality, and since it must be incomprehension whose field is unreality, then we need to find out if there is in fact something which falls between incomprehension and knowledge,   b whose field is this intermediate, don't we?'

'Yes.'

'Now, we acknowledge the existence of belief, don't we?'

'Of course.'

'Is it a different faculty from knowledge, or is it the same?'

'Different.'

'Every faculty has its own distinctive abilities, so belief and knowledge must have different domains.'

'Yes.'

'Now, since the natural field of knowledge is reality – its function is to know reality as reality . . . Actually, I think there's something else we need to get clear about first.'

'What?'

'Shall we count as a distinct class of things the faculties which give hu-   c man beings and all other creatures their abilities? By "faculties" I mean things like sight and hearing. Do you understand the type of thing I have in mind?'

'Yes, I do,' he said.

'Let me tell you something that strikes me about them. I can't distinguish one faculty from another the way I commonly distinguish other things, by looking at their colours or shapes or anything like that, because faculties don't have any of those sorts of qualities for me to look at. The only aspect of a faculty I can look at is its field, its effect. This is what enables me to identify   d each of them as a particular faculty. Where I find a single domain and a single effect, I say there is a single faculty; and I distinguish faculties which have different fields and different effects. What about you? What do you do?'

'The same as you,' he said.

'Let's go back to where we were before, then, Glaucon,' I said. 'Do you think that knowledge is a faculty, or does it belong in your opinion to some other class?'

'I think it belongs to that class,' he said, 'and is the most powerful of all the faculties.'

'And shall we classify belief as a faculty, or what?'   e

'As a faculty,' he said. 'Belief is precisely that which enables us to entertain beliefs.'

'Not long ago, however, you agreed that knowledge and belief were different.'

'Of course,' he said. 'One is infallible and the other is fallible, so anyone with any sense would keep them separate.'

'Good,' I said. 'There can be no doubt of our position: knowledge and 478a belief are different.'

'Yes.'

'Since they're different faculties, then, they have different natural fields, don't they?'[2]

'Necessarily.'

'The field of knowledge is reality, isn't it? Its function is to know the reality of anything real?'

'Yes.'

'And the function of belief, we're saying, is to entertain beliefs?'

'Yes.'

'Does it entertain beliefs about the same thing which knowledge knows? Will what is accessible to knowledge and what is accessible to belief be identical? Or is that out of the question?'

'It's ruled out by what we've already agreed,' he said. 'If different faculties naturally have different fields, and if both knowledge and belief are b faculties, and different faculties too, as we said, then it follows that it is impossible for what is accessible to knowledge and what is accessible to belief to be identical.'

'So if it is reality that is accessible to knowledge, then it is something else, not reality, that is accessible to belief, isn't it?'

'Yes.'

'Does it entertain beliefs about what is unreal? Or is it also impossible for that to happen? Think about this: isn't it the case that someone who is entertaining a belief is bringing his believing mind to bear on something? I mean, is it possible to have a belief, and to be believing nothing?'

'That's impossible.'

'In fact, someone who has a belief has some single thing in mind, doesn't he?'

'Yes.'

'But the most accurate way to refer to something unreal would be to say c that it is nothing, not that it is a single thing, wouldn't it?'

'Yes.'

'Didn't we find ourselves forced to relate incomprehension to unreality and knowledge to reality?'

'That's right,' he said.

'So the field of belief is neither reality nor unreality?'

'No.'

'Belief can't be incomprehension or knowledge, then?'

'So it seems.'

'Well, does it lie beyond their limits? Does it shed more light than knowledge or spread more obscurity than incomprehension?'

'It does neither.'

'Alternatively, does belief strike you as more opaque than knowledge and more lucid than incomprehension?'

'Considerably more,' he said.

'It lies within their limits?'   d

'Yes.'

'Then belief must fall between them.'

'Absolutely.'

'Now, didn't we say earlier that something which is simultaneously real and unreal (were such a thing to be shown to exist) would fall between the perfectly real and the wholly unreal, and wouldn't be the field of either knowledge or incomprehension, but of an intermediate (again, if such a thing were shown to exist) between incomprehension and knowledge?'

'Right.'

'And now we've found that what we call belief is such an intermediate, haven't we?'

'We have.'

'So the only thing left for us to discover, apparently, is whether there's   e anything which partakes of both reality and unreality, and cannot be said to be perfectly real or perfectly unreal. If we were to come across such a thing, we'd be fully justified in describing it as the field of belief, on the principle that extremes belong together, and so do intermediates. Do you agree?'

'Yes.'

'Let's return, on this basis, to the give and take of conversation with that   479a fine fellow who doesn't acknowledge the existence of beauty itself or think that beauty itself has any permanent and unvarying character, but takes the plurality of beautiful things as his norm – that sightseer who can't under any circumstances abide the notion that beauty, morality, and so on are each a single entity. What we'll say to him is, "My friend, is there one beautiful thing, in this welter of beautiful things, which won't turn out to be ugly? Is there one moral deed which won't turn out to be immoral? Is there one just act which won't turn out to be unjust?"'

'No, there isn't,' he said. 'It's inevitable for these things to turn out to   b be both beautiful and ugly, in a sense, and the same goes for all the other qualities you mentioned in your question.'

'And there are doubles galore – but they turn out to be halves just as much as doubles, don't they?'

'Yes.'

'And do things which are large, small, light, and heavy deserve these attributes any more than they deserve the opposite attributes?'

'No, each of them is bound to have both qualities,' he said.

'So isn't it the case, then, that any member of a plurality no more *is* whatever it is said to be than it *is not* whatever it is said to be?'

c   '. . . it is impossible to form a stable conception of any of them as either being what it is, or not being what it is, or being both, or being neither.'

'How are you going to cope with them, then?' I asked. 'Can you find a better place to locate them than between real being and unreality? I mean, they can't turn out to be more opaque and unreal than unreality, or more

d   lucid and real than reality.'

'True,' he said.

'So there we are. We've discovered that the welter of things which the masses conventionally regard as beautiful and so on mill around somewhere between unreality and perfect reality.'

'Yes, we have.'

'But we have a prior agreement that were such a thing to turn up, we'd have to call it the field of belief, not of knowledge, since the realm which occupies some uncertain intermediate point must be accessible to the intermediate faculty.'

'Yes, we do.'

e   'What shall we say about those spectators, then, who can see a plurality of beautiful things, but not beauty itself, and who are incapable of following if someone else tries to lead them to it, and who can see many moral actions, but not morality itself, and so on? That they only ever entertain beliefs, and do not *know* any of the things they believe?'

'That's what we have to say,' he said.

'As for those who can see each of these things in itself, in its permanent and unvarying nature, we'll say they have knowledge and are not merely entertaining beliefs, won't we?'

'Again, we have to.'

480a   'And won't our position be that they're devoted to and love the domain of knowledge, as opposed to the others, who are devoted to and love the domain of belief? I mean, surely we haven't forgotten our claim that these others love and are spectators of beautiful sounds and colours and so on, but can't abide the idea that there is such a thing as beauty itself?'

'No, we haven't forgotten.'

'They won't think us nasty if we refer to them as "lovers of belief" rather than as philosophers, who love knowledge, will they? Are they going to get very cross with us if we say that now?'

'Not if they listen to me,' he replied. 'It's not right to get angry at the truth.'

'But the term "believers" is inappropriate for those who are devoted to everything that is real: they should be called philosophers, shouldn't they?'

'Absolutely.' . . .

. . . 'Socrates,' said Glaucon, '. . . We'd be happy with the kind of description of goodness that you gave of morality, self-discipline, and so on.'   506d

'So would I, Glaucon,' I said, 'very happy. But I'm afraid it'll be more than I can manage, and that my malformed efforts will make me ridiculous. What I suggest, my friends, is that we forget about trying to define goodness itself for the time being. You see, I don't at the moment think   e
that our current impulse is enough to take us to where I'd like to see us go. However, I am prepared to talk about something which seems to me to be the child of goodness and to bear a very strong resemblance to it. Would you like me to do that? If not, we can just forget it.'

'Please do,' he said. 'You can settle your account by discussing the father another time.' . . .

'First I want to make sure that we're not at cross purposes,' I said, 'and   507a
to remind you of something that came up earlier, though you've often heard it on other occasions as well.'

'What?' he asked.   b

'As we talk,' I said, 'we mention and differentiate between a lot of beautiful things and a lot of good things and so on.'

'Yes, we do.'

'And we also talk about beauty itself, goodness itself and so on. All the things we refer to as a plurality on those occasions we also conversely count as belonging to a single class by virtue of the fact that they have a single particular character, and we say that the *x* itself is "what really is".'

'True.'

'And we say that the first lot is visible rather than intelligible, whereas characters are intelligible rather than visible.'

'Absolutely.'

'With what aspect of ourselves do we see the things we see?'   c

'With our sight,' he replied.

'And we use hearing for the things we hear, and so on for all the other senses and the things we perceive. Yes?'

'Of course.'

'Well, have you ever stopped to consider', I asked, 'how generous the creator of the senses was when he created the domain of seeing and being seen?'

'No, not really,' he said.

'Look at it this way. Are hearing and sound deficient? Do they need an
d   extra something to make the one hear and the other be heard – some third
thing without which hearing won't hear and sound won't be heard?'

'No,' he answered.

'And in my opinion', I went on, 'the same goes for many other domains,
if not all: they don't need anything like this. Or can you point to one that
does?'

'*I* can't,' he said.

'But do you realize that sight and the visible realm *are* deficient?'

'How?'

'Even if a person's eyes are capable of sight, and he's trying to use it, and
what he's trying to look at is coloured, the sight will see nothing and the
colours will remain unseen, surely, unless there is also present an extra third
thing which is made specifically for this purpose.'

'What is this thing you're getting at?' he asked.

'It's what we call light,' I said.

'You're right,' he said.

'So if light has value, then because it links the sense of sight and the
508a   ability to be seen, it is far and away the most valuable link there is.'

'Well, it certainly does have value,' he said.

'Which of the heavenly gods would you say is responsible for this? Whose
light makes it possible for our sight to see and for the things we see to be
seen?'

'My reply will be no different from what yours or anyone else's would
be,' he said. 'I mean, you're obviously expecting the answer, "the sun".'

'Now, there are certain conclusions to be drawn from comparing sight
to this god.'

'What?'

'Sight and the sun aren't to be identified: neither the sense itself nor its
b   location – which we call the eye – is the same as the sun.'

'True.'

'Nevertheless, there's no sense-organ which more closely resembles the
sun, in my opinion, than the eye.'[3]

'The resemblance is striking.'

'Moreover, the eye's ability to see has been bestowed upon it and chan-
nelled into it, as it were, by the sun.'

'Yes.'

'So the sun is not to be identified with sight, but is responsible for sight
and is itself within the visible realm. Right?'

'Yes,' he said.

'The sun is the child of goodness I was talking about, then,' I said. 'It is a counterpart to its father, goodness. As goodness stands in the intelligible realm to intelligence and the things we know, so in the visible realm the sun stands to sight and the things we see.'   c

'I don't understand,' he said. 'I need more detail, please.'

'As you know,' I explained, 'when our eyes are directed towards things whose colours are no longer bathed in daylight, but in artificial light instead, then they're less effective and seem to be virtually blind, as if they didn't even have the potential for seeing clearly.'

'Certainly,' he said.

'But when they're directed towards things which are lit up by the sun,   d
then they see clearly and obviously do have that potential.'

'Of course.'

'Well, here's how you can think about the mind as well. When its object is something which is lit up by truth and reality, then it has – and obviously has – intelligent awareness and knowledge. However, when its object is permeated with darkness (that is, when its object is something which is subject to generation and decay), then it has beliefs and is less effective, because its beliefs chop and change, and under these circumstances it comes across as devoid of intelligence.'

goodness gives us know-ledge

'Yes, it does.'

'Well, what I'm saying is that it's goodness which gives the things we know   e
their truth and makes it possible for people to have knowledge. It is responsible for knowledge and truth, and you should think of it as being within the intelligible realm, but you shouldn't identify it with knowledge and truth, otherwise you'll be wrong: for all their value, it is even more valuable. In the other realm, it is right to regard light and sight as resembling the sun, but not   509a
to identify either of them with the sun; so in this realm it is right to regard knowledge and truth as resembling goodness, but not to identify either of them with goodness, which should be rated even more highly.'

'You're talking about something of inestimable value,' he said, 'if it's not only the source of knowledge and truth, but is also more valuable than them. I mean, you certainly don't seem to be identifying it with pleasure!'

'How could you even think it?' I exclaimed. 'But we can take our analogy even further.'

'How?'   b

'I think you'll agree that the ability to be seen is not the only gift the sun gives to the things we see. It is also the source of their generation, growth, and nourishment, although it isn't actually the process of generation.'

'Of course it isn't.'

'And it isn't only the known-ness of the things we know which is conferred upon them by goodness, but also their reality and their being, although goodness isn't actually the state of being, but surpasses being in majesty and might.'

c   'It's way beyond human comprehension, all right,' was Glaucon's quite amusing comment.

'It's your fault for forcing me to express my views on the subject,' I replied.

'Yes, and please don't stop,' he said. 'If you've left anything out of your explanation of the simile of the sun, then the least you could do is continue with it.'

'There are plenty of omissions, in fact,' I said.

'Don't leave any gaps,' he said, 'however small.'

'I think I'll have to leave a lot out,' I said, 'but I'll try to make it as complete as I can at the moment.'

'All right,' he said.

d   'So bear in mind the two things we've been talking about,' I said, 'one of which rules over the intelligible realm and its inhabitants, while the other rules over the visible realm . . . . Anyway, do you understand this distinction between visible things and intelligible things?'

'Yes.'

'Well, picture them as a line [Figure 1] cut into two unequal sections and, following the same proportion, subdivide both the section of the visible realm and that of the intelligible realm.

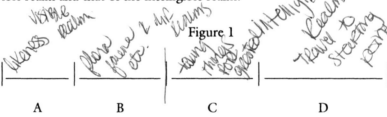

Figure 1

A   B   C   D

e   Now you can compare the sections in terms of clarity and unclarity. The first section [A] in the visible realm consists of likenesses, by which I mean a number of things: shadows, reflections (on the surface of water or on anything else which is inherently compact, smooth, and bright), and so on. Do you see what I'm getting at?'

510a

'I do.'

'And you should count the other section [B] of the visible realm as consisting of the things whose likenesses are found in the first section: all the flora and fauna there are in the world, and every kind of artefact too.'

'All right.'

'I wonder whether you'd agree,' I said, 'that truth and lack of truth have been the criteria for distinguishing these sections, and that the image stands to the original as the realm of beliefs stands to the realm of knowledge?'

'Yes,' he said, 'I certainly agree.'

b

'Now have a look at how to subdivide the section which belongs to the intelligible realm.'

'How?'

'Like this. If the mind wants to explore the first subdivision [C] it can do so only by using those former originals as likenesses and by taking things for granted on its journey, which leads it to an end-point, rather than to a starting-point. If it wants to explore the second subdivision [D], however, it takes things for granted in order to travel to a starting-point where nothing needs to be taken for granted, and it has no involvement with likenesses, as before, but makes its approach by means of types [or Forms] alone, in and of themselves.'

'I don't quite understand what you're saying,' he said.

'You will if I repeat it,' I said, 'because this preamble will make it easier to understand. I'm sure you're aware that practitioners of geometry, arithmetic, and so on take for granted things like numerical oddness and evenness, the geometrical figures, the three kinds of angle, and any other things of that sort which are relevant to a given subject. They act as if they know about these things, treat them as basic, and don't feel any further need to explain them either to themselves or to anyone else, on the grounds that there is nothing unclear about them. They make them the starting-points for their subsequent investigations, which end after a coherent chain of reasoning at the point they'd set out to reach in their research.'

c

d

'Yes, I'm certainly well aware of this,' he said.

'So you must also be aware that in the course of their discussions they make use of visible forms, despite the fact that they're not interested in visible forms as such, but in the things of which the visible forms are likenesses: that is, their discussions are concerned with what it is to be a square, and with what it is to be a diagonal (and so on), rather than with the diagonal (and so on) which occurs in their diagrams. They treat their models and diagrams as likenesses, when these things have likenesses themselves, in fact (that is, shadows and reflections on water); but they're actually trying to see squares and so on in themselves, which only thought can see.'[4]

e

511a

'You're right,' he said.

'So it was objects of this type that I was describing as belonging to the intelligible realm, with the rider that the mind can explore them only by taking things for granted, and that its goal is not a starting-point, because it is incapable of changing direction and rising above the things it is taking for granted. And I went on to say that it used as likenesses those very things which are themselves the originals of a lower order of likenesses, and that relative to the likenesses, the originals command respect and admiration for their distinctness.'

b 'I see,' he said. 'You're talking about the objects of geometry and related occupations.'

'Now, can you see what I mean by the second subdivision [D] of the intelligible realm? It is what reason grasps by itself, thanks to its ability to practise dialectic. When it takes things for granted, it doesn't treat them as starting-points, but as basic in the strict sense – as platforms and rungs, for example. These serve it until it reaches a point where nothing needs to be taken for granted, and which is the starting-point for everything. Once it has grasped this starting-point, it turns around and by a process of depending on the things which depend from the starting-point, it descends to an end-point. It makes absolutely no use of anything perceptible by the senses:

c it aims for types by means of types alone, in and of themselves, and it ends its journey with types.'

'I don't quite understand,' he said. 'I mean, you're talking about crucial matters here, I think. I do understand, however, that you want to mark off that part of the real and intelligible realm which is before the eyes of any-one who knows how to practise dialectic as more clear than the other part, which is before the eyes of practitioners of the various branches of exper-tise, as we call them. The latter make the things they take for granted their starting-points, and although they inevitably use thought, not the senses, to observe what they observe, yet because of their failure to ascend to a

d starting-point – because their enquiries rely on taking things for granted – you're saying that they don't understand these things, even though they are intelligible, when related to a starting-point. I take you to be describing what geometers and so on do as thinking rather than knowing, on the grounds that thinking is the intermediate state between believing and know-ing.'

'There's nothing wrong with your understanding,' I said. 'And you should appreciate that there are four states of mind, one for each of the four sec-tions. There's knowledge for the highest section and thought for the sec-

e ond one; and you'd better assign confidence to the third one and conjecture to the final one.[5] You can make an orderly progression out of them, and you should regard them as possessing as much clarity as their objects pos-sess truth.'

'I see,' he said. 'That's fine with me: I'll order them in the way you suggest.'

'Next,' I said, 'here's a situation which you can use as an analogy for the 514a
human condition – for our education or lack of it. Imagine people living in
a cavernous cell down under the ground; at the far end of the cave, a long
way off, there's an entrance open to the outside world. They've been there
since childhood, with their legs and necks tied up in a way which keeps b
them in one place and allows them to look only straight ahead, but not to
turn their heads. There's firelight burning a long way further up the cave
behind them, and up the slope between the fire and the prisoners there's a
road, beside which you should imagine a low wall has been built – like the
partition which conjurors place between themselves and their audience and
above which they show their tricks.'

'All right,' he said.

'Imagine also that there are people on the other side of this wall who are
carrying all sorts of artefacts. These artefacts, human statuettes, and animal
models carved in stone and wood and all kinds of materials stick out over c
the wall; and as you'd expect, some of the people talk as they carry these 515a
objects along, while others are silent.'

'This is a strange picture you're painting,' he said, 'with strange prisoners.'

'They're no different from us,' I said. 'I mean, in the first place, do you
think they'd see anything of themselves and one another except the shadows cast by the fire on to the cave wall directly opposite them?'

'Of course not,' he said. 'They're forced to spend their lives without
moving their heads.' b

'And what about the objects which were being carried along? Won't
they only see their shadows as well?'

'Naturally.'

'Now, suppose they were able to talk to one another: don't you think
they'd assume that their words applied to what they saw passing by in front
of them?'

'They couldn't think otherwise.'

'And what if sound echoed off the prison wall opposite them? When any
of the passers-by spoke, don't you think they'd be bound to assume that
the sound came from a passing shadow?'

'I'm absolutely certain of it,' he said.

'All in all, then,' I said, 'the shadows of artefacts would constitute the c
only reality people in this situation would recognize.'

'That's absolutely inevitable,' he agreed.

'What do you think would happen, then,' I asked, 'if they were set free
from their bonds and cured of their inanity? What would it be like if they
found that happening to them? Imagine that one of them has been set free

and is suddenly made to stand up, to turn his head and walk, and to look towards the firelight. It hurts him to do all this and he's too dazzled to be capable of making out the objects whose shadows he'd formerly been look-

d   ing at. And suppose someone tells him that what he's been seeing all this time has no substance, and that he's been seeing all this time has no substance, and that he's now closer to reality and is seeing more accurately, because of the greater reality of the things in front of his eyes – what do you imagine his reaction would be? And what do you think he'd say if he were shown any of the passing objects and had to respond to being asked what it was? Don't you think he'd be bewildered and would think that there was more reality in what he'd been seeing before than in what he was being shown now?'

'Far more,' he said.

e   'And if he were forced to look at the actual firelight, don't you think it would hurt his eyes? Don't you think he'd turn away and run back to the things he could make out, and would take the truth of the matter to be that these things are clearer than what he was being shown?'

'Yes,' he agreed.

'And imagine him being dragged forcibly away from there up the rough, steep slope,' I went on, 'without being released until he's been pulled out

516a   into the sunlight. Wouldn't this treatment cause him pain and distress? And once he's reached the sunlight, he wouldn't be able to see a single one of the things which are currently taken to be real, would he, because his eyes would be overwhelmed by the sun's beams?'

'No, he wouldn't,' he answered, 'not straight away.'

'He wouldn't be able to see things up on the surface of the earth, I suppose, until he'd got used to his situation. At first, it would be shadows that he could most easily make out, then he'd move on to the reflections of people and so on in water, and later he'd be able to see the actual things themselves. Next, he'd feast his eyes on the heavenly bodies and the heav-

b   ens themselves, which would be easier at night: he'd look at the light of the stars and the moon, rather than at the sun and sunlight during the day-time.'

'Of course.'

'And at last, I imagine, he'd be able to discern and feast his eyes on the sun – not the displaced image of the sun in water or elsewhere, but the sun on its own, in its proper place.

'Yes, he'd inevitably come to that,' he said.

'After that, he'd start to think about the sun and he'd deduce that it is the source of the seasons and the yearly cycle, that the whole of the visible

c   realm is its domain, and that in a sense everything which he and his peers used to see is its responsibility.'

'Yes, that would obviously be the next point he'd come to,' he agreed.

'Now, if he recalled the cell where he'd originally lived and what passed for knowledge there and his former fellow prisoners, don't you think he'd feel happy about his own altered circumstances, and sorry for them?'

'Definitely.'

'Suppose that the prisoners used to assign prestige and credit to one another, in the sense that they rewarded speed at recognizing the shadows as they passed, and the ability to remember which ones normally come earlier and later and at the same time as which other ones, and expertise at using this as a basis for guessing which ones would arrive d next. Do you think our former prisoner would covet these honours and would envy the people who had status and power there, or would he much prefer, as Homer describes it, "being a slave labouring for someone else – someone without property" [*Odyssey*. II.489], and would put up with anything at all, in fact, rather than share their beliefs and their life?'

'Yes, I think he'd go through anything rather than live that way,' he said. e

'Here's something else I'd like your opinion about,' I said. 'If he went back underground and sat down again in the same spot, wouldn't the sudden transition from the sunlight mean that his eyes would be overwhelmed by darkness?'

'Certainly,' he replied.

'Now, the process of adjustment would be quite long this time, and suppose that before his eyes had settled down and while he wasn't seeing well, he had once again to compete against those same old prisoners at $517a$ identifying those shadows. Wouldn't he make a fool of himself? Wouldn't they say that he'd come back from his upward journey with his eyes ruined, and that it wasn't even worth trying to go up there? And wouldn't they – if they could – grab hold of anyone who tried to set them free and take them up there and kill him?'

'They certainly would,' he said.

'Well, my dear Glaucon,' I said, 'you should apply this allegory, as a whole, to what we were talking about before. The region which is accessi- b ble to sight should be equated with the prison cell, and the firelight there with the light of the sun. And if you think of the upward journey and the sight of things up on the surface of the earth as the mind's ascent to the intelligible realm, you won't be wrong – at least, *I* don't think you'd be wrong, and it's my impression that you want to hear. Only God knows if it's actually true, however. Anyway, it's my opinion that the last thing to be seen – and it isn't easy to see either – in the realm of knowledge is good- c ness; and the sight of the character of goodness leads one to deduce that it is responsible for everything that is right and fine, whatever the circumstances, and that in the visible realm it is the progenitor of light and of the source of light, and in the intelligible realm it is the source and provider of truth and knowledge. And I also think that the sight of it is a prerequisite for intelligent conduct either of one's own private affairs or of public business.'

'I couldn't agree more,' he said.

'All right, then,' I said. 'I wonder if you also agree with me in not finding it strange that people who've travelled there don't want to engage in human business: there's nowhere else their minds would ever rather be than in the upper region – which is hardly surprising, if our allegory has got this aspect right as well.'

'No, it's not surprising,' he agreed.

'Well, what about this?' I asked. 'Imagine someone returning to the human world and all its misery after contemplating the divine realm. Do you think it's surprising if he seems awkward and ridiculous while he's still not seeing well, before he's had time to adjust to the darkness of his situation, and he's forced into a contest (in a lawcourt or wherever) about the shadows of morality or the statuettes which cast the shadows, and into a competition whose terms are the conceptions of morality held by people who have never seen morality itself?'

'No, that's not surprising in the slightest,' he said.

'In fact anyone with any sense,' I said, 'would remember that the eyes can become confused in two different ways, as a result of two different sets of circumstances: it can happen in the transition from light to darkness, and also in the transition from darkness to light. If he took the same facts into consideration when he also noticed someone's mind in such a state of confusion that it was incapable of making anything out, his reaction wouldn't be unthinking ridicule. Instead, he'd try to find out whether this person's mind was returning from a mode of existence which involves greater lucidity and had been blinded by the unfamiliar darkness, or whether it was moving from relative ignorance to relative lucidity and had been overwhelmed and dazzled by the increased brightness. Once he'd distinguished between the two conditions and modes of existence, he'd congratulate anyone he found in the second state, and feel sorry for anyone in the first state. If he did choose to laugh at someone in the second state, his amusement would be less absurd than when laughter is directed at someone returning from the light above.'

'Yes,' he said, 'you're making a lot of sense.'

'Now, if this is true,' I said, 'we must bear in mind that education is not capable of doing what some people promise. They claim to introduce knowl-

edge into a mind which doesn't have it, as if they were introducing sight
into eyes which are blind.'   c
'Yes, they do,' he said.

'An implication of what we're saying at the moment, however,' I pointed
out, 'is that the capacity for knowledge is present in everyone's mind. If
you can imagine an eye that can turn from darkness to brightness only if
the body as a whole turns, then our organ of understanding is like that. Its
orientation has to be accompanied by turning the mind as a whole away
from the world of becoming, until it becomes capable of bearing the sight
of real being and reality at its most bright, which we're saying is goodness.
Yes?'   d
'Yes.'

Notes

1 The meaning seems to be that beauty, say, is not something that a person
  either 'perfectly' ('unqualifiably') has or 'perfectly' ('unqualifiably') lacks,
  since not only do people change but attributions of such qualities presuppose comparisons. Helen is more beautiful than her grandfather, but less so
  than some goddess.
2 The translator prefers 'fields' to 'objects', on the grounds that fields – of
  expertise, for instance – can overlap. Hence it is not excluded that something can be both known and believed.
3 The translator notes that, among the Greeks, 'the eye was commonly regarded as containing a good proportion of fire – it flashes and twinkles'
  (*Republic*, tr. Waterfield, p. 420).
4 Since a diagram can be viewed as a mere physical object, but also serve as a
  tool for mathematical thinking, this shows that B and C on the line do not
  represent different objects (nor indeed do A and D) but, as Plato puts it,
  different degrees of 'clarity' or 'unclarity' with which things may be considered.
5 The four Greek words here translated as 'knowledge', 'thought', 'confidence'
  and 'conjecture' are *noesis, dianoia, pistis* and *eikasia*. The best rendition of
  the last three is a disputed matter. 'Reflective belief', 'unreflective belief'
  and 'illusion' respectively have sometimes been suggested.

Aristotle, *Posterior Analytics*, Book I, 1–4, 31 and Book II, 19

From *The Oxford Translation of Aristotle*, ed. W. D. Ross, Vol. 1, tr. G. R. G. Mure. Oxford: Oxford University Press, 1928 [most notes and part of chapter 4 omitted; asterisked note is the translator's]; reprinted by permission of Oxford University Press.

'All men by nature desire to know' is the famous beginning of Aristotle's (384–322 BCE) greatest work, *Metaphysics*. Given that, in his view, it is this desire which best distinguishes humans from all other creatures, it is perhaps surprising that Aristotle devoted relatively little attention to the notion of knowledge. But, like his teacher Plato and unlike later Greek philosophers, he was not unduly vexed either by the threat of general scepticism or by any alleged opacity in the meaning of 'A knows that *p*'. With an important caveat, to which I return, the interesting issues, for Aristotle, surround the things we know, not our knowledge of them.

However, having in *Prior Analytics* articulated his theory of 'pure' logic and the syllogism, Aristotle turns in *Posterior Analytics*, to discussing the nature of a peculiarly important form of knowledge, *episteme*, or what we might call scientific knowledge or understanding. The work belongs, therefore, as much to the philosophies of science and mathematics (lumped together by Aristotle) as to epistemology. Indeed, in one well-known general commentary on Aristotle, the work is discussed not under the heading of 'The theory of knowledge', but of 'The logic of science'.[1]

Unlike the 'accidental' knowledge which the non-scientist may have of triangles, cows or whatever, scientific knowledge of them is 'demonstrable', incorporating an understanding of why they have to be as they are. It must be deducible from 'basic premisses' or principles that are 'true, primary, immediate, better known than and prior to the conclusion', which is related to the premisses as 'effect to cause' (71b). These premisses include the basic axioms of a science and 'definitions', statements of what things in their essence are.

In order to avoid a regress (ch. 3), Aristotle must hold that these basic prem-

[1] W. D. Ross, *Aristotle*, London: Methuen, 1949, pp. 43ff.

isses, while indisputably true, need not, and cannot, themselves be demonstrated, though the question of how, in that case, they are known is postponed until the final chapter of the work. Aristotle, therefore, is perhaps the first to have unequivocally advanced a 'foundationalist' view of knowledge – however much it differs from later versions where, typically, it is only something general like immediate sense-experience or universal logical truths, and not axioms or definitions peculiar to a science, that is foundational.[2] The distance between Aristotelian foundationalism and later, empiricist versions is visible in Aristotle's insistence that knowledge 'is not possible through the act of perception' (87b). In effect, this is a tautology given his definition of *episteme*: for scientific knowledge involves an ability to explain and to recognize something's necessity that unaided perception could never confer.

Earlier, I qualified my remark that Aristotle sees no general *problem* with the nature of knowledge. That caveat concerned the issue of how knowledge ever arises, and this is one that Aristotle addresses, in rather different guises, in the opening and closing chapters of the work. In the former, he considers the issue of 'innate' knowledge, raised by Plato in his *Meno*. How do we ever learn anything? – since, if we already know it, we cannot *learn* it, and if we don't already know it, we can't recognize it as the right answer to our enquiry. In Book II, 19, Aristotle considers the (to him) more urgent issue of how we acquire knowledge of 'basic premisses', solving it in a manner which was to provide some, but not total, satisfaction to both empiricists and rationalists of later times. While such knowledge presupposes a process of perception, memory and inductive generalization, it requires as well a capacity for intellectual 'intuition' (*nous*) that does not itself belong to any such developmental process. The implication, found paradoxical by some, is that scientific knowledge rests on a kind of knowledge of a quite different order.

There exist more literal translations of *Posterior Analytics* than the one I have chosen:[3] but while the former may be better suited to classical scholars, their very fidelity to Aristotle's tortuous style renders his views barely intelligible to the more general reader in the absence of a whole battery of explanatory notes.

Book I

1   All instruction given or received by way of argument proceeds from   71a
pre-existent knowledge. This becomes evident upon a survey of all the

---

[2] See Terence Irwin, 'Aristotle', in *A Companion to Epistemology*, ed. J. Dancy and E. Sosa, Oxford: Blackwell, 1992, p. 28.
[3] See especially, Jonathan Barnes (tr.), *Aristotle's Posterior Analytics*, Oxford: Clarendon Press, 1975. Barnes does provide the required battery of extremely helpful notes.

species of such instruction. The mathematical sciences and all other speculative disciplines are acquired in this way, and so are the two forms of dia-
5   lectical reasoning, syllogistic and inductive; for each of these latter makes
use of old knowledge to impart new, the syllogism assuming an audience
that accepts its premisses, induction exhibiting the universal as implicit in
the clearly known particular. Again, the persuasion exerted by rhetorical
arguments is in principle the same, since they use either example, a kind of
10   induction, or enthymeme [deduction in a rhetorical context], a form of
syllogism.

The pre-existent knowledge required is of two kinds. In some cases admission of the fact must be assumed, in others comprehension of the meaning of the term used, and sometimes both assumptions are essential.[1] Thus,
we assume that every predicate can be either truly affirmed or truly denied
of any subject, and that 'triangle' means so and so; as regards 'unit' we
have to make the double assumption of the meaning of the word and the
15   existence of the thing. The reason is that these several objects are not equally
obvious to us. Recognition of a truth may in some cases contain as factors
both previous knowledge and also knowledge acquired simultaneously with
that recognition – knowledge, this latter, of the particulars actually falling
under the universal and therein already virtually known. For example, the
20   student knew beforehand that the angles of every triangle are equal to two
right angles; but it was only at the actual moment at which he was being
led on to recognize this as true in the instance before him that he came to
know 'this figure inscribed in the semicircle' to be a triangle. For some
things (viz. the singulars finally reached which are not predicable of anything else as subject) are only learnt in this way, i.e. there is here no recognition through a middle of a minor term as subject to a major. Before he
25   was led on to recognition or before he actually drew a conclusion, we should
perhaps say that in a manner he knew, in a manner not.

If he did not in an unqualified sense of the term *know* the existence of
this triangle, how could he *know* without qualification that its angles were
equal to two right angles? No: clearly he *knows* not without qualification
but only in the sense that he *knows* universally. If this distinction is not
drawn, we are faced with the dilemma in [Plato's] *Meno*: either a man will
30   learn nothing or what he already knows; for we cannot accept the solution
which some people offer. A man is asked, 'Do you, or do you not, know
that every pair is even?' He says he does know it. The questioner then
produces a particular pair, of the existence, and so *a fortiori* of the evenness, of which he was unaware. The solution which some people offer is to
assert that they do not know that every pair is even, but only that every-
71b   thing which they know to be a pair is even: yet what they know to be even

is that of which they have demonstrated evenness, i.e. what they made the subject of their premiss, viz. not merely every triangle or number which they know to be such, but any and every number or triangle without reservation. For no premiss is ever couched in the form 'every number which you know to be such', or 'every rectilinear figure which you know to be such': the predicate is always construed as applicable to any and every instance of the thing. On the other hand, I imagine there is nothing to pre-   5
vent a man in one sense knowing what he is learning, in another not knowing it. The strange thing would be, not if in some sense he knew what he was learning, but if he were to know it in that precise sense and manner in which he was learning it.

2   We suppose ourselves to possess unqualified scientific knowledge of a thing, as opposed to knowing it in the accidental way in which the sophist knows⌈when we think that we know the cause on which the fact depends,   10
as the cause of that fact and of no other, and, further, that the fact could not be other than it is. Now that scientific knowing is something of this sort is evident⌉– witness both those who falsely claim it and those who actually possess it, since the former merely imagine themselves to be, while the latter are also actually, in the condition described. Consequently the proper object of unqualified scientific knowledge is something which can-   15
not be other than it is.

   There may be another manner of knowing as well – that will be discussed later. What I now assert is that at all events we do know by demonstration. By demonstration I mean a syllogism productive of scientific knowledge, a ‧ syllogism, that is, the grasp of which is *eo ipso* such knowledge. Assuming then that my thesis as to the nature of scientific knowing is correct, the premisses of demonstrated knowledge must be true, primary, immediate,   20
better known than and prior to the conclusion, which is further related to them as effect to cause. Unless these conditions are satisfied, the basic truths will not be 'appropriate' to the conclusion. Syllogism there may indeed be without these conditions, but such syllogism, not being productive of scientific knowledge, will not be demonstration. The premisses must be true: 25
for that which is non-existent cannot be known – we cannot know, e.g., that the diagonal of a square is commensurate with its side. The premisses must be primary and indemonstrable; otherwise they will require demonstration in order to be known, since to have knowledge, if it be not accidental knowledge, of things which are demonstrable, means precisely to have a demonstration of them. The premisses must be the causes of the conclusion, better known than it, and prior to it; its causes, since we pos-   30
sess scientific knowledge of a thing only when we know its cause; prior, in

order to be causes; antecedently known, this antecedent knowledge being not our mere understanding of the meaning, but knowledge of the fact as well. Now 'prior' and 'better known' are ambiguous terms, for there is a difference between what is prior and better known in the order of being and what is prior and better known to man. I mean that objects nearer to sense are prior and better known to man; objects without qualification prior and better known are those further from sense. Now the most universal causes are furthest from sense and particular causes are nearest to sense, and they are thus exactly opposed to one another. In saying that the premisses of demonstrated knowledge must be primary, I mean that they must be the 'appropriate' basic truths, for I identify primary premiss and basic truth. A 'basic truth' in a demonstration is an immediate proposition. An immediate proposition is one which has no other proposition prior to it. A proposition is either part of an enunciation, i.e. it predicates a single attribute of a single subject. If a proposition is dialectical, it assumes either part indifferently; if it is demonstrative, it lays down one part to the definite exclusion of the other because that part is true. The term 'enunciation' denotes either part of a contradiction indifferently. A contradiction is an opposition which of its own nature excludes a middle. The part of a contradiction which conjoins a predicate with a subject is an affirmation; the part disjoining them is a negation. I call an immediate basic truth of syllogism a 'thesis' [or 'posit'] when, though it is not susceptible of proof by the teacher, yet ignorance of it does not constitute a total bar to progress on the part of the pupil: one which the pupil must know if he is to learn anything whatever is an axiom. I call it an axiom because there are such truths and we give them the name of axioms *par excellence*. If a thesis assumes one part or the other of an enunciation, i.e. asserts either the existence or the non-existence of a subject, it is a hypothesis;* if it does not so assert, it is a definition. Definition *is* a 'thesis' or a 'laying something down', since the arithmetician lays it down that to be a unit is to be quantitatively indivisible; but it is not a hypothesis, for to define what a unit is is not the same as to affirm its existence.

Now since the required ground of our knowledge – i.e. of our conviction – of a fact is the possession of such a syllogism as we call demonstration, and the ground of the syllogism is the facts constituting its premisses, we must not only know the primary premisses – some if not all of them – beforehand, but know them better than the conclusion: for the cause of an attribute's inherence in a subject always itself inheres in the subject more

---

* 'Hypothesis' to Aristotle and Plato means an assumption not calling for proof within the sphere of the special science in which it functions, not a 'working hypothesis'.

firmly than that attribute; e.g. the cause of our loving anything is dearer to us than the object of our love. So since the primary premisses are the cause of our knowledge – i.e. of our conviction – it follows that we know them better – that is, are more convinced of them – than their consequences, precisely because our knowledge of the latter is the effect of our knowledge of the premisses. Now a man cannot believe in anything more than in the things he knows, unless he has either actual knowledge of it or something better than actual knowledge. But we are faced with this paradox if a student whose belief rests on demonstration has not prior knowledge; a man must believe in some, if not in all, of the basic truths more than in the conclusion. Moreover, if a man sets out to acquire the scientific knowledge that comes through demonstration, he must not only have a better knowledge of the basic truths and a firmer conviction of them than of the connexion which is being demonstrated: more than this, nothing must be more certain or better known to him than these basic truths in their character as contradicting the fundamental premisses which lead to the opposed and erroneous conclusion. For indeed the conviction of pure science must be unshakable.

3   Some hold that, owing to the necessity of knowing the primary premisses, there is no scientific knowledge. Others think there is, but that all truths are demonstrable. Neither doctrine is either true or a necessary deduction from the premisses. The first school, assuming that there is no way of knowing other than by demonstration, maintain that an infinite regress is involved, on the ground that if behind the prior stands no primary, we could not know the posterior through the prior (wherein they are right, for one cannot traverse an infinite series): if on the other hand – they say – the series terminates and there are primary premisses, yet these are unknowable because incapable of demonstration, which according to them is the only form of knowledge. And since thus one cannot know the primary premisses, knowledge of the conclusions which follow from them is not pure scientific knowledge nor properly knowing at all, but rests on the mere supposition that the premisses are true. The other party agree with them as regards knowing, holding that it is only possible by demonstration, but they see no difficulty in holding that all truths are demonstrated, on the ground that demonstration may be circular and reciprocal.

Our own doctrine is that not all knowledge is demonstrative: on the contrary, knowledge of the immediate premisses is independent of demonstration. (The necessity of this is obvious; for since we must know the prior premisses from which the demonstration is drawn, and since the regress must end in immediate truths, those truths must be indemonstrable.) Such,

30

35

72b

5

10

15

20

then, is our doctrine, and in addition we maintain that besides scientific knowledge there is its originative source which enables us to recognize the definitions.

25 Now demonstration must be based on premisses prior to and better known than the conclusion; and the same things cannot simultaneously be both prior and posterior to one another: so circular demonstration is clearly not possible in the unqualified sense of 'demonstration', but only possible if 'demonstration' be extended to include that other method of argument which rests on a distinction between truths prior to us and truths without qualification prior, i.e. the method by which induction produces knowledge. But if we accept this extension of its meaning, our definition of unqualified knowledge will prove faulty; for there seem to be two kinds of it. Perhaps, however, the second form of demonstration, that which proceeds from truths better known to us, is not demonstration in the unqualified sense of the term.

The advocates of circular demonstration are not only faced with the difficulty we have just stated: in addition their theory reduces to the mere statement that if a thing exists, then it does exist – an easy way of proving anything. That this is so can be clearly shown by taking three terms, for to constitute the circle it makes no difference whether many terms or few or even only two are taken. Thus by direct proof, if A is, B must be; if B is, C must be; therefore if A is, C must be. Since then – by the circular proof – if

73a A is, B must be, and if B is, A must be, A may be substituted for C above. Then 'if B is, A must be' = 'if B is, C must be', which above gave the conclusion 'if A is, C must be': but C and A have been identified. Consequently the upholders of circular demonstration are in the position of say-

5 ing that if A is, A must be – a simple way of proving anything. Moreover, even such circular demonstration is impossible except in the case of attributes that imply one another, viz. 'peculiar' properties.

Now, it has been shown that the positing of one thing – be it one term or one premiss – never involves a necessary consequent: two premisses consti-

10 tute the first and smallest foundation for drawing a conclusion at all and therefore *a fortiori* for the demonstrative syllogism of science. If, then, A is implied in B and C, and B and C are reciprocally implied in one another and in A, it is possible, as has been shown in my writings on the syllogism [*Prior Analytics*], to prove all the assumptions on which the original con-

15 clusion rested, by circular demonstration in the first figure. But it has also been shown that in the other figures either no conclusion is possible, or at least none which proves both the original premisses. Propositions the terms of which are not convertible cannot be circularly demonstrated at all, and since convertible terms occur rarely in actual demonstrations, it is clearly

frivolous and impossible to say that demonstration is reciprocal and that
therefore everything can be demonstrated.   20

4   Since the object of pure scientific knowledge cannot be other than it is,
the truth obtained by demonstrative knowledge will be necessary. And since
demonstrative knowledge is only present when we have a demonstration, it
follows that demonstration is an inference from necessary premises. So we
must consider what are the premises of demonstration – i.e. what is their
character: and as a preliminary, let us define what we mean by an attribute   25
'true in every instance of its subject', an 'essential' attribute, and a 'commensurate and universal' attribute. I call 'true in every instance' what is
truly predicable of all instances – not of one to the exclusion of others –
and at all times, not at this or that time only; e.g. if animal is truly predica- 30
ble of every instance of man, then if it be true to say 'this is a man', 'this is
an animal' is also true, and if the one be true now the other is true now. A
corresponding account holds if point is in every instance predicable as contained in line. There is evidence for this in the fact that the objection we
raise against a proposition put to us as true in every instance is either an
instance in which, or an occasion on which, it is not true. Essential attributes are (1) such as belong to their subject as elements in its essential   35
nature (e.g. line thus belongs to triangle, point to line; for the very being
or 'substance' of triangle and line is composed of these elements, which are
contained in the formulae defining triangle and line): (2) such that, while
they belong to certain subjects, the subjects to which they belong are contained in the attribute's own defining formula. Thus straight and curved
belong to line, odd and even, prime and compound, square and oblong, to   40
number; and also the formula defining any one of these attributes contains   73b
its subject – e.g. line or number as the case may be.
   Extending this classification to all other attributes, I distinguish those
that answer the above description as belonging essentially to their respective subjects; whereas attributes related in neither of these two ways to
their subjects I call accidents or 'coincidents'; e.g. musical or white is a
'coincident' of animal. . . .

                                                                            87b
31   Scientific knowledge is not possible through the act of perception.
Even if perception as a faculty is of 'the such [and such], and not merely of
a 'this somewhat', yet one must at any rate actually perceive a 'this somewhat', and at a definite present place and time: but that which is commen-   30
surately universal and true in all cases one cannot perceive, since it is not
'this' and it is not 'now'; if it were, it would not be commensurately universal – the term we apply to what is always and everywhere. Seeing, therefore,

35 that demonstrations are commensurately universal and universals imperceptible, we clearly cannot obtain scientific knowledge by the act of perception: nay, it is obvious that even if it were possible to perceive that a triangle has its angles equal to two right angles, we should still be looking for a demonstration – we should not (as some say) possess knowledge of it; for perception must be of a particular, whereas scientific knowledge involves the recognition of the commensurate universal. So if we were on the

40 moon, and saw the earth shutting out the sun's light, we should not know

88a the cause of the eclipse: we should perceive the present fact of the eclipse, but not the reasoned fact at all, since the act of perception is not of the commensurate universal. I do not, of course, deny that by watching the frequent recurrence of this event we might, after tracking the commensurate universal, possess a demonstration, for the commensurate universal is elicited from the several groups of singulars.

5 The commensurate universal is precious because it makes clear the cause; so that in the case of facts like these which have a cause other than themselves universal knowledge is more precious than sense-perceptions and than intuition. (As regards primary truths there is of course a different account to be given [see Book II, ch. 19].) Hence it is clear that knowledge of things demonstrable cannot be acquired by perception, unless the

10 term perception is applied to the possession of scientific knowledge through demonstration. Nevertheless certain points do arise with regard to connexions to be proved which are referred for their explanation to a failure in sense-perception: there are cases when an act of vision would terminate our inquiry, not because in seeing we should be knowing, but because we should have elicited the universal from seeing; if, for example, we saw

15 the pores in the glass and the light passing through, the reason of the kindling would be clear to us because we should at the same time see it in each instance and intuit that it must be so in all instances.

Book II

99b 15 . . . As regards syllogism and demonstration, the definition of, and the conditions required to produce each of them, are now clear, and with that also the definition of, and the conditions required to produce, demonstrative knowledge, since it is the same as demonstration. As to the basic premisses, how they become known and what is the developed state of knowledge of them is made clear by raising some preliminary problems. 19

20 We have already said that scientific knowledge through demonstration is impossible unless a man knows the primary immediate premisses. But there

are questions which might be raised in respect of the apprehension of these immediate premises: one might not only ask whether it is of the same kind as the apprehension of the conclusions, but also whether there is or is not scientific knowledge of both; or scientific knowledge of the latter, and of the former a different kind of knowledge; and, further, whether the developed states of knowledge are not innate but come to be in us, or are innate 25
but at first unnoticed. Now it is strange if we possess them from birth; for it means that we possess apprehensions more accurate than demonstration and fail to notice them. If on the other hand we acquire them and do not previously possess them, how could we apprehend and learn without a basis of pre-existent knowledge? For that is impossible, as we used to find 30
[Book I, ch. 1], in the case of demonstration. So it emerges that neither can we possess them from birth, nor can they come to be in us if we are without knowledge of them to the extent of having no such developed state at all. Therefore we must possess a capacity of some sort, but not such as to rank higher in accuracy than these developed states. And this at least is an obvious characteristic of all animals, for they possess a congenital discriminative capacity which is called sense-perception. But though sense- 35
perception is innate in all animals, in some the sense-impression comes to persist, in others it does not. So animals in which this persistence does not come to be have either no knowledge at all outside the act of perceiving, or no knowledge of objects of which no impression persists; animals in which it does come into being have perception and can continue to retain the sense-impression in the soul: and when such persistence is frequently re- 100a
peated a further distinction at once arises between those which out of the persistence of such sense-impressions develop a power of systematizing them and those which do not. So out of sense-perception comes to be what we call memory, and out of frequently repeated memories of the same thing develops experience; for a number of memories constitute a single experi- 5
ence. From experience again – i.e. from the universal now stabilized in its entirety within the soul, the one beside the many which is a single identity within them all – originate the skill of the craftsman and the knowledge of the man of science, skill in the sphere of coming to be and science in the sphere of being.

We conclude that these states of knowledge are neither innate in a determinate form, nor developed from other higher states of knowledge, but 10
from sense-perception. It is like a rout in battle stopped by first one man making a stand and then another, until the original formation has been restored. The soul is so constituted as to be capable of this process.

Let us now restate the account given already, though with insufficient clearness. When one of a number of logically indiscriminable particulars 15

has made a stand, the earliest universal is present in the soul: for though the
act of sense-perception is of the particular, its content is universal – is man,
for example, not the man Callias. A fresh stand is made among these rudi-
mentary universals, and the process does not cease until the indivisible
concepts, the true universals, are established: e.g. such and such a species
of animal is a step towards the genus animal, which by the same process is
a step towards a further generalization.

Thus it is clear that we must get to know the primary premisses by induction; for the method by which even sense-perception implants the universal is inductive. Now of the thinking states by which we grasp truth,
some are unfailingly true, others admit of error – opinion, for instance, and
calculation, whereas scientific knowing and intuition are always true: further, no other kind of thought except intuition is more accurate than scientific knowledge, whereas primary premisses are more knowable than
demonstrations, and all scientific knowledge is discursive. From these considerations it follows that there will be no scientific knowledge of the primary premisses, and since except intuition nothing can be truer than
scientific knowledge, it will be intuition that apprehends the primary premisses – a result which also follows from the fact that demonstration cannot
be the originative source of demonstration, nor, consequently, scientific
knowledge of scientific knowledge. If, therefore, it is the only other kind of
true thinking except scientific knowing, intuition will be the originative
source of scientific knowledge. And the originative source of science grasps
the original basic premiss, while science as a whole is similarly related as
originative source to the whole body of fact.

Note

1 Aristotle can hardly mean that we only *sometimes* require 'comprehension of
 the meaning of the term[s] used' in statements. His point, presumably, is
 that we are often entitled to take their meaning for granted, so that only
 sometimes – in the case of ambiguous words, say – do we need *explicitly* to
 assume that a term means such-and-such.

Sextus Empiricus, *Outlines of Pyrrhonism*, Book I, Sections 1–16, 18–27

From The Skeptic Way: Sextus Empiricus's Outlines of Pyrrhonism by Benson Mates, tr. Benson Mates. Oxford: Oxford University Press, Inc., 1996, pp. 89–94, 110–17 [most of Section 14 omitted]; translation copyright © 1996 by Benson Mates. Used by permission of Oxford University Press, Inc.

Greek philosophy did not grind to a halt after Aristotle, and in recent years there has been a welcome revival of interest, subdued since Renaissance times, in thinkers of the Hellenistic period that followed the death of Alexander the Great in 323 BCE. These three centuries were lively ones during which battle on many issues, including epistemological ones, was joined by warring schools – most famously, the Stoics, Epicureans and Sceptics. Common to these schools, however, was an ideal of tranquillity or 'freedom from disturbance (*ataraxia*)', of what is now popularly called a 'philosophical attitude to life'. For the Stoics and Epicureans, this was to be achieved through arriving at a true and satisfying account of reality, but for the sceptical followers of Pyrrho of Elis (*c.* 365–270 BCE) tranquillity comes with 'suspension of judgement (*epochē*)', a gentle refusal to attach oneself to any beliefs whatsoever about how things really are, as distinct from how they may seem to one. Pyrrho, it is said, maintained that 'nothing is honourable or base, or just or unjust, and that . . . nothing exists in truth': allegedly, he followed his principles by 'taking no precautions, facing everything that came, wagons, precipices, dogs', trusting nothing.[1]

Pyrrho, it seems, was more intent on advocating this sceptical lifestyle than on providing reasons for 'suspension of judgement', this latter task being taken up by later sceptics like Aenesidemus (first century BCE), who is credited with formulating the famous 'tropes' or 'modes' of sceptical argument. It is their views which were chronicled with clarity and detail by a second-century physician, Sextus Empiricus, an otherwise obscure figure. I have omitted most of § 14 where all ten 'tropes' are described, since some of them – like their support-

[1] Diogenes Laertius, quoted in A. A. Long and D. N. Sedley, *The Hellenistic Philosophers*, Vol. 1, Cambridge: Cambridge University Press, 1987, p. 13.

ing examples – are too fanciful to take seriously (the more plausible of the arguments are distilled in §§ 15–16.) Suffice it to say that they 'include practically all the ingredients of what nowadays is called "the argument from illusion" ',[2] and that their thrust is to show that there is 'equipollence' between conflicting beliefs about reality, that there is never reason to adopt one such belief in preference to a rival one.

An intriguing feature of Pyrrhonian scepticism was its resolutely self-referential nature. Sextus says many times that he himself is not committed to the arguments and evidence marshalled in favour of the sceptical stance. They merely seem to him to be plausible and therefore result in it seeming to him that no belief deserves credence. The point of such remarks, of course, is to divert the familiar objection that the sceptic refutes himself when employing reason and evidence in order to discredit their authority. The sceptic, as Sextus portrays him, does not end up with a sceptical doctrine: rather, he suspends his faculty of belief and judgement, emulating, one might say, the condition of an animal or young child who acts naturally and without the mediation of beliefs.[3] (Students of Taoism will recognize similarities with the position of Chuang Tzu.)

Sextus' writings were an important discovery for Renaissance scholars and hence influenced such philosophers as Montaigne and, through them, the founder of modern scepticism, Descartes (see chapter 7 below). Pyrrhonian scepticism, though, was at once more and less radical than Cartesian scepticism: more radical in that, first, the sceptical position is not merely a tactical, methodological one to be provisionally adopted but then overcome and, second, the Pyrrhonian urges something stronger than the dubitability of our beliefs. It is not doubt but *aporia* – bafflement as to the very sense of making objective claims – that the tropes or modes are intended to induce. It is less radical, however, than Cartesian doubt – though some commentators would contest this – in that Sextus does not call into question the very existence of an external world. The point, rather, is that we should (undogmatically, of course) suspend all judgement as to what that world beyond our 'feelings' (*pathē*) is like.

1. The Main Difference between the Philosophies

When people search for something, the likely outcome is that either they find it or, not finding it, they accept that it cannot be found, or they con-

---

[2] Benson Mates, *The Skeptic Way*, p. 57.
[3] See William Jordan, *Ancient Concepts of Philosophy*, London: Routledge, 1992, pp. 162ff.

tinue to search. So also in the case of what is sought in philosophy, I think, some people have claimed to have found the truth, others have asserted 2 that it cannot be apprehended, and others are still searching. Those who think that they have found it are the Dogmatists, properly so called – for 3 example, the followers of Aristotle and Epicurus, the Stoics, and certain others. The followers of Cleitomachus and Carneades, as well as other Academics, have asserted that it cannot be apprehended. The Skeptics continue to search. Hence it is with reason that the main types of philosophy 4 are thought to be three in number: the Dogmatic, the Academic, and the Skeptic. Concerning the first two it will best become others to speak; but concerning the Skeptic Way we shall now give an outline account, stating in advance that as regards none of the things that we are about to say do we firmly maintain that matters are absolutely as stated, but in each instance we are simply reporting, like a chronicler, what now appears to us to be the case.

2. The Accounts of Skepticism

One account of the Skeptic philosophy is called "general"; the other, "spe- 5 cific." In the general account we set forth the characteristic traits of Skepticism, stating its basic idea, its origins, arguments, criterion and goal, as well as the modes of *epochē* [suspension of judgment], and how we take the Skeptic statements, and the distinction between Skepticism and the competing philosophies. In the specific account we state objections to each part of so-called "philosophy." Let us, then, first take up the general ac- 6 count, beginning the exposition with the various terms for the Skeptic Way.

3. The Nomenclature of the Skeptic Way

The Skeptic Way is called Zetetic ["questioning"] from its activity in ques- 7 tioning and inquiring, Ephectic ["suspensive"] from the *pathos* that arises concerning the subject of inquiry, Aporetic ["inclined to *aporia*"] either, as some say, from its being puzzled and questioning about everything or from its being at a loss as to whether to assent or dissent, and Pyrrhonean because it appears to us that Pyrrho applied himself to Skepticism more vigorously and conspicuously than his predecessors did.

4. What Skepticism Is

8   The Skeptic Way is a disposition to oppose phenomena and noumena to one another in any way whatever,[1] with the result that, owing to the equipollence among the things and statements thus opposed, we are brought
9   first to *epochē* and then to *ataraxia*. We do not apply the term "disposition" in any subtle sense, but simply as cognate with "to be disposed." At this point we are taking as phenomena the objects of sense perception, thus contrasting them with the noumena. The phrase "in any way whatever" can modify both the word "disposition" (so as to make us take that word in a plain sense, as we said) and the phrase "to oppose phenomena and noumena"; for since we oppose these in various ways – phenomena to phenomena, noumena to noumena, or *alternando* phenomena to noumena, we say "in any way whatever" in order to include all such oppositions. Or we can apply "in any way whatever" to "phenomena and noumena," in order that we may not have to inquire how the phenomena appear or the
10   noumena are thought, but may take these terms in their plain senses. By "opposed" statements we simply mean inconsistent ones, not necessarily affirmative and negative. By "equipollence" we mean equality as regards credibility and the lack of it, that is, that no one of the inconsistent statements takes precedence over any other as being more credible. *Epochē* is a state of the intellect on account of which we neither deny nor affirm anything. *Ataraxia* is an untroubled and tranquil condition of the soul. In our remarks on the goal of Skepticism we shall come back to the question of how *ataraxia* enters the soul along with *epochē*.

5. The Skeptic

11   The definition of the Pyrrhonean philosopher is implicitly contained in that of the Skeptic Way: he is the person who has the aforementioned disposition.

6. The Origins of Skepticism

12   We say that the causal origin of the Skeptic Way is the hope of attaining *ataraxia*. Certain talented people, upset by anomaly in "the facts" and at a loss as to which of these "facts" deserve assent, endeavored to discover what is true in them and what is false, expecting that by settling this they would achieve *ataraxia*. But the main origin of Skepticism is the practice of

opposing to each statement an equal statement; it seems to us that doing this brings an end to dogmatizing.

7. Does the Skeptic Dogmatize?

When we say that the Skeptic does not dogmatize we are not using the 13 term "dogma" as some do, in its more common meaning, "something that one merely agrees to", for the Skeptic does give assent to the *pathē* [feelings, affects] that are forced upon him by a *phantasia* [impression]: for example, when feeling hot (or cold) he would not say "I seem not to be hot (or cold)." But when we assert that he does not dogmatize, we use "dogma" in the sense, which others give it, of assent to one of the non-evident matters investigated by the sciences. For the Pyrrhonist assents to nothing that is non-evident. Not even in putting forward the Skeptic 14 slogans about non-evident things does he dogmatize – slogans like "Nothing more" or "I determine nothing" or any of the others of which we shall speak later. For the dogmatizer propounds as certainty the things about which he is said to be dogmatizing, but the Skeptic does not put forward these slogans as holding absolutely. He considers that, just as the "All things are false" slogan says that together with the other things it is itself false, as does the slogan "Nothing is true," so also the "Nothing more" slogan says that it itself is no more the case than its opposite, and thus it applies to itself along with the rest. We say the same of the other Skeptic slogans. So that since the dogmatizer is one who posits the con- 15 tent of his dogmas as being true, while the Skeptic presents his skeptical slogans as implicitly self-applicable, the Skeptic should not be said to dogmatize thereby. But the most important point is that in putting forward these slogans he is saying what seems to him to be the case and is reporting his *pathos* without belief, not firmly maintaining anything concerning what exists externally.

8. Does the Skeptic Have a System?

We proceed in the same way when asked whether the Skeptic has a system. 16 If one defines a system as an attachment to a number of dogmas that agree with one another and with appearances, and defines a dogma as an assent to something non-evident, we shall say that the Skeptic does not have a system. But if one says that a system is a way of life that, in accordance with 17 appearances, follows a certain rationale, where that rationale shows how it is possible to seem to live rightly ("rightly" being taken, not as referring only to virtue, but in a more ordinary sense) and tends to produce the disposition to suspend judgment, then we say that he does have a system. For we do follow a certain rationale that, in accord with appearances, points us toward a life in conformity with the customs of our country and its laws and institutions, and with our own particular *pathē*.

9. Does the Skeptic Theorize about Nature?

18 We reply in the same vein if asked whether the Skeptic needs to theorize about nature. On the one hand, if there is a question of making an assertion with firm confidence about any of the matters dogmatically treated in physical theory, we do not theorize; but, on the other hand, in the course of opposing to every statement an equal statement, and in connection with *ataraxia*, we do touch upon physical theory. This, too, is the way we approach the logical and ethical parts of so-called "philosophy."

10. Do the Skeptics Deny Appearances?

19 Those who claim that the Skeptics deny appearances seem to me not to have heard what we say. For, as we stated above, we do not reject the things that lead us involuntarily to assent in accord with a passively received *phantasia*, and these are appearances. And when we question whether the external object is such as it appears, we grant that it does appear, and we are not raising a question about the appearance but rather about what is said about the appearance; this is different from raising a
20 question about the appearance itself. For example, the honey appears to us to be sweet. This we grant, for we sense the sweetness. But whether it *is* sweet we question insofar as this has to do with the [philosophical] theory, for that theory is not the appearance, but something said about the appearance. And even when we do present arguments in opposition to the appearances, we do not put these forward with the intention of denying the appearances but by way of pointing out the precipitancy of the Dogmatists; for if the theory is so deceptive as to all but snatch away the appearances from under our very eyes, should we not distrust it in regard to the non-evident, and thus avoid being led by it into precipitate judgments?

11. The Criterion of the Skeptic Way

That we hold to the appearances is obvious from what we say about the   21
criterion of the Skeptic Way. The word "criterion" is used in two ways: first,
for the criterion that is assumed in connection with belief about existence or
nonexistence, and that we shall discuss in our objections; and second, for
the criterion of action, by attention to which in the conduct of daily life we
do some things and not others; it is of the latter that we are now speaking.
Accordingly, we say that the criterion of the Skeptic Way is the appearance –   22
in effect using that term here for the *phantasia* – for since this appearance
lies in feeling and involuntary *pathos* it is not open to question. Thus nobody, I think, disputes about whether the external object appears this way
or that, but rather about whether it is such as it appears to be.

Holding to the appearances, then, we live without beliefs but in accord   23
with the ordinary regimen of life, since we cannot be wholly inactive. And
this ordinary regimen of life seems to be fourfold: one part has to do with
the guidance of nature, another with the compulsion of the *pathē*, another
with the handing down of laws and customs, and a fourth with instruction
in arts and crafts. Nature's guidance is that by which we are naturally capa-   24
ble of sensation and thought; compulsion of the *pathē* is that by which
hunger drives us to food and thirst makes us drink; the handing down of
customs and laws is that by which we accept that piety in the conduct of life
is good and impiety bad; and instruction in arts and crafts is that by which
we are not inactive in whichever of these we acquire. And we say all these
things without belief.

12. What Is the Goal of Skepticism?

After these remarks, our next task is to explain the goal of the Skeptic Way.   25
Now the goal or end is that for the sake of which everything is done or
considered, while it, in turn, is not done or considered for the sake of
anything else; or, it is the ultimate object of the desires. We always say that
as regards belief the Skeptic's goal is *ataraxia*, and that as regards things
that are unavoidable it is having moderate *pathē*. For when the Skeptic set   26
out to philosophize with the aim of assessing his *phantasiai* – that is, of
determining which are true and which are false so as to achieve *ataraxia* –
he landed in a controversy between positions of equal strength, and, being
unable to resolve it, he suspended judgment. But while he was thus suspending judgment there followed by chance the sought-after *ataraxia* as   27

regards belief. For the person who believes that something is by nature good or bad is constantly upset; when he does not possess the things that seem to be good, he thinks he is being tormented by things that are by nature bad, and he chases after the things he supposes to be good; then, when he gets these, he falls into still more torments because of irrational

28   and immoderate exultation, and, fearing any change, he does absolutely everything in order not to lose the things that seem to him good. But the person who takes no position as to what is by nature good or bad neither avoids nor pursues intensely. As a result, he achieves *ataraxia*.[2]

Indeed, what happened to the Skeptic is just like what is told of Apelles the painter. For it is said that once upon a time, when he was painting a horse and wished to depict the horse's froth, he failed so completely that he gave up and threw his sponge at the picture – the sponge on which he used to wipe the paints from his brush – and that in striking the picture the sponge produced the desired effect. So, too, the Skeptics were hoping to

29   achieve *ataraxia* by resolving the anomaly of phenomena and noumena, and, being unable to do this, they suspended judgment. But then, by chance as it were, when they were suspending judgment the *ataraxia* followed, as a shadow follows the body. We do not suppose, of course, that the Skeptic is wholly untroubled, but we do say that he is troubled only by things unavoidable. For we agree that sometimes he is cold and thirsty and has

30   various feelings like those. But even in such cases, whereas ordinary people are affected by two circumstances – namely by the *pathē* themselves and not less by its seeming that these conditions are by nature bad – the Skeptic, by eliminating the additional belief that all these things are naturally bad, gets off more moderately here as well. Because of this we say that as regards belief the Skeptic's goal is *ataraxia*, but in regard to things unavoidable it is having moderate *pathē*. But some notable Skeptics have added "suspension of judgment during investigations" to these.

13. The General Modes of *Epochē*

31   Since we have been saying that *ataraxia* follows on suspending judgment about everything, the next thing would be to explain how we reach this suspension. Roughly speaking, one may say that it comes about through the opposition of things. We oppose phenomena to phenomena or noumena

32   to noumena, or *alternando*. For instance, we oppose phenomena to phenomena when we say that the same tower appears round from a distance but square from close up; and noumena to noumena when, in reply to one

33   who infers the existence of divine providence from the order of the heav-

enly bodies, we oppose the fact that often the good fare ill and the bad fare well, and deduce from this that divine providence does not exist; and noumena to phenomena, as when Anaxagoras argued, in opposition to snow's being white, that snow is frozen water and water is dark in color, and therefore snow is dark in color. Or, with a different concept of opposition, we sometimes oppose present things to present things, as in the foregoing examples, and sometimes present things to things past or to things future; for example, when somebody brings up an argument that we are not able to refute, we say to him: "Just as before the birth of the person who introduced the system which you follow, the argument supporting that system did not yet appear sound although it really was, so also it is possible that the opposite of the argument you now advance is really sound despite its not yet appearing so to us, and hence we should not yet assent to this argument that now seems so strong." 34

But in order that we may more accurately understand these oppositions, I shall set down the modes or arguments by means of which suspension of judgment is brought about, without, however, maintaining anything about their number or their force. For they may well be unsound, and there may be more than the ones I shall mention. 35

14. The Ten Modes

The older Skeptics, according to the usual account, have handed down some modes, ten in number, through which it seems that suspension of judgment is brought about, and which they also synonymously call 'arguments' or 'points.' And these modes are as follows: first, there is the one based on the variety of animals; second, the one based on the differences among human beings; third, that based on the differences in constitution of the sense organs; fourth, on the circumstances; fifth, on positions, distances and locations; sixth, on admixtures; seventh, on the quantity and constitution of the external objects; eighth, on relativity; ninth, on the frequency or infrequency of occurrence; and tenth, on ways of life, customs and laws, mythic beliefs and dogmatic opinions . . . 36 37 38

15. The Five Modes

The more recent Skeptics hand down the following five modes of *epochē*: the first is the mode based on disagreement; the second is that based on infinite regress; the third, that based on relativity; the fourth, on hypoth- 164

165   esis; and the fifth is the circularity mode. The one based on disagreement is that according to which we find that, both in ordinary life and among philosophers, with regard to a given topic there has been reached an unresolvable impasse on account of which we are unable to reach a verdict one way or the other, and we end up with suspension of judgment. The

166   one based on infinite regress is that in which we say that what is offered as support for believing a given proposition is itself in need of such support, and that support is in need of other support, and so on ad infinitum, so that, since we have no place from which to begin to establish anything,

167   suspension of judgment follows. The one based on relativity is, as we said before, that in which the external object appears this way or that way in relation to the judging subject and the things observed at the same time,

168   but we suspend judgment as to how it is in its nature. And the one based on hypothesis comes into play when the Dogmatists, involved in an infinite regress, begin with something that they do not establish but that they deem worthy of acceptance as agreed upon without question or demonstration.

169   And the circularity mode occurs when what ought to make the case for the matter in question has need of support from that very matter; whence, being unable to assume either in order to establish the other, we suspend judgment about both.

      That every matter of inquiry can be brought under these modes we shall

170   show in brief as follows. Anything proposed for consideration is either a sense object or a thought object, but whichever it is, there is a disagreement concerning it. For some people say that only the sense objects are true, others that only the thought objects, and still others that some of each. Now, will they say that the disagreement can be decided or that it cannot? If it cannot, we have the conclusion that one must suspend judgment, for concerning disagreements that are not decidable one cannot make an assertion. On the other hand, if it is decidable, then we want to know

171   how it is to be decided. Shall we decide about a sense object, for example (for first we shall base the argument on this case) by a sense object or a thought object? If by a sense object, then, since the sense objects are what our inquiry is about, this object too will need something else as support. And if that also is a sense object, it again will need support from another

172   one, and so on ad infinitum. But if we are to decide about the sense object by a thought object, then, since there is a disagreement about the thought objects, too, and this is a thought object, it also will be in need of decision and support. But by what will it be supported? If by a thought object, it will similarly involve an infinite regress; but if by a sense object, then, since a thought object was used as support for a sense object and a sense object for a thought object, the circularity mode of *epochē* comes in.

But if, to avoid these points, our interlocutor should think to assume 173
something, by consent and without demonstration, as a basis for demonstrating what follows, the hypothesis mode comes into play and allows no
way out. For if the hypothesizer is worthy of credence, we shall be no less
worthy of credence whenever we hypothesize the opposite. And if what
the hypothesizer hypothesizes is true, he makes it suspect by taking it as a
hypothesis instead of establishing it; but if it is false, the underpinnings of
the things being established will be rotten. Further, if hypothesizing con- 174
tributes something to credibility, we might as well hypothesize what is in
question and not something else from which the hypothesizer is going to
establish the point at issue; and if it is absurd to hypothesize what is in
question, it will also be absurd to hypothesize a proposition superordinate
to this.

That all sense objects are relative is evident, for they are relative to who- 175
ever does the sensing. It is therefore plain that any sense object that is
proposed to us is easily brought under the five modes. And we reason in
the same way about thought objects. For if it is said that the dispute is not
decidable, the necessity of suspending judgment about it will be granted
us. And if the dispute is going to be decided, then if by means of a thought 176
object, we shall produce an infinite regress, while if by means of a sense
object, a circular inference. For when the dispute is about the sense object
and cannot be decided by means of a sense object because of an infinite
regress, there will be need of a thought object, just as for the thought
object there will be need of a sense object. For these reasons, again, anyone 177
who assumes something as a hypothesis will be acting absurdly. Furthermore, the thought objects, too, are relative; for they are so named with
respect to the people who think them, and if they were in nature as they are
said to be, there would be no dispute about them. Hence the thought
objects, too, are brought under the five modes, so that in all cases it is
necessary for us to suspend judgment about any matter proposed for consideration.

Such, then, are the five modes handed down by the later Skeptics; they
are not put forward by way of throwing out the ten modes, but in order to
combat the precipitancy of the Dogmatists in greater detail by means of
both together.

16. The Two Modes

They also hand down two other modes of *epochē*. For since everything that 178
is apprehended is either apprehended through itself or through something

else, by pointing out that what is apprehended is apprehended neither through itself nor through anything else they produce *aporiai*, as they suppose, about everything. That nothing is apprehended through itself is apparent, they say, from the dispute among the physical scientists concerning not only all sense objects but also, I think, all thought objects – a dispute that is not decidable since we cannot use either a sense object or a thought object as a criterion, for anything we take will be in dispute and hence not credible. And the following is the reason why they do not agree that something can be apprehended through something else. If that through which something is apprehended must in every case be apprehended through something else, they encounter the circularity or infinite regress modes of *epochē*. But if somebody should wish to take as apprehended through itself something through which something else is apprehended, he runs up against the fact that for the aforementioned reasons nothing is apprehended through itself. So we are at a loss as to how the thing in question could be apprehended either on the basis of itself or on that of something else, since there is no apparent criterion of truth or of apprehension and since signs, even apart from proof, are eliminated, as we shall show later.

It will suffice for the present to have said thus much about the modes leading to suspension of judgment.

. . .

18. The Skeptic Slogans

187

Since, in using each of these modes and those leading to suspension of judgment, we utter certain slogans expressive of the Skeptic temper of mind and of our *pathē* – for example, "not more," "nothing is to be determined," and the like – it would be reasonable to take up these next. Let us begin with "not more."

19. The "Not More" Slogan

188

We say this sometimes in the form I have just mentioned, but sometimes in the form "nothing more"; for we do not, as some people suppose, employ the "not more" in specific investigations and the "nothing more" in general ones; rather, we say either "not more" or "nothing more" indifferently, and now we shall discuss them as though they were identical. This slogan, then, is elliptical. Just as when we say "a duplex" we are saying in effect "a duplex house," and when we say "a wide [*plateia*, a square]" we are saying in effect "a wide street,' so also when we say "not more" we are saying in effect "not more this than that, up than down." Some of the Skeptics, however, in place of the "not" adopt "what" – "what more this   189 than that" – taking the "what" to refer to the cause, so that the meaning is "because of what [i.e., why] this more than that?" For it is common practice to use questions instead of assertions, as in the line

What mortal doesn't know the bride of Zeus?
Euripides, *Hercules* 1

and assertions instead of questions, such as "I want to know where Dion lives" and "I ask why one should marvel at a poetic person." Also, the use of "what" instead of "why" [i.e., "because of what"] is found in Menander:

[Because of] what was I left behind?
Frag. 900 Kock

And the slogan "not more this than that" also makes evident our *pathos*   190 with respect to which we reach equilibrium through the equipollence of the opposed things–where we use the term "equipollence" for equality as regards what appears persuasive to us, and "opposed things" in the everyday sense of things that conflict, and "equilibrium" for the absence of assent to either alternative.

Even if the slogan "nothing more" exhibits the character of assent or   191 denial, we do not use it in that way, but rather we take it in an imprecise and not strictly correct sense, either in place of a question or instead of saying "I don"t know to which of these I ought to assent and to which I ought not to assent." For our goal is to make evident what appears to us, and we do not care with what expression we do it. And this also should be noticed: that in uttering the "nothing more" slogan we are not maintaining that it is entirely true and firm, but in its case, too, we are speaking in accord with what appears to us.

20. "Non-assertion" (*Aphasia*)

Concerning non-assertion we say the following. The term "assertion" has   192 two senses, a wider and a narrower. In the wider sense an assertion is an expression indicating affirmation or denial, such as "It is day," "It is not day"; whereas in the narrower sense it is an expression indicating affirmation only; in this sense people do not call negative statements "assertions."

Non-assertion, then, is the avoidance of assertion in the wider sense, in which we say that both affirmation and negation are covered; so that non-assertion is a *pathos* of ours in view of which we say that we do not affirm or deny anything. From this it is evident that we adopt the "non-assertion" slogan, too, not on the assumption that things are in their nature such as to produce non-assertion in every case, but simply as making evident that we, now, when we are uttering it, and in the case of the particular matters in question, are experiencing this *pathos*. And this, too, must be kept in mind: it is dogmatic statements about the non-evident that we say we neither affirm nor deny; we grant the things that stir our *pathē* and drive us by force to assent.

21. "Perhaps," "It Is Possible," "Maybe"

194   The slogans "perhaps" and "perhaps not," and "possibly" and "possibly not," and "maybe" and "maybe not" we take in place of "perhaps it is the case" and "perhaps it is not the case," and "possibly it is the case" and "possibly it is not the case," and "maybe it is the case" and "maybe it is not the case" – for brevity's sake using "possibly not" for "possibly it is not the case" and "maybe not" for "maybe it is not the case," and "per-

195   haps not" for "perhaps it is not the case." But here again we do not fight over words, nor are we raising the issue of whether the slogans make evident the nature of these matters; rather, as I said before, we employ them imprecisely. Nevertheless, I think, it is evident that these slogans are expressive of non-assertion. Certainly the person who says "perhaps it is the case," by not firmly maintaining that it is the case, is in effect also asserting the seemingly inconsistent "perhaps it is not the case", similarly for the remaining slogans.

22. "I Withhold Assent"

196   We use "I withhold assent" as short for "I am unable to say which of the alternatives proposed I ought to believe and which I ought not believe," indicating that the matters appear equal to us as regards credibility and incredibility. As to whether they are equal, we maintain no firm opinion, but we do state what appears to us to be the case about them when that appearance affects us. And withholding assent [*epochē*] is so called from the intellect's being held back [*epechesthai*] in such a way as neither to assert nor deny, because of the equipollence of the matters in question.

23. "I Determine Nothing"

Concerning "I determine nothing" we say the following. We think that   197
"determining" is not simply saying something but rather is putting forward and assenting to something non-evident. Thus, I suppose, the Skeptic
will be found not to be determining anything, not even the slogan "I determine nothing" itself. For that slogan is not a dogmatic opinion, that is,
an assent to the non-evident, but rather it makes evident our *pathos*. Whenever the Skeptic says "I determine nothing," he is saying this: "I am now in
such a state of mind as neither dogmatically to affirm nor deny any of the
matters in question." And this he says, reporting what appears to him concerning the matters at hand, not dogmatically and confidently, but just as a
description of his state of mind, his *pathos*.

24. "Everything Is Indeterminate"

Indeterminateness is a *pathos* of the intellect in accord with which we take   198
neither a negative nor an affirmative position on the matters of dogmatic
inquiry, that is, the non-evident. Whenever the Skeptic says "Everything is
indeterminate," he uses "is" in place of "appears to me to be," and with
"everything" he does not refer simply to all there is, but rather to the
Dogmatists' non-evident objects that are under his consideration; and by
"indeterminate" he means "not standing out as superior, as regards credibility and incredibility, among the things that are opposite or mutually
inconsistent." And just as the person who says "I'm walking around" is in   199
effect saying "I am walking around," so, according to us, the one who is
saying "Everything is indeterminate" means also "as relates to me" or "as
appears to me"; consequently, what is said comes down to this: "all the
matters of dogmatic inquiry that I have considered appear to me to be such
that not one of them seems to me superior, as regards credibility and incredibility, to anything inconsistent with it."

25. "Everything Is Non-apprehensible"

And we adopt a similar stance, too, when we say "Everything is non-   200
apprehensible." For we explain "everything" in the same way, and we
add "to me," so that what is said amounts to this: "All of the non-evident
matters of dogmatic inquiry that I have considered appear to me to be

non-apprehensible." This is not the assertion of one who is firmly maintaining that the things investigated by the Dogmatists are of such a nature as to be non-apprehensible, but rather of one who is reporting his own *pathos*, in accord with which he says: "I take it that up to now, because of the equipollence of the opposites, I have apprehended none of them; and consequently everything that is brought forward by way of refutation seems to me to be irrelevant to what we are reporting."

26. "I Am Non-apprehensive" and "I Do Not Apprehend"

201   Both of the slogans "I am non-apprehensive" and "I do not apprehend" express a personal *pathos*, in accord with which the Skeptic declines for the present to take an affirmative or negative position on any of the non-evident matters of inquiry, as is evident from what we have previously said about the other slogans.

27. "To Every Argument an Equal Argument Is Opposed"

202   When we say "To every argument an equal argument is opposed," by "every argument" we mean "every argument that has been considered by us," and we use "argument" not in its ordinary sense but for that which establishes something dogmatically, that is to say, concerning the non-evident, and which establishes it in any way at all, not necessarily by means of premises and conclusion. We say "equal" as regards credibility and the lack of it, and we use "opposed" in its common meaning of "conflicting"; and we tacitly
203   supply "as appears to me." Thus, when I say "To every argument an equal argument is opposed," I say in effect this: "for every argument that I have examined and that establishes something dogmatically, there appears to me to be opposed another argument that establishes something dogmatically and is equal to it as regards credibility and lack of credibility," so that the utterance of the statement is not dogmatic but is just a report of a human *pathos*, which is apparent to the person experiencing it.
204   But also some people state the slogan thus: "To every argument an equal argument is to be opposed," intending to give this admonition: "To every argument establishing something dogmatically let us oppose some conflicting argument that proceeds dogmatically and is equal to it as regards credibility and lack of credibility"; they are addressing the statement to the Skeptic, although they use the infinitive "to be opposed" in place of the
205   imperative "let us oppose." And they address this admonition to the Skeptic

lest he be tricked somehow by the Dogmatist into ceasing to raise questions about the arguments and through precipitancy should miss out on the *ataraxia* that appears to them and that they, as we mentioned before, think follows on suspension of judgment about everything.

Notes

1 Phenomena and noumena are, roughly, the objects of sense-experience and of thought respectively.
2 The capacity of the sceptic way to engender *ataraxia* is, of course, questionable. Some people, one might think, would end up in a state of neurotic uncertainty. One might wonder, too, if the goal of *ataraxia* is compatible with Sextus' insistence, in §1, that the sceptic is someone who continues to search for truth. For discussion of these and related issues, see M. F. Burnyeat, 'Can the sceptic live his scepticism?', in *Doubt and Dogmatism*, ed. M. Schofield et al., Oxford: Clarendon Press, 1980.

4 ▶ The Book of Chuang Tzu, Chapter 2

From The Book of Chuang Tzu, tr. M. Palmer. Harmondsworth: Penguin, 1996, pp. 8–20 [notes omitted]. Reprinted by permission of the publisher.

In the previous chapter we saw that, for Pyrrho and his followers, 'the sceptic way' was attractive primarily because it secured a good and tranquil life. In the Chinese tradition, where practical philosophy was always the main interest, questions about knowledge and its limits were similarly set within a broadly ethical context. Indeed, it is difficult to identify, within that tradition, a single sustained discussion of epistemological matters which is not tied to reflections on the good life. Certainly this ethical context sets what is, perhaps, the most famous Chinese discussion of the limits of knowledge, chapter 2 of *The Book of Chuang Tzu*, its 'most philosophically acute and challenging' chapter.[1]

Chuang Tzu (*c.*369–286 BCE) was the foremost architect of that tendency of thought we now know as Taoism. (Lao Tzu, 'author' of the best-known Taoist text, was almost certainly a legendary figure.) A central aspect of that tendency was rejection of the Confucian insistence on obedience to 'conventional' morality. In a previous volume in this series, *Ethics: The Classic Readings*, the selections from Chuang Tzu exhibit his hostility to convention, largely on the ground that it *was* just convention or artifice, and hence militated against the 'natural' life of 'the true man', one led in harmony with the *tao* (Way), the 'source' and 'sustainer' of the world. (Chuang Tzu practised what he preached. Offered a position at court, he turned it down with the remark that he preferred to enjoy himself in the mud rather than serve a ruler of a kingdom (ch. 32).)

It is in chapter 2 of his Book that Chuang Tzu makes the epistemological preparations for his attack on convention and artifice and, in so doing, 'substantially contributed to China's long tradition of scepticism'.[2] Unfortunately, his unsystematic, anecdotal style precludes confident interpretation of his overall

---

[1] Ewing Y. Chinn, 'Zhuangzi and relativistic scepticism', *Asian Philosophy*, 7, 1997, p. 207.
[2] Wing-Tsit Chan, *A Source Book in Chinese Philosophy*, Princeton, NJ: Princeton University Press, 1963, p. 188.

position. There is, however, general agreement that he is denying that any of our everyday judgements amount to knowledge of, or even warranted, rational belief about, reality – though in the Pyrrhonian manner, he is hesitant about the denial itself. 'Then does nothing know anything?' – 'How could I know that?'

It is not obvious, however, that Chuang Tzu should be classed as a sceptic. Two other possibilities are, first, that he was a 'mystic', for whom there can be genuine knowledge of reality (the *tao*), but only of an ineffable kind, and second, that he was a 'relativist', one who is not so much questioning whether our judgements 'fit' reality as denying sense to the notion of a reality beyond our merely conventional 'perspectives'.[3]

Be that as it may, Chuang Tzu certainly marshals a number of considerations designed to show that our everyday judgements do not constitute knowledge of reality (if such there be). Like Sextus Empiricus and Montaigne, he likes to assemble examples of seemingly irresolvable disagreements in judgement and taste, arguing that attempts to resolve them always presuppose some prior prejudice. He also deploys a somewhat strange version of 'the argument from dreaming'. 'I . . . dreamt that I was a butterfly . . . . But I could not tell, had I been Chuang Tzu dreaming I was a butterfly, or a butterfly dreaming I was now Chuang Tzu?'

But his most original and interesting argument revolves around the role of language and is prescient of both Nietzsche's 'perspectivism' and what, in our century, has been called 'linguistic relativism'. For Chuang Tzu, it seems, the languages we speak are simply convenient artifices, whose utility for purposes of communication need not and should not be taken to imply any correspondence between our statements and an independent reality. The distinctions we make among things are merely conventional and these things are what they are in virtue of how they are called. Unfortunately, we take these distinctions to be real ones and hence too seriously, like the monkeys in the anecdote told on p. 66 below. The true sage, recognizing that 'the great *tao* is not named' and something seamless, will confine himself to speaking for simple, practical purposes, eschewing 'speech which enables argument' by purporting to express knowledge of how things are.

Chapter 2: Working Everything Out Evenly

Master Chi of the Southern District sat leaning forward on his chair, staring up at Heaven and breathing steadily, as if in a trance, forgetful of all around him. Master Yen Cheng Yu stood beside him and said, 'What is it? Is it true that you can make the body like a shrivelled tree, the heart like

---

[3] See Chinn, 'Zhuangzi and relativistic scepticism', and Chad Hansen, *A Daoist Theory of Chinese Thought*, Oxford: Oxford University Press, 1992.

cold, dead ashes? Surely the man here now is not the same as the one who was here yesterday.'

Master Chi said, 'Yen, this is a good point to make, but do you really understand?

'I have lost myself, do you understand?
You hear the pipes of the people, but not the pipes of earth.
Even if you hear the pipes of earth, you don't hear the pipes of Heaven!'

'Please explain this,' said Master Yu.
Master Chi replied,

'The vast breath of the universe, this is called Wind.
Sometimes it is unmoving;
when it moves it makes the ten thousand openings resound
    dramatically.
Have you not heard it,
like a terrifying gale?
Mountains and forests are stormed by it,
great trees, a hundred spans round with dips and hollows,
are like noses, like mouths, like ears, like sockets,
like cups, like mortars, like pools, like gulleys;
sounding like a crashing wave, a whistling arrow, a screech;
    sucking, shouting, barking, wailing, moaning,
the winds ahead howling *yeeh*,
those behind crying *yooh*,
light breezes making gentle sounds,
while the typhoon creates a great din.
When the typhoon has passed, all goes quiet again.
Have you not witnessed this disturbance settle down again?'

Master Yu said, 'What you've just described are the notes of the earth, while the notes of humanity come from wind instruments, but you have said nothing about the notes of Heaven.'

'The role of these forces on all forms of living things is not the same,' said Master Chi. 'For each is different, using what they need to be, not influenced by any other force!'

*   *   *

True depth of understanding is wide and steady,
Shallow understanding is lazy and wandering,
Words of wisdom are precise and clear,
Foolish words are petty and mean.

When we sleep, our spirits roam the earth,
when awake our bodies are alert,
whatever we encounter captures us,
day by day our hearts are struggling.

Often simple,
often deep,
often intimate.

Minor troubles make them unsettled, anxious,
Major troubles are plain and simple.

They fly off like an arrow,
convinced that they know right from wrong;
it is like one who makes a sacred promise,
standing sure and true and on their way to victory.
They give way, like autumn and winter,
decaying away with the ebb and flow of each day;
it is like a stream of water, it cannot be brought back;
they stagnate, because they are like old blocked drains,
brought on by old age,
which makes their minds closed as if near death,
and there is nothing which can draw their hearts into the power
   of the yang[1] –
the life-giving light.

Joy and anger,
sadness and delight,
hope and disappointment;
faithlessness and certainty,
forcefulness and sloth,
eagerness and reticence,
like notes from an empty reed,
or mushrooms growing in dampness,
day and night follow each other before our very eyes and we
   have no idea why.

Enough, enough!
Morning and night exist,
we cannot know more about the Origin than this!

Without them, we don't exist,
Without us, they have no purpose.
This is close to our meaning,
but we cannot know what creates things to be thus.
It is as if they have a Supreme Guidance, but there is no way of
    grasping such a One.
He can certainly act, of that there is no doubt,
but I cannot see his body.
He has desires, but no body.
A hundred parts and nine orifices and six organs,
are parts that go to make up myself,
but is any part more noble than another?
You say I should treat all parts as equally noble:
But shouldn't I also treat some as better than other?
Don't they all serve me as well as each others?
If they are all servants, then aren't they all as bad as each other?
Or are there rulers amongst these servants?
There must be some Supreme Ruler who is over them all.
Though it is doubtful that you can find his true form,
and even if it were possible,
is it not meaningless to his true nature?
When someone is born in this body, doesn't life continue until
    death?
Either in conflict with others or in harmony with them,
we go through life like a runaway horse, unable to stop.
Working hard until the end of his life,
unable to appreciate any achievement,
worn out and incapable of resting,
isn't he a pathetic sight?
He may say, 'I'm still alive,' but so what?
When the body rots, so does the mind – is this not tragic?
Is this not ridiculous, or is it just me that is ridiculous and
    everyone else is sane?
If you allow your mind to guide you,
who then can be seen as being without a teacher?
Why is it thought that only the one who understands change and
    whose heart approves this can be the teacher?

Surely the fool is just the same.
But if you ignore your mind but insist you know right from
     wrong, you are like the saying,
'Today I set off for Yueh and arrived yesterday.'
This is to claim that what is not, is;
That what is not, does exist –
why, even the holy sage [emperor] Yu cannot understand this,
let alone poor old me!

*   *   *

Our words are not just hot air. Words work because they say something, but the problem is that, if we cannot define a word's meaning, it doesn't really say anything. Is it possible that there really is something here? Or does it really mean nothing? Is it possible to make a proper case for it being any different from the chirruping of chicks? How is it that we have the Tao so obscured that we have to distinguish between true and false? What has clouded our words so that we can have both what is and what is not? How can it be that the Tao goes off and is no longer? How can it be that words are found but are not understood? When the Tao is obscured by pettiness and the words are obscured by elaboration, then we end up having the 'this is, this is not' of the Confucians and Mohists, with what one of them calls reality being denied by the other, and what the other calls real disputed by the first. If we want to confound what they call right and confirm what they call wrong, we need to shed light on both of them.

Nothing exists which is not 'that', nothing exists which is not 'this'. I cannot look at something through someone else's eyes, I can only truly know something which I know. Therefore 'that' comes out of 'this' and 'this' arises from 'that'. That is why we say that 'that' and 'this' are born from each other, most definitely.

Compare birth with death, compare death with life; compare what is possible with what is not possible and compare what is not possible with what is possible; because there is, there is not, and because there is not, there is.

Thus it is that the sage does not go down this way, but sheds the light of Heaven upon such issues. This is also that and that is also this. The 'that' is on the one hand also 'this', and 'this' is on the other hand also 'that'. Does this mean he still has a this and that? Does this mean he does not have a this and that?

When 'this' and 'that' do not stand against each other, this is called the pivot of the Tao. This pivot provides the centre of the circle, which is without end, for it can react equally to that which is and to that which is not. This is why it is best to shed light on such issues. To use a finger to show that a finger is not a finger, is not really as good as using something that is not a finger to show that a finger is not a finger; to use a horse to show a horse is not a horse is not as good as using something other than a horse to show that a horse is not a horse. Heaven and Earth are as one as a finger is, and all of creation is as one as a horse is.

What is, is, what is not, is not.
The Tao is made because we walk it,
things become what they are called.
Why is this so? Surely because this is [called] so.
Why is this not so? Surely because this is not [called] so.
Everything has what is innate,
everything has what is necessary.
Nothing is not something,
nothing is not so.
Therefore, take a stalk of wheat and a pillar,
a leper or a beauty like Hsi-shih,
the great and the insecure,
the cunning and the odd:
all these are alike to the Tao.
In their difference is their completeness;
in their completeness is their difference.

Through the Tao they are all seen as one, regardless of their completeness or difference, by those who are capable of such extended vision. Such a person has no need for distinctions but follows the ordinary view. The ordinary view is firmly set on the ground of usefulness. The usefulness of something defines its use; the use is its flexibility; its flexibility is its essence and from this it comes to a stop. We stop but do not know why we stop, and this is called Tao.

To tax our spirits and our intellect in this way without realizing that everything is the same is called 'Three in the Morning'. And what is 'Three in the Morning'? A monkey trainer was giving out acorns and he said, 'In the morning I will give you each three acorns and in the evening you will get four.' The monkeys were very upset at this and so he said, 'All right, in the morning you will get four and in the evening, three.' This pleased the monkeys no end. His two statements were essentially the same, but got different reactions from the monkeys. He gained what he wanted by his skill. So it is with the sage, who manages to harmonize right and wrong and is content to abide by the Natural Equality of Heaven. This is called walking two roads.

*   *   *

The men of old understood a great deal. How much?

In the beginning they did not know that anything existed; this is virtually perfect knowledge, for nothing can be added. Later, they knew that some things existed but they did not distinguish between them. Next came those who distinguished between things, but did not judge things as 'being' or 'not being'. It was when judgements were made that the Tao was damaged, and because the Tao was damaged, love became complete. Is anything complete or damaged? Is anything not complete or damaged? There is completion and damage, just as Chao Wen played the lute. There is nothing which is complete or damaged, just as Chao Wen did not play the lute.

> Chao Wen played the lute,
> Shih Kuang conducted,
> Hui Tzu debated.

The understanding of these three was almost perfect and they followed it to the end of their years. They cared about this because it was different, and they wanted to teach others about it. But it was not possible to make things clear, though they tried to make things simple. They ended up instead with the folly of the 'hard' and the 'white'.[2]

Wen's son ended up continuing to play Wen's lute and achieved nothing for himself. If someone like this is called complete, then am I not also? And if someone like this is called incomplete, then surely neither I nor anyone else has ever been complete. Also, by the light shining out of chaos, the sage is guided; he does not make use of distinctions but is led on by the light.

*   *   *

Now, however, I have something to say. Do I know whether this is in the same sort of category as what is said by others? I don't know. At one level, what I say is not the same. At another level, it most definitely is, and there is no difference between what I say and what others say. Whatever the case, let me try and tell you what I mean.

There is the beginning; there is not as yet any beginning of the beginning; there is not as yet beginning not to be a beginning of the beginning. There is what is, and there is what is not, and it is not easy to say whether what is not, is not; or whether what is, is.

I have just made a statement, yet I do not know whether what I said has been real in what I said or not really said.

Under Heaven there is nothing greater than the tip of a hair, but Mount Tai is smaller; there is no one older than a dead child, yet Peng Tsu [who supposedly lived for centuries] died young.

Heaven and Earth and I were born at the same time, and all life and I are one.

As all life is one, what need is there for words? Yet I have just said all life is one, so I have already spoken, haven't I? One plus one equals two, two plus one equals three. To go on from here would take us beyond the understanding of even a skilled accountant, let alone the ordinary people. If going from 'no-thing' to 'some-thing' we get to three, just think how much further we would have to go if we went from 'some-thing' to something!

Don't even start, let's just stay put.

The great Tao has no beginning, and words have changed their meaning from the beginning, but because of the idea of a 'this is' there came to be limitations. I want to say something about these limitations. There is right and left, relationships and their consequences, divisions and disagreements, emulations and contentions. These are known as the eight Virtues.

The sage will not speak of what is beyond the boundaries of the universe – though he will not deny it either. What is within the universe, he says something about but does not pronounce upon. Concerning the record of the past actions of the kings in the *Spring and Autumn Annals*, the sage discusses but does not judge. When something is divided, something is not divided; when there is disagreement there are things not disagreed about.

You ask, what does this mean? The sage encompasses everything, while ordinary people just argue about things. This is why I say that disagreement means you do not understand at all.

The great Way is not named,
the great disagreement is unspoken,
great benevolence is not benevolent,
great modesty is not humble,
great courage is not violent.
The Tao that is clear is not the Tao,
speech which enables argument is not worthy,
benevolence which is ever present does not achieve its goal,
modesty if flouted, fails,
courage that is violent is pointless.

These five are fine: they are, as it were, rounded. But if they lose this they can become awkward. This is why the one who knows how to stop at what he knows is best. Who knows the argument that needs no words, and the Tao that cannot be named? To those who do, this is called the Treasury of Heaven. Pour into it and it is never full; empty it and it is never empty. We do not know where it comes from originally, and this is called our Guiding Light.

*   *   *

In the olden days Yao said to Shun [two emperors], 'I want to attack Tsung, Kuai and Hsu Ao. I have wanted to do this since I became king. What do you think?'

Shun replied, 'These three rulers are just primitives living in the backwoods – why can't you just forget them? In ancient times, ten suns rose and all life was illuminated. But how much more does Virtue illuminate life than even these suns!'

*   *   *

Yeh Chueh said to Wang Ni, 'Do you know, Master, what everything agrees upon?'

'How can I possibly know?' said Wang Ni.

'Do you know, Master, what you do not know?'

'How can I know?' he replied.

'Then does nothing know anything?'

'How could I know that?' said Wang Ni. 'Nevertheless, I want to try and say something. How can I know that what I say I know is not actually what I don't know? Likewise, how can I know that what I think I don't know is not really what I do know? I want to put some questions to you:

'If someone sleeps in a damp place, he will ache all over and he will be half paralysed, but is it the same for an eel? If someone climbs a tree, he will be frightened and shaking, but is it so for a monkey? Out of these three, which is wisest about where to live?

'Humans eat meat, deer consume grass, centipedes devour snakes and owls and crows enjoy mice. Of these four, which has the best taste?

'Monkeys mate with each other, deer go with deer. People said that Mao Chiang and Li Chi were the most beautiful women in the world, but fish seeing them dived away, birds took off into the air and deer ran off. Of these four, who really knows true beauty? As I see it, benevolence and righteousness, also the ways of right and wrong, are completely interwoven. I do not think I can know the difference between them!'

Yeh Chueh said: 'Master, if you do not know the difference between that which is good and that which is harmful, does this mean the perfect man is also without such knowledge?'

'The perfect man is pure spirit,' replied Wang Ni. 'He does not feel the heat of the burning deserts nor the cold of the vast waters. He is not frightened by the lightning which can split open mountains, nor by the storms that can whip up the seas. Such a person rides the clouds and mounts upon the sun and moon, and wanders across and beyond the four seas. Neither death nor life concern him, nor is he interested in what is good or bad!'

*   *   *

Chu Chiao Tzu asked Chang Wu Tzu,

'I have heard from the Master [Confucius]
that the sage does not labour at anything,
does not look for advantage,
does not act benevolently,
does not harm,
does not pursue the Tao;
He speaks without speaking,
and does not speak when he speaks,
and looks beyond the confines of this dusty world.

'The Master sees all this as an endless stream of words, but to me they are like the words of the mysterious Tao. Master, what do you think?'

Chang Wu Tzu said, 'Such a saying as this would have confused even the Yellow Emperor [a legendary sage], so how could Confucius be able to understand them! However, you are getting ahead of yourself, counting your chickens before your eggs are hatched and looking at the bowl, imagining the roasted fowl. I will try to speak to you in a random way, so you listen to me likewise. How can the wise one sit beside the sun and moon and embrace the universe? Because he brings all things together in harmony, he rejects difference and confusion and ignores status and power. While ordinary people rush busily around, the sage seems stupid and ignorant, but to him all life is one and united. All life is simply what it is and all appear to him to be doing what they rightly should.

'How do I know that the love of life is not a delusion? Or that the fear of death is not like a young person running away from home and unable to find his way back? The Lady Li Chi was the daughter of a border warden, Ai. When the state of Chin captured her, she wept until she had drenched her robes; then she came to the King's palace, shared the King's bed, ate his food, and repented of her tears. How do I know whether the dead now repent for their former clinging to life?

'Come the morning, those who dream of the drunken feast may weep and moan; when the morning comes, those who dream of weeping and moaning go hunting in the fields. When they dream, they don't know it is a dream. Indeed, in their dreams they may think they are interpreting dreams, only when they awake do they know it was a dream. Eventually there comes the day of reckoning and awakening, and then we shall know that it was all a great dream. Only fools think that they are now awake and that they really know what is going on, playing the prince and then playing the servant. What fools! The Master and you are both living in a dream. When I say a dream, I am also dreaming. This very saying is a deception. If after ten thousand years we could once meet a truly great sage, one who understands, it would seem as if it had only been a morning.

'Imagine that you and I have a disagreement, and you get the better of me, rather than me getting the better of you, does this mean that you are automatically right and I am automatically wrong? Suppose I get the better of you, does it follow that I am automatically right and you are therefore wrong? Is it really that one of us is right and the other wrong? Or are we both right and both wrong? Neither you nor I can really know and other people are even more in the dark. So who can we ask to give us the right answer? Should you ask someone who thinks you are right? But how then can that person give a fair answer? Should we ask someone who thinks I am right? But then if he agrees with me, how can he make a fair judgement? Then again, should we ask someone who agrees with both of us? But again, if he agrees with both of us, how can he make a true judgement? Should we ask someone who disagrees with both of us? But here again, if he disagrees with both of us, how can he make an honest judgement? It is clear that neither you, I nor anyone else can make decisions like this amongst ourselves. So should we wait for someone else to turn up?

'To wait for one voice to bring it all together is as pointless as waiting for no one. Bring all things together under the Equality of Heaven, allow their process of change to go on unimpeded, and learn to grow old. What do I mean by bringing everything together under the Equality of Heaven? With regard to what is right and wrong, I say not being is being and being is not being. But let us not get caught up in discussing this. Forget about life, forget about worrying about right and wrong. Plunge into the unknown and the endless and find your place there!'

*   *   *

The Outline said to the Shadow, 'First you are on the move, then you are standing still; you sit down and then you stand up. Why can't you make up your mind?'

Shadow replied, 'Do I have to look to something else to be what I am? Does this something else itself not have to rely upon yet another something? Do I have to depend upon the scales of a snake or the wings of a cicada? How can I tell how things are? How can I tell how things are not?'

Once upon a time, I, Chuang Tzu, dreamt that I was a butterfly, flitting around and enjoying myself. I had no idea I was Chuang Tzu. Then suddenly I woke up and was Chuang Tzu again. But I could not tell, had I been Chuang Tzu dreaming I was a butterfly, or a butterfly dreaming I was now Chuang Tzu? However, there must be some sort of difference between Chuang Tzu and a butterfly! We call this the transformation of things.

Notes

1 One of the famous polarity of *yin* and *yang*, two opposed, but interdependent, principles – 'dark', 'feminine', 'hidden' *versus* 'bright', 'masculine', 'open' – whose balance sustains the universe.
2 A reference to Chuang Tzu's friend and intellectual sparring partner, Hui Tzu's, penchant for discussing abstract issues about the existence and identity of universals, such as 'hardness' and 'whiteness'.

The Nyāya-Sūtras, from Book I, Chapter 1 and Book II, Chapter 1, with Vātsyāyana's Commentary

From *The Nyāya-Sūtras of Gotama*, tr. S. C. Vidyabhusana, ed. N. Sinha. Motilal Banarsidass: Delhi, 1981, pp. 1–6, 32, 34–7, 48–9, 232–7, 248–51, 255–6 [notes and some passages omitted; bracketed commentary is the editor's]; reprinted by permission of the publisher.

In contrast to the Chinese philosophical tradition, epistemological issues represented a central concern of the Indian one. During a remarkably fertile period from around 500 BCE to 1000 CE, thinkers belonging to the many Indian 'schools' (*darśanas*) formulated and debated competing positions on almost every epistemological question familiar in modern Western philosophy. Several of those positions, indeed, almost exactly prefigure ones later adopted by Western epistemologists. In the theory of perception, for example, positions closely akin to Berkeley's idealism, phenomenalism, and direct and indirect realism all had their champions and critics.

As the opening sections of the *Nyāya-Sūtras* ('logical sayings', roughly) indicate, however, this epistemological focus was closely related to a practical purpose, albeit one of a very different kind from that which informed the much scantier Chinese discussions of knowledge. Common to all the Indian Schools – whether 'orthodox' (in virtue of accepting the authority of Vedic scripture) or 'unorthodox' – was a soteriological purpose of gaining knowledge, and hence of articulating an understanding of what truly counts as knowledge. The purpose was 'release' from a cycle of rebirth, from a world of 'suffering', through dispelling the ignorance (*avidyā*) which binds men and women to it. Western epistemologists who do not share such soteriological concerns should not be put off for, as the bulk of the *Nyāya-Sūtras* demonstrates, these concerns barely intrude once the discussions of knowledge, reason, doubt, evidence etc. are underway. Anyway, one should recall that soteriological concerns also inspired the epistemological interests of important figures in the Western tradition, including St Augustine and Descartes.

The primary topic of Indian epistemological debate was the *pramāṇas*. Usually translated as 'means of knowledge (or cognition)', the term is triply ambiguous, referring at once to the causally effective instruments for acquiring knowledge, the ways of proving things and (most importantly) the authoritative grounds on which to make knowledge-claims.[1] Two main questions were raised about the *pramāṇas*. First, assuming that there *are* such 'means of knowledge', what are they? Answers varied widely, but perhaps the most enduring is the one offered by the Nyāya School, according to which there are four irreducible 'means' – perception, inference, comparison (or analogy) and 'word' (or verbal testimony). These last two deserve comment. The thoughts seem to be that (1) a capacity for recognizing similarities is required for knowledge gained through perception and inductive inference to be extended to novel cases and (2) the reliability of some people, and so their testimony, is a *sui generis* source of knowledge, irreducible to inductive warrant. This second thought is especially important for a school like the Nyāya which, as 'orthodox', accepts the 'word' of the Vedic scriptures. It is, perhaps, the Indian attention to 'word' (*śabda*) which most distinguishes that tradition from a Western one in which, until very recently, the epistemic role of testimony has been strangely neglected.[2]

The second main question about the *pramāṇas* was how they might be validated as legitimate grounds for knowledge-claims. In Book II, ch.1, §§17 ff, the author of the Sūtras considers an objection to the effect that any attempt to validate them must either be circular or involve an infinite regress. (In fact, as we will see in chapter 6 below, just such an objection was raised by the Buddhist philosopher Nāgārjuna.) Whether or not the reply to this criticism, in terms of the 'self-illuminating' character of the *pramāṇas*, is satisfying, readers must judge for themselves.

The Nyāya School is of great antiquity and the life of the supposed author of the *Nyāya-Sūtras*, Akṣapāda Gotama, is cloudy. He has been placed anywhere between 400 BCE and 100 CE. The most important commentator on the Sūtras, Vātsyāyana, can be located rather more definitely, around 300 CE. His main commentary, the *Nyāyabhāsya*, is not simply exegesis and interpretation of the Sūtras since, at crucial places, it presents different messages from the original – for example, on the question of the 'self-illuminating' character of the *pramāṇas*.

In this chapter, I have selected the general statement of the *pramāṇas* theory from Book I of the Sūtras and the attempt, in Book II, to respond to various objections to that theory. I have included some of the editor's explanatory comments and following the selections from Books I and II are the corresponding sections from Vātsyāyana's commentary.[3]

[1] See Bimal Krishna Matilal, *Perception: An Essay on Classical Indian Theories of Knowledge*, Oxford: Clarendon Press, 1991, pp. 35ff.
[2] J. N. Mohanty, 'Indian epistemology', in *A Companion to Epistemology*, ed. J. Dancy and E. Sosa, Oxford: Blackwell, 1992. See also Ernest Sosa, 'Testimony', in the same volume.
[3] Detailed accounts of Nyāya epistemology may be found in Matilal, *Perception*, J. N. Mohanty, *Reason and Tradition in Indian Thought*, Oxford: Clarendon Press, 1992, and S. Radhakrishnan, *Indian Philosophy*, Vol. 2, Delhi: Oxford University Press, 1989.

The Nyāya-Sūtras

Book I, Chapter I

1. **Supreme felicity** is attained by the knowledge about the true nature of the sixteen categories, [such as] means of right knowledge (pramāṇa), object of right knowledge (prameya), doubt (saṃśaya), and purpose (prayojana). . . .

> *Knowledge about the true nature of the sixteen categories* means true knowledge by the 'enunciation,' 'definition' and 'critical examination' of the categories. . . . The attainment of supreme felicity is preceded by the knowledge of four things, *viz.*, (1) that which is fit to be abandoned (*viz.*, pain), (2) that which produces what is fit to be abandoned (*viz.*, misapprehension, etc.), (3) complete destruction of what is fit to be abandoned and (4) the means of destroying what is fit to be abandoned (*viz.*, true knowledge).

2. Pain, birth, activity, faults and misapprehension – on the successive annihilation of these in the reverse order, there follows **release**.

> Misapprehension, faults, activity, birth and pain – these in their uninterrupted course constitute the "world." Release, which consists in the soul's getting rid of the world, is the condition of supreme felicity marked by perfect tranquillity and not tainted by any defilement. A person, by the true knowledge of the sixteen categories, is able to remove his misapprehensions. When this is done, his faults, *viz.*, affection, aversion and stupidity, disappear. He is then no longer subject to any activity and is consequently freed from transmigration and pains. This is the way in which his release is effected and supreme felicity secured.

3. Perception, inference, comparison and word (verbal testimony – these are the **means of right knowledge**. . . .

4. **Perception** is that knowledge which arises from the contact of a sense with its object, and which is determinate, unnameable and non-erratic.

> *Determinate* – This epithet distinguishes perception from indeterminate knowledge; as, for instance, a man looking from a distance cannot ascertain whether there is smoke or dust.
> *Unnameable* – Signifies that the knowledge of a thing derived through perception has no connection with the name which the thing bears.[1]

Non-erratic – In summer the sun's rays coming in contact with earthly heat quiver and appear to the eyes of men as water. The knowledge of water derived in this way is not perception. To eliminate such cases the epithet non-erratic has been used. . . .

5.   **Inference** is knowledge which is preceded by perception, and is of three kinds, *viz.*, a priori, a posteriori and 'commonly seen.'

A priori is the knowledge of effect derived from the perception of its cause, *e.g.*, one seeing clouds infers that there will be rain.

A posteriori is the knowledge of cause derived from the perception of its effects, *e.g.*, one seeing a river swollen infers that there was rain.

'*Commonly seen*' is the knowledge of one thing derived from the perception of another thing with which it is commonly seen, *e.g.*, one seeing a beast possessing horns, infers that it possesses also a tail, or one seeing smoke on a hill infers that there is fire on it.

6.   **Comparison** is the knowledge of a thing through its similarity to another thing previously well known.

A man, hearing from a forester that a *bos gavaeus* is like a cow, resorts to a forest where he sees an animal like a cow. Having recollected what he heard he institutes a comparison, by which he arrives at the conviction that the animal which he sees is *bos gavaeus*. This is knowledge derived through comparison Some hold that comparison is not a separate means of knowledge, for when one notices the likeness of a cow in a strange animal one really performs an act of perception. In reply, it is urged that we cannot deny comparison as a separate means of knowledge, for how does otherwise the name *bos gavaeus* signify the general notion of the animal called *bos gavaeus*? That the name *bos gavaeus* signifies one and all members of the *bos gavaeus* class is not a result of perception, but the consequence of a distinct knowledge, called comparison.

7.   **Word (verbal testimony)** is the instructive assertion of a reliable person.

A reliable person is one . . . who as an expert in a certain matter is willing to communicate his experiences of it.

[Suppose a young man coming to the side of a river cannot ascertain whether the river is fordable or not, and immediately an old experienced man of the locality, who has no enmity against him, comes and tells him that the river is easily fordable: the word of the old man is to be accepted as a means of right knowledge, called verbal testimony].

8.   It is of two kinds, *viz.*, that which refers to *matter which is seen*, and that which refers to *matter which is not seen*.

> The first kind involves matter which can be actually verified. Though we are incapable of verifying the matter involved in the second kind, we can somehow ascertain it by means of inference.
>
> [*Matter which is seen, e.g.*, a physician's assertion that physical strength is gained by taking butter].
>
> [*Matter which is not seen, e.g.*, a religious teacher's assertion that one conquers heaven by performing horse-sacrifices].

9.   Soul, body, senses, objects of sense, intellect, mind, activity, fault, transmigration, fruit, pain and release – are the **objects of right knowledge**. . . .[2]

Vātsyāyana's Commentary on Book I, Chapter 1

. . . False knowledge, faults, activity, birth and pain, ever following without interruption, constitute saṃsāra or the wheel of life. Knowledge of truth removes false knowledge. On the removal of false knowledge faults disappear. On the disappearance of faults activity ceases. On the cessation of activity birth does not take place. In the absence of birth there is no pain. In the absence of pain absolute success, *i.e.* release, which is the supreme good, is attained.

Knowledge of truth is the opposite of the false notions mentioned above. And therefore just as food mixed with honey and poison is unacceptable so is also pleasure tainted with pain.

The method of the Nyāya-Sūtras is threefold: enumeration, definition and examination. First is given the division of the subject enumerated, and then the definition of each division. Next is given the subdivision of the subject enumerated and defined.

The subdivisions of Pramāṇa are Pratyakṣa (perception), Anumāna (inference), Upamāna (comparison) and Śabda (word).

Pratyakṣa is the vṛtti (modification) of each sense according to each object appropriate to it. Vṛtti is proximity or knowledge. Whenever there is proximity there is knowledge of reality. The consequence of knowledge is the idea of avoidance or acquisition or indifference.

Anumāna is the knowledge of the object after the observation of the previously known mark.

Upamāna is the knowledge of an object by means of its resemblance to a known object.

Śabda is that by which an object is designated, *i.e.*, made known as such and such.

The four pramāṇas sometimes operate conjointly and sometimes individually according to the nature of the prameya. Thus: the existence of the soul is known from testimony, by inference, and by perception through a particular conjunction of the internal organ with the soul brought about by the power of meditation of a Yogī. In the case of heaven there can be neither the observation of a mark nor perception. When the rumbling of a cloud is heard, the cloud is not an object of perception or of testimony, but of inference from the sound. In the case of one's own hand there is neither inference nor testimony.

Pramiti, knowledge, which is thus the result of the pramāṇas, ultimately rests on perception. The object of enquiry which is obtained from testimony, is sought to be known by means of the observation of the mark; that which is inferred from the observation of the mark, is sought to be seen by perception; and when the object is realised in perception the enquiry ceases.

Definition of Pramāṇas: Sūtras 3–8

Gotama now proceeds to give the definition of each of the four pramāṇas.

Perception is the knowledge which is produced from the contact of the sense with the object. The contact of the soul with the mind and of the mind with the sense is not mentioned, because it is common to cognitions produced by all the pramāṇas. The definition only gives the specific cause of perceptual knowledge. The knowledge of the object produced from the contact of the sense with the object takes the form of "colour," "taste," etc. The words, colour, taste, etc. are the names of the viṣayas or contents of the knowledge. But the name-words have no operation at the time of the production of the knowledge of the object; they operate only when use has to be made of the knowledge. Hence the knowledge of the object produced from the contact of the sense with the object is independent of words. Again, mirage is also produced from the contact of the sense with the object. But it is not perception, because it is erratic, unreal. Perceptual knowledge must be unerring, real. For the same reason doubt or uncertain knowledge, *e.g.* be that a post or a man, a cloud of smoke or of dust, is not perceptual knowledge. Moreover, the latter must be discrete, specific, particular, and not general such as is produced from the contact of the soul with the mind alone.

The soul, etc. as well as pleasure, etc. are also objects of perception. But their perception is not produced from the contact of the sense with the object.

Manas, the mind, is a sense, but it has been separately mentioned because of its distinctive character. The senses are constituted by the elements, are restricted each to its own province, and possess attributes. The mind, on the other hand, is not constituted by the elements, and is all-extensive and without attribute. Hence it is said that perceptual knowledge of the soul, etc., which is produced from a particular conjunction of the soul and the mind, is not produced from the contact of the sense with the object. . . .

Inference is the knowledge the antecedents of which are the observation of the connection between the mark and the thing marked, and the observation of the mark (liṅga, sign). Recollection of the mark follows from the observation of the mark and the thing marked as connected. By means of recollection and the observation of the mark an unperceived object is inferred.

Inference of succession is of three kinds: (1) from cause to effect, (2) from effect to cause, and (3) from change of position, as, *e.g.*, the inference of the movement of the sun from its change of position in the sky. Inference of co-existence is as of the fire by smoke; that is, when two objects have been previously known as co-existent, the presence of one, though not perceived, is inferred from the presence of the other. Inference also takes place by the method of exhaustion or residue. Again, where the connection of the mark and the thing marked is not an object of perception, inference of the thing marked which is unperceived, may yet take place through the resemblance of the mark to some other object *e.g.*, the inference of the soul by means of desire, etc.; desire, etc. are attributes, attributes reside in substances, the substance in which desire, etc. reside, is the soul.

The sphere of perception is the present; that of inference is the present, past and future.

Comparison makes an object known through its resemblance to a known object, *e.g.* as the cow so the *bos gavaeus*. Comparison subserves perception. It enables one to know an object designated by a particular name.

Testimony is the direction of an Āpta, *i.e.* of one, be he a seer or a man of culture or a savage, who possesses true knowledge and is truthful. The object of testimony may be of this world or of the other world. The testimony of common people is confined to the things of this world; the testimony of seers embraces things of the other world also. Both kinds of testimony are pramāṇa: the former is based on actual experience; the latter, on inference.

It is by means of these four pramāṇas and not otherwise, that the affairs of gods, men and lower animals are conducted.

Definition of Prameya *(knowable):* Sūtra 9

The pramāṇas make known the soul, the body, the senses, object, cognition, the mind, activity, faults, re-birth, the fruit, pain and release. The soul is the seer of all, the experience of all, the all-knower, the all-reacher. The body is the field of its experience. The senses are the instruments of its experience. The objects of the senses are the things to be experienced. The experience is cognition. The senses do not extend to all objects. That which embraces all objects is the inner sense, the mind. Activity and faults are the causes which accomplish the soul's experiences of the body, the senses, the objects, cognition and pleasure. This body is neither its first nor its last. There is no beginning of its past bodies. Its future bodies will end only when release is attained. This is re-birth. The fruit is the action of pleasure and pain with their causes on the soul. Pain is a constant companion of pleasure and enters as an element in its experience. For this reason, and not to ignore the experience of pleasure as an agreeable feeling, pleasure has not been separately mentioned. Release is the negation of all possibility of births and deaths, the total annihilation of all pain. It is the final fruit of a process of self-culture of which the successive stages are withdrawal from the world and concentration upon the self, meditation, thoughtfulness and dispassion.

There are innumerable prameyas such as substance, attribute, action, genus, species, combination and their varieties. In the Nyāya-Sūtras twelve prameyas have been specially taught, because knowledge of the truth about them leads to release, while false knowledge about them leads to the stream of births and deaths. . . .

The Nyāya-Sūtras

Book II, Chapter 1

. . . 69.   Perception and other means of knowledge, says an objector, are invalid, as they are impossible at all the three times. – 8.

> According to the objector, perception is impossible at the present, past and future times, or, in other words, perception can neither be prior to, nor posterior to, nor simultaneous with, the objects of sense.[3]

...73.   In reply, it is stated that if perception and other means of right knowledge are impossible, the denial of them is also impossible. – 12.

Owing to absence of the matter to be denied, the denial is inoperative.

74.   Moreover, the denial itself cannot be established, if you deny all means of right knowledge. – 13.

If you are to establish anything (*e.g.*, denial), you can do so only by one or more of the means of right knowledge, *viz.*, perception, inference, comparison, etc. If you deny them, there will be left nothing which will lead you to the establishment of the thing. Hence you will not be able to establish the denial itself.[4]

75.   If you say that your denial is based on a certain means of right knowledge, you do there by acknowledge the validity of the means. – 14.

Suppose you deny a thing, because it is not perceived. You do thereby acknowledge that perception is a means of right knowledge. Similarly, inference, etc., are also to be acknowledged as means of right knowledge.

76.   The means of right knowledge cannot, therefore, be denied. They are established in the manner that a drum is proved by its sound. – 15. . . .

77.   The character of an object of right knowledge resembles that of a balance by which a thing is weighed. – 16.

Just as a balance is an instrument for measuring weight, but is a measured object when it is itself weighed in another balance, so the senses, etc., are said to be instruments of right knowledge from one point of view, and objects of right knowledge from another point of view. The eye, for instance, is an instrument of perception as well as an object of perception. So also the means of right knowledge may, if occasion arises, be also regarded as objects of right knowledge.

78.   If an object of right knowledge, continues the objector, is to be established by a means of right knowledge, this latter needs also to be established by another means of right knowledge. – 17.

The objection stands thus: –
You say that an object of right knowledge is to be established by a means of right knowledge. I admit this, and ask how you establish the means of right knowledge itself. Since a means of right knowledge may also be regarded as

an object of right knowledge, you are required to establish the so-called means of right knowledge by another means of right knowledge, and so on.

79.   Or, he continues, if a means of right knowledge does not require another means of right knowledge for its establishment, let an object of right knowledge be also established without any means of right knowledge. – 18.

A means of right knowledge stands in the same category as an object of right knowledge, if you are to establish either of them. If the means of right knowledge is accepted as self-established, the object of right knowledge must also, according to the objector, be accepted as self-established. In such a contingency perception, inference, etc., will be superfluous.

80.   It is not so: the means of right knowledge are established like the illumination of a lamp. – 19.

A lamp illumines a jar and our eye illumines the lamp. Though it is sometimes the lamp, and sometimes the eye, that illumines, you are bound to admit a general notion of illuminator. Similarly, you must admit a general notion of the means of right knowledge as distinguished from that of the objects of right knowledge. The means will not, of course, be regarded as such when included under the category of an object.

[The aphorism is also interpreted as follows: – Just as a lamp illumines itself and the other objects, the means of right knowledge establish themselves and the objects of right knowledge. Hence perception establishes itself and the objects of sense]. . . .

. . . 110.   **Verbal testimony,** say some, is inference, because the object revealed by it is not perceived but inferred. – 49.

Inference gives us the knowledge of an unperceived object, through the knowledge of an object which is perceived. Similarly, verbal testimony enables us to acquire the knowledge of an unperceived object, through the knowledge of a word which is perceived. The verbal testimony is, therefore, supposed by some to be inference, as the object revealed by both is unperceived.

111.   In respect of perceptibility the two cases are not, continues the objector, different. – 50.

In inference as well as in verbal testimony we pass to an unperceived object through an object which is perceived. In respect of perceptibility of the object through which we pass, the inference does not, continues the objector, differ from the verbal testimony.

112.   There is, moreover, adds the objector, the same connection. –
51.

> Just as in inference there is a certain connection between a sign (*e.g.* smoke)
> and the thing signified by it (*e.g.*, fire), so in verbal testimony there is con-
> nection between a word and the object signified by it. So inference, says the
> objector, is not different from verbal testimony.

113.   In reply, we say that there is reliance on the matter signified by a
word, because the word has been used by a reliable person. – 52.

> In reference to the objections raised in aphorisms 49 and 50, we say that we
> rely on unseen matter, not simply because it is signified by words, but be-
> cause they are spoken by a reliable person. There are, some say, paradise,
> nymphs, . . . seven islands, ocean human settlements, etc. We accept them as
> realities, not because they are known through words, but because they are
> spoken of by persons who are reliable. Hence verbal testimony is not infer-
> ence. The two agree in conveying knowledge of an object through its sign,
> but the sign in one is different from the sign in the other. In the case of
> verbal testimony, the special point is to decide whether the sign (word) comes
> from a reliable person. . . .

Vātsyāyana's Commentary on Book II, Chapter I

The Pramāṇas *in General:* Sūtras 8, 12–19

Some thinkers maintain that Perception, Inference, Comparison and Word
are not pramāṇas (sources of knowledge) because it cannot be shown that
they exist before, after, or along with, the prameyas (objects of knowledge). If Perception, *e.g.* cognition of smell, etc. by the senses, exists as a
pramāṇa before the existence of the smell, etc., then the definition of Perception as cognition produced from the contact of the senses and objects
does not hold good. On the other hand, if Perception as a pramāṇa comes
after the cognition of the prameya, then it is useless as the prameya has
already been otherwise cognised. Lastly, if the pramāṇas co-exist with the
prameyas then there would be simultaneity of several cognitions and the
inference of the mind by the non-simultaneity of cognitions would be de-
molished.

To the above objection, we reply as follows:

The fallacy of the objector's reasoning lies in this that he has distributed
the pramāṇas, and has compounded the prameyas, in respect of time. The

prameyas (like the pramāṇas) do come some before, some after, and some along with, the pramāṇas. Thus, the sun's rays appear before their effect, the blooming of the lotus; a lamp which illumines an object in a dark room comes after the object; where the existence of fire is inferred by the existence of the smoke the cause and object of cognition appear at the same time. There is therefore no hard and fast rule as to the relative position of the pramāṇas and the prameyas in time. Moreover, pramāṇa and prameya are correlative terms as the cause and the object of cognition. Where the pramāṇa follows the prameya the correlation still exists, as a "cook" is always a cook even when he is not actually cooking.

Then, what does the objection establish? Is it the negation of the existence of the pramāṇas or the knowledge of their non-existence? It cannot be the former because when you proceed to negate their existence you thereby admit their existence, for what is non-existent cannot be negated. It cannot be the latter, because your very argument becomes a pramāṇa as it makes known the non-existence of the pramāṇas, Perception, etc.

The reason advanced by the objector again can be turned equally against himself. The reason is "non-existence in the past, future and present." The negation cannot precede the thing to be negated, *i.e.* the pramāṇas, because there is then nothing to be negated. If it follows, then in the absence of the negation, the pramāṇas cannot be called the thing to be negated. If it co-exists with the pramāṇas, then the existence of the thing to be negated being admitted the negation becomes useless.

Again, the opponent's reasoning is invalid if he cannot cite a familiar instance in support of the reason. If he cites a familiar instance then this being an object of perception, Perception as a pramāṇa is admitted by him and his negation of all pramāṇas falls to the ground. The reason thus becomes what is known as the fallacy of the contradictory reason.

Further, we have already shown that in the reasoning of five members all the pramāṇas are combined. The opponent cannot say that the pramāṇas are valid in his reasoning and not in the reasoning of others.

The reason, "non-existence in the past, future and present," advanced by the opponent, does not also stand scrutiny. For pramāṇas do operate subsequently as when the existence of a flute is inferred by its tune.

The pramāṇas are thus established. Pramāṇa and prameya are, however, correlative terms. Whatever is the cause of cognition is pramāṇa; whatever is the object of cognition is prameya. When the nature, character and strength of a pramāṇa is under examination it is a prameya, just as scales and weights by which things are measured may themselves be objects of measurement. Thus the soul, being the object of cognition, is a prameya (knowable); as it is an independent agent in the act of cognition, it is the knower. Cognition, being the cause of apprehension, is pramāṇa; as an object of apprehension, it is a prameya. Where it is neither pramāṇa nor a prameya it is pramiti (knowledge).

Now, admitting all this, asks the opponent, are the pramāṇas, Perception, etc., established by other pramāṇas or are they independent of any pramāṇa? Our answer is that to admit the need of other pramāṇas would entail infinite regression which is illogical, while to say that the pramāṇas do not stand in need of establishment would imply that the soul and other prameyas also do not require to be established and that the pramāṇas themselves are futile. Our reply therefore is that just as a lamp which is a cause of perception is itself made known by the contact of the eye which is also a cause of perception, in other words, just as Perception is the pramāṇa of Perception, so the pramāṇas, Perception, etc., are established by themselves mutually. It is not necessary that pramāṇa and prameya should belong to different classes of objects. It is seen that the soul knows itself by itself in such cases as "I feel pleasure, I feel pain." So also is the mind inferred by the mind, non-simultaneity of heterogeneous cognitions being the mark of its inference. Moreover, nothing is known to exist which cannot be cognised by the four pramāṇas. There is therefore no reason to assume other pramāṇas.

Some are of opinion that just as a lamp reveals itself as well an object without the aid of another lamp so the pramāṇas reveal themselves as well as their objects and do not require the aid of other pramāṇas. This view cannot be accepted.[5] For there are objects such as a pot which do not reveal themselves but require pramāṇas. Is there any special reason to account for the difference in the two cases? If there is no such reason, the example cited leads to no conclusion but stands by itself. If there is such a reason then the example presents a special case and does not establish a general rule.

Of the Word in General: Sūtras *49–52*

The opponent says that Testimony is not different from Inference, because (1) the meaning which is not known and which is not an object of perception is known by means of the word which is known, as in Inference the unknown is known by means of the known, (2) cognition from Testimony does not, as does cognition from Comparison, differ from cognition from Inference, and (3) there is universal concomitance of the word and its meaning. To this we reply that in Testimony the word by itself is not competent to produce cognition of truth, and that it derives the force to produce such a cognition only from its being spoken by an āpta or truth-knowing benevolent person, as in the case of "heaven," "seven islands and seven oceans," and so on. Inference is not so dependent upon an āpta. This also constitutes the difference of cognition from Testimony to cognition from Inference. Again, the relation of the word and the meaning is that of the signifier and the significate, and is not natural (dependent on and following from a law of nature). Natural concomitance exists between two objects when both are perceptible to the senses, as in the case of fire and smoke. But objects denoted by words are not perceived by Hearing, and there are objects denoted by words which are not perceptible by any sense. Therefore the supposed natural connection of the word aud meaning cannot be established by any means. It cannot be said that the meaning always accompanies the word, for in that case whenever the words food, fire, and sword are uttered the mouth should be filled with food, burnt with fire and cut with sword. Neither can it be said that the word always accompanies the meaning, for in that case the vocal apparatus should be found near the pot and other objects. It is true there is a uniformity in the relation of the word and the meaning. But this uniformity is due to convention created by the will of man and handed down from generation to generation. This is clear from the fact that the same word conveys different meanings among different races of mankind.

Notes

1 The point, as Vātsyāyana explains, is that, contrary to the opinion of some recent philosophers, one can have perceptual knowledge of something without that thing being conceptualized or linguistically represented.
2 'Fruit' here refers to the karmic effects of actions.
3 See Vātsyāyana's commentary for an explanation of this point about 'the three times'. A point the objector seems to assume is that cognitions always come singly and in succession and cannot, therefore, correspond in any obvious way to the objects of cognition, which can occur simultaneously.
4 The reply being made in this and the following Sūtras is of just the kind that Nāgārjuna in turn responds to in chapter 6 below.
5 Here Vātsyāyana appears to distance himself from the position of the *Nyāya-Sūtras* themselves. His view is that the *pramāṇas* are not 'self-illuminating': rather, they serve to support one another so as, together, to constitute a coherent epistemic system.

Nāgārjuna, *Vigrahavyāvartanī*, Verses 5–6, 30–51

6

From The Dialectical Method of Nāgārjuna: Vigrahavyāvartanī, tr. Kamaleswar Bhattacharya. Delhi: Motilal Banarsidass, 1978, pp. 99–100, 114–24 [notes omitted]; reprinted by permission of the publisher.

Nāgārjuna was a second-century CE Buddhist monk from southern India and the most renowned exponent of the Mādhyamika ('middle way') tendency within Mahāyana ('great vehicle') Buddhism. In his best-known work, the *Mādhyamika-kārikā*, he advances the apparently startling view that everything is 'empty' or 'void' (or lacking in 'own-being') on the basis of the central Buddhist doctrines of 'not-self' and 'conditioned co-origination'. Extracts from that work are included in the forthcoming *Metaphysics: The Classic Readings* and I will say nothing about the 'emptiness' view here except for noting an implication that Nāgārjuna draws from it. This is that none of our claims about objects, persons or whatever can possess more than relative truth, and therefore register genuinely objective knowledge.

In his *Vigrahavyāvartanī* ('End to Discussions'), Nāgārjuna is concerned to rebut various objections to the 'emptiness' view, such as that it is self-defeating because it presents itself as possessing more than relative truth. But it is the objection he puts in the mouths of critics in verses 5–6 which inspires the most important verses (30–51) of the book. The imagined objection is that Nāgārjuna has himself relied upon various 'means of knowledge' (*pramāṇas*) in order even to identify the objects he then pronounces 'empty', and so cannot consistently deny all objective knowledge. Nāgārjuna bluntly replies that he has not relied on these 'means' and then proceeds to launch a 'brilliant criticism of the *pramāṇas*' and of the philosophers, especially those of the Nyāya School (encountered in chapter 5 above), who defend the existence of these 'means of knowledge'.[1] (It is very probably Nāgārjuna whom Vātsyāyana had in mind when responding to criticisms of Nyāya epistemology.)

Nāgārjuna raises several objections to *pramāṇa* theory, challenging, for

---

[1] Kamaleswar Bhattacharya, Introduction to *The Dialectical Method of* Nāgārjuna, p. 89.

example, the cogency of regarding the 'means of knowledge', in the style of the *Nyāya-Sūtras*, as self-illuminating in the manner of a torch. But his most important charges are ones of circularity. If, he argues, all objects of knowledge (*prameyas*) are ascertained through the 'means of knowledge', then, since these latter must themselves be objects of knowledge (why else rely on them?), some objects of knowledge are ascertained on the basis of themselves – which is circular. The alternative is an infinite regress, with each *pramāṇa* being validated on the basis of a further one, which in turn is validated by another, and so on (see verse 32).

Beginning at verse 40, Nāgārjuna detects a further circularity in *pramāṇa* theory. Advocates of that theory, like the Nyāya School, typically define the *pramāṇas* in terms of their enabling us to ascertain *prameyas*, objects of knowledge such as physical bodies, colours, souls, etc. But the existence of such objects is then asserted solely on the evidence of the *pramāṇas*. The *pramāṇa* theorist, concludes Nāgārjuna, is caught in a circle: 'neither the *prameyas* nor the *pramāṇas* are [independently] established' (verse 46).

Both of Nāgārjuna's circularity charges raise issues familiar in contemporary epistemological debate.[2] The first invites such questions as (1) is there any alleged 'means of knowledge' or epistemic ground – sense-perception, say – which, *pace* Nāgārjuna, it would be incoherent to challenge?, and (2) is it *viciously* circular to invoke 'means of knowledge' in one another's support? Might it not be, instead, that the mutual support these 'means' offer is good reason to trust our general epistemic apparatus?

The second charge will remind readers of such currently 'hot' issues as those of the relationship between theory and data, and of the impossibility, alleged by Rorty and others, of jumping 'out of our skins' so as to compare an objective domain of objects with our ways of thinking and talking.[3] It is one mark of Nāgārjuna's brilliance that he was, arguably, the first philosopher to have raised, in an acute and precise manner, doubts as to the very sense of a correspondence between two supposedly independent terms, thought and the world – doubts, of course, which have come to shape much modern epistemological debate.

 V.   Now, if [you (Nāgārjuna) say that] you deny the things after having apprehended them through perception, [we reply:] that perception through which the things are apprehended does not exist.

You cannot say that you deny all things in the statement 'All things are

[2] See Bimal Krishna Matilal, *Perception: An Essay on Classical Indian Theories of Knowledge*, Oxford: Claresdon Press, 1991, pp. 49ff. See also the article on Nāgārjuna in *Encyclopedia of Asian Philosophy*, ed. B. Carr and I. Mahalingam, London: Routledge, 1997.
[3] Richard Rorty, *Philosophy and the Mirror of Nature*, Princeton, NJ: Princeton University Press, 1980.

void', after having apprehended them through perception. – Why? – Because even perception, an instrument of true cognition (*pramāṇa*), is void, being included in all things. The person who apprehends the things is also void. Thus, there is no such thing as apprehension through perception, an instrument of true cognition; and a negation of that which is not apprehended is a logical impossibility. In these circumstances, your statement that all things are void is not valid.

You think, perhaps, that you deny all things after having apprehended them through inference, verbal testimony and comparison.

To this we [i.e. the objectors] reply:

VI. In our refutation of perception, we have [already] refuted inference, verbal testimony and comparison, as well as the objects to be established by inference, verbal testimony and example.

We have [already] refuted inference, comparison and verbal testimony, in our refutation of the 'instrument of true cognition' (*pramāṇa*), perception. Just as perception, an 'instrument of true cognition', is void because all things are void, so also are inference, comparison and verbal testimony void because all things are void. Those objects which are to be established by inference, verbal testimony and comparison are also void because all things are void. The person who apprehends the things through inference, comparison and verbal testimony, is also void. Thus, there is no apprehension of things, and a negation of the intrinsic nature of things that are not apprehended is a logical impossibility. In these circumstances, your [Nāgārjuna's] statement that all things are void is not valid.

. . . [Refutation of the third objection; see vv. V, VI above].[1]
XXX. If I apprehended something with the help of perception, etc., then I would either affirm or deny. [But] since that thing does not exist, I am not to blame.

If I apprehended something with the help of the four *pramāṇas*, viz., perception, inference, comparison and verbal testimony, or with the help of one of these, then only would I either affirm or deny. [But] since I do not even apprehend an object of any kind, I neither affirm nor deny. In these circumstances, your criticism: 'If [you say that] you deny the things after having apprehended them through one of the *pramāṇas*, viz., perception, etc., [we reply:] those *pramāṇas* do not exist, nor do exist the objects to be apprehended through them', does not concern me at all.

Furthermore:

XXXI.   If such and such objects are established for you through the *pramāṇas*, tell me how those *pramāṇas* are established for you.

If you think that such and such 'objects of true cognition' are established through the 'instruments of true cognition' (*pramāṇa*), just as the things to be measured (*meya*) are established through the measuring instruments (*māna*), [we ask:] How are those 'instruments of true cognition', viz., perception, inference, comparison and verbal testimony, established? If [you say that] the *pramāṇas* are established without the help of *pramāṇas*, then [your] proposition that [all] objects are established through *pramāṇas* is abandoned.

XXXII a–b.   If the *pramāṇas* are established through other *pramāṇas*, then there is an infinite series.

If you think that the 'objects of true cognition' (*prameya*) are established through the 'means of true cognition' (*pramāṇa*) and that those 'means of true cognition' are established through other 'means of true cognition', then there follows an infinite series. – What harm is there if there is an infinite series? –

XXXII c–d.   Neither the beginning nor the middle nor the end can then be established.

If there is an infinite series, the beginning cannot be established. – Why? – Because those *pramāṇas* are established through other *pramāṇas*, and those others again through other *pramāṇas*. Thus there is no beginning. [And] if there is no beginning, how can there be a middle? how can there be an end?

Consequently, the statement that those *pramāṇas* are established through other *pramāṇas* is not valid.

XXXIII.   Now, if [you think that] those *pramāṇas* are established without *pramāṇas*, then your philosophic position is abandoned. There is a discordance, and you should state the special reason for that.

Now, if you think: those *pramāṇas* are established without *pramāṇas*, the objects to be cognized, however, are established through the *pramāṇas*, then your position that [all] objects are established through *pramāṇas* is abandoned. There is, moreover, a discordance, namely that some objects are established through *pramāṇas*, while some others are not. And you should state the special reason why some objects are established through *pramāṇas*, while some others are not. But you have not stated that. Thus this assumption, too, is not valid.

The opponent replies: The *pramāṇas* establish themselves as well as other things. As it is said:

'Fire illuminates itself as well as other things. Likewise, the *pramāṇas* establish themselves as well as other things'.[2]

Here we observe:

XXXIV. This is a defective proposition. Fire does not illuminate itself, for its non-perception is not seen to be comparable to that of a pot in darkness.

Your proposition that the *pramāṇas* establish themselves as well as other things like fire [that illuminates itself as well as other things] is defective. For fire does not illuminate itself. A pot, not illuminated by fire, is first not perceived in darkness. Then, being illuminated by fire, it is perceived. If, in the same manner, fire, not being illuminated, first existed in darkness and then were illuminated, it would be possible to say: it illuminates itself. This, however, is not the case. Thus this assumption, too, is not valid.

Furthermore:

XXXV. If, as you say, fire illuminates itself as it illuminates other things, then it will also burn itself.

If, as you say, fire illuminates itself just as it illuminates other things, then it will also burn itself just as it burns other things. This, however, is not the case. In these circumstances, your statement that fire illuminates itself as it illuminates other things, is not valid.

Besides:

XXXVI. If, as you say, fire illuminates both other things and itself, then darkness will cover both other things and itself.

If in your opinion fire illuminates both other things and itself, then its opposite, darkness, too, would cover both other things and itself. This, however, is not seen. In these circumstances, your statement that fire illuminates both other things and itself is not valid.

And again:

XXXVII. There is no darkness in fire nor in something else in which fire stands. How can it [then] illuminate? For illumination is destruction of darkness.

Here, in fire, there is no darkness. Nor is there any darkness where fire is. Now, illumination is obstruction caused to darkness. But since there is no darkness in fire nor where fire is, what is that darkness which is obstructed by fire, and by virtue of whose obstruction it illuminates both other things and itself?

The opponent replies: But is it not true that fire illuminates both other things and itself, for this very reason that there is no darkness in fire nor where fire is? For, in the very process of its origination, fire obstructs darkness. If there is no darkness in fire nor where fire is, it is because in the very process of its origination fire illuminates both other things and itself.

Here we observe:

XXXVIII. It is wrong to say that fire illuminates in the very process of its origination. For, in the very process of its origination, fire does not come in contact with darkness.

The opinion that fire, in the very process of its origination, illuminates both other things and itself, is not tenable. – Why? – Because, in the very process of its origination, fire does not come in contact with darkness; since it does not come in contact with it, it does not destroy it; and since darkness is not destroyed, there is no illumination.

XXXIX. Or, if fire destroyed darkness even without coming in contact with it, then this fire, standing here, would destroy darkness in all the worlds.

Or, if you think that fire destroys darkness even without coming in contact with it, then this fire, standing here at this moment, will equally destroy the darkness existing in all the worlds, without coming in contact with it. This, however, is not seen to be the case. Thus, your opinion that fire destroys darkness even without coming in contact with it, is not valid.

Furthermore:

XL. If the *pramāṇas* are self-established, then the 'means of true cognition' are established for you independently of the 'objects of true cognition'. For self-establishment does not require another thing.

The opponent replies: What defect will ensue if the means of true cognition do not require the objects to be cognized?

Here we observe:

XLI. If you think that the 'means of true cognition' (*pramāṇa*) are established independently of the 'objects of true cognition', then those *pramāṇas* are [*pramāṇas*] of nothing.

If [you think that] the 'means of true cognition' are established independently of the 'objects of true cognition', then those *pramāṇas* are *pramāṇas* of nothing. Thus there is a defect. If, however, the *pramāṇas* are *pramāṇas* of something, they do not then become 'means of true cognition' independently of the 'objects of true cognition'.

XLII. [The opponent may reply:] If it is admitted that they are established in relation [to the objects to be cognized], what defect is there? – [The defect is that] what is [already] established is established [again]. For something that is not established does not require something else.[3]

If it is admitted that the 'means of true cognition' are established in relation to the 'objects of true cognition', then the four 'means of true cognition', which are [already] established, are established [anew]. – Why? – Because an object that is not established does not require [something else]. For instance, Devadatta, who is not [yet] established, does not require anything whatever. But it is not admissible that something that is [already] established be established [anew]. One does not do something that is [already] done.

Besides:

XLIII. If the *pramāṇas* are at all events established in relation to the *prameyas*, the *prameyas* are not established in relation to the *pramāṇas*.

If the *pramāṇas* are established in relation to the *prameyas*, then the *prameyas* are not established in relation to the *pramāṇas*. – Why? – Because the object to be established does not establish the instrument by which it is established. The *pramāṇas*, however, it is said, are the instruments by which the *prameyas* are established.

XLIV. And if the *prameyas* are established even independently of the *pramāṇas*, what do you gain by establishing the *pramāṇas*? That whose purpose they serve is [already] established.

XLV. Besides, if you establish the *pramāṇas* in relation to the *prameyas*, then there is certainly an interchange of *pramāṇas* and *prameyas*.

Moreover, if you think, in order to avoid the defect stated before [XLI], that the 'means of true cognition' exist only in relation to the 'objects of true cognition', then there is an interchange of *pramāṇas* and *prameyas*. Your *pramāṇas* become *prameyas*, because they are established by the *prameyas*. And the *prameyas* become *pramāṇas*, because they establish the *pramāṇas*.

XLVI. Now, if you think that through the establishment of the *pramāṇas* are established the *prameyas*, and that through the establishment of the *prameyas* are established the *pramāṇas*, then neither the *prameyas* nor the *pramāṇas* are established for you.

Now, if you think that through the establishment of the *pramāṇas* are established the *prameyas* – because the *prameyas* require the *pramāṇas* – and that through the establishment of the *prameyas* are established the *pramāṇas* – because the *pramāṇas* require the *prameyas* – then neither the *prameyas* nor the *pramāṇas* are established – Why? –

XLVII. Because, if the *prameyas* owe their establishment to the *pramāṇas*, and if those *pramāṇas* are to be established by the very *prameyas*, how will the *pramāṇas* establish [the *prameyas*]?

Because, if the *prameyas* owe their establishment to the *pramāṇas*, and if those *pramāṇas* are to be established by those very *prameyas*, [we encounter the following difficulty:] the *prameyas* not having been established, the *pramāṇas* are not established, for their cause is not established.[4] How, then, will the *pramāṇas* establish the *prameyas*?

XLVIII. And if the *pramāṇas* owe their establishment to the *prameyas*, and if those *prameyas* are to be established by those very *pramāṇas*, how will the *prameyas* establish [the *pramāṇas*]?

And if the *pramāṇas* owe their establishment to the *prameyas*, and if those *prameyas* are to be established by those very *pramāṇas*, [we encounter the following difficulty:] the *pramāṇas* not having been established, the *prameyas* are not established, for their cause is not established. How, then, will the *prameyas* establish the *pramāṇas*?

XLIX. If the son is to be produced by the father, and if that father is to be produced by that very son, tell me which of these produces which other.

Supposing somebody said: the son is to be produced by the father, and that father is to be produced by that very son, tell me who is to be produced by whom. In exactly the same manner you say: the *prameyas* are to be established by the *pramāṇas*, and those very *pramāṇas* in turn are to be established by those very *prameyas*. Now, which of these are to be established for you by which others?

L. Tell me which of these is the father, and which other the son. Both of them bear, indeed, the mark of a father and that of a son, wherefore we have a doubt here.

Of that father and that son, mentioned before, which is the son, and which other the father? Both of them, as producers, bear the mark of a father, and, as produced, the mark of a son. We have a doubt here: which of these is the father, and which other the son? In just the same manner, of these *pramāṇas* and *prameyas* of yours, which are the *pramāṇas*, and which others the *prameyas*? For both of these, as those which establish, are *pramāṇas*, and as those which are to be established, *prameyas*. We have a doubt here as to which of these are the *pramāṇas*, and which others the *prameyas*.

LI.   The *pramāṇas* are not established by themselves or by one another or by other *pramāṇas*. Nor are they established by the *prameyas*, or accidentally.

Perception is not established by that very perception, inference is not established by that very inference, comparison is not established by that very comparison, and testimony is not established by that very testimony. Nor are they established by one another, i.e., perception by inference, comparison and testimony, inference by perception, comparison and testimony, comparison by perception, inference and testimony, and testimony by perception, inference and comparison. Nor are perception, inference, comparison and testimony established, respectively, by another perception, another inference, another comparison, and another testimony. Nor are the *pramāṇas* established by the *prameyas*, taken collectively or severally, included in their own field or in those of the other *pramāṇas* as well. Nor are they established accidentally. Nor again are they established by a combination of the causes mentioned before whatever their number . . . – In these circumstances, your statement: 'Because the things to be cognized are to be apprehended through the means of true cognition, those things to be cognized exist as well as those means of true cognition through which those things to be cognized are apprehended', is not valid.

Notes.

1 From this verse on, Nāgārjuna is speaking in his own voice and 'you' refers to his opponents. In verse XXX, we get a hint of Nāgārjuna's seemingly paradoxical insistence, developed elsewhere in the book, that he is not making assertions at all, not even when saying that all things are 'void'. One might compare this manoeuvre with that of the Pyrrhonian sceptic (see chapter 3 above).
2 See the *Nyāya-Sūtras*, Book II, ch. 1, §19 in chapter 5 above. Nāgārjuna will argue that the comparison of the *pramāṇas* with a self-illuminating fire is unhelpful since, in fact, fire does not illuminate itself at all.

3 The obscurely put point is, perhaps, this: if the reliability of the *pramāṇas* does not require justification in terms of anything independent of them, but is a matter, say, of the internal coherence among the claims they warrant, then it is incoherent to try to justify ('establish') them on the basis of a reality independent of them.

4 'Ground' or 'basis' might be better than 'cause' in this and the following verses.

René Descartes, *Meditations on First Philosophy*, I–III and 'Objections and Replies' (Selections)

From Descartes: Selected Philosophical Writings, tr. J. Cottingham, R. Stoothoff and D. Murdoch. Cambridge: Cambridge University Press, 1988, pp. 76–88, 123–9 [notes and latter part of Meditation III omitted]; reprinted by permission of Cambridge University Press and the translators.

Renaissance philosophy received its stimulus from the rediscovery, accelerated by the fall of Constantinople in 1453, of long-lost Greek texts, most famously many of Plato's dialogues. But of equal importance for future developments was the reemergence of works, like Sextus Empiricus' (see chapter 3 above), chronicling Greek sceptical thought: for, as one historian puts it, with only slight exaggeration, '*modern* philosophy from Descartes to Kant can be seen as [so many] attempts to answer the challenge of modern scepticism, or to live with it'.[1] The most famous attempt of the former kind was, of course, the first, that of René Descartes (1596–1650), 'the father of modern philosophy'.

For Descartes, it was imperative to scotch the sceptical temper of his times for at least two reasons. Not only did scepticism stand as an obstacle to acceptance of the fledgling cosmology and physics being developed by Galileo, but worse, it threatened belief in God and personal immortality. It is one of the great ironies in the history of ideas that Descartes' strategy for scotching scepticism should have served only to make its challenge seem all the more powerful. For in Meditation I, he articulates with great clarity and force a radically sceptical stance towards virtually all our received beliefs – in the existence of an external world, in the truths of mathematics, and so on. By general consensus, his attempts in Meditation III to recover much of the ground conceded to the sceptic for purely 'methodological' reasons are a failure.

The following extract from *Meditations* ends at the point where Descartes

---

[1] Richard H. Popkin, 'Scepticism and modernity', in *The Rise of Modern Philosophy*, ed. T. Sorell, Oxford: Clarendon Press, 1993, p. 15.

stands poised to prove the existence of a non-deceiving God, a proof which is to enable us once again to accept many of the beliefs previously surrendered to the sceptic. That proof belongs more in the annals of the philosophy of religion than of epistemology. I append to the *Meditations* extract some of Descartes' replies to some sharp objections raised against that work by, among others, Thomas Hobbes.

Even in this extract, Descartes' contributions to epistemology is not exhausted by his rehearsal of the sceptics' position and by the famous *cogito* argument, establishing the certainty of his own existence as 'a thinking thing' and hence placing a limit on sceptical doubt. For in the discussion in Meditation II of the piece of wax, one finds an important and typically 'rationalist' case made out for holding that it is through the intellect, not the senses, that the existence of substances is recognized. More generally, the criterion of knowledge laid down (in Meditation III), though left unelaborated, by Descartes, in terms of the 'clearness and distinctness' of our ideas was to become a distinctive tenet of 'rationalist' thought.

There has been much debate in recent years about the originality or otherwise of Descartes' position. Certainly he relies, especially in his attempt to prove God's existence, on well-worn (and dubious) principles of scholastic philosophy (such as 'what is more perfect cannot be produced by what is less perfect'). Nor is his proof of the existence of the mind as something distinct from anything bodily an original one. A very similar argument – known as 'the flying (or floating) man argument' – was produced by the Persian philosopher Ibn Sina (Avicenna) in the eleventh century.[2] Nor, to readers of Vedantic thought is there anything new in the idea that, provisionally at least, we can think of the external world as a dream or illusion. Perhaps, however, Descartes was the first who, for good or ill, articulated in detail and rendered plausible the idea of the mind as something logically self-contained, as an inner arena of thoughts and experiences which can at least be imagined to take place in the absence of an objective order to which, ordinarily, we take them to be related.[3] This 'methodological solipsism', with its accompanying problem of how anyone breaks out of his or her private mental enclosure so as to gain knowledge of anything external, was to set the stamp upon philosophical enquiry during the centuries which followed, as several further chapters in this volume will confirm.

[2] See L. E. Goodman, *Avicenna*, London: Routledge, 1992, pp. 155ff.
[3] See John McDowell, 'Singular thought and the extent of inner space', in *Subject, Thought and Context*, ed. P. Pettit and J. McDowell, Oxford: Clarendon Press, 1986.

Meditations on First Philosophy *in which are Demonstrated the Existence of God and the Distinction between the Human Soul and the Body*

First Meditation: What Can Be Called Into Doubt

Some years ago I was struck by the large number of falsehoods that I had accepted as true in my childhood, and by the highly doubtful nature of the whole edifice that I had subsequently based on them. I realized that it was necessary, once in the course of my life, to demolish everything completely and start again right from the foundations if I wanted to establish anything at all in the sciences that was stable and likely to last. But the task looked an enormous one, and I began to wait until I should reach a mature enough age to ensure that no subsequent time of life would be more suitable for tackling such inquiries. This led me to put the project off for so long that I would now be to blame if by pondering over it any further I wasted the time still left for carrying it out. So today I have expressly rid my mind of all worries and arranged for myself a clear stretch of free time. I am here quite alone, and at last I will devote myself sincerely and without reservation to the general demolition of my opinions.

18

But to accomplish this, it will not be necessary for me to show that all my opinions are false, which is something I could perhaps never manage. Reason now leads me to think that I should hold back my assent from opinions which are not completely certain and indubitable just as carefully as I do from those which are patently false. So, for the purpose of rejecting all my opinions, it will be enough if I find in each of them at least some reason for doubt. And to do this I will not need to run through them all individually, which would be an endless task. Once the foundations of a building are undermined, anything built on them collapses of its own accord; so I will go straight for the basic principles on which all my former beliefs rested.

Whatever I have up till now accepted as most true I have acquired either from the senses or through the senses. But from time to time I have found that the senses deceive, and it is prudent never to trust completely those who have deceived us even once.

Yet although the senses occasionally deceive us with respect to objects which are very small or in the distance, there are many other beliefs about which doubt is quite impossible, even though they are derived from the senses – for example, that I am here, sitting by the fire, wearing a winter dressing-gown, holding this piece of paper in my hands, and so on. Again, how could it be denied that these hands or this whole body are mine?

19   Unless perhaps I were to liken myself to madmen, whose brains are so damaged by the persistent vapours of melancholia that they firmly maintain they are kings when they are paupers, or say they are dressed in purple when they are naked, or that their heads are made of earthenware, or that they are pumpkins, or made of glass. But such people are insane, and I would be thought equally mad if I took anything from them as a model for myself.

A brilliant piece of reasoning! As if I were not a man who sleeps at night, and regularly has all the same experiences while asleep as madmen do when awake – indeed sometimes even more improbable ones. How often, asleep at night, am I convinced of just such familiar events – that I am here in my dressing-gown, sitting by the fire – when in fact I am lying undressed in bed! Yet at the moment my eyes are certainly wide awake when I look at this piece of paper; I shake my head and it is not asleep; as I stretch out and feel my hand I do so deliberately, and I know what I am doing. All this would not happen with such distinctness to someone asleep. Indeed! As if I did not remember other occasions when I have been tricked by exactly similar thoughts while asleep! As I think about this more carefully, I see plainly that there are never any sure signs by means of which being awake can be distinguished from being asleep. The result is that I begin to feel dazed, and this very feeling only reinforces the notion that I may be asleep.

Suppose then that I am dreaming, and that these particulars – that my eyes are open, that I am moving my head and stretching out my hands – are not true. Perhaps, indeed, I do not even have such hands or such a body at all. Nonetheless, it must surely be admitted that the visions which come in sleep are like paintings, which must have been fashioned in the likeness of things that are real, and hence that at least these general kinds of

20   things – eyes, head, hands and the body as a whole – are things which are not imaginary but are real and exist. For even when painters try to create sirens and satyrs with the most extraordinary bodies, they cannot give them natures which are new in all respects; they simply jumble up the limbs of different animals. Or if perhaps they manage to think up something so new that nothing remotely similar has ever been seen before – something which is therefore completely fictitious and unreal – at least the colours used in the composition must be real. By similar reasoning, although these general kinds of things – eyes, head; hands and so on – could be imaginary, it must at least be admitted that certain other even simpler and more universal things are real. These are as it were the real colours from which we form all the images of things, whether true or false, that occur in our thought.

This class appears to include corporeal nature in general, and its extension; the shape of extended things; the quantity, or size and number of these things; the place in which they may exist, the time through which they may endure, and so on.

So a reasonable conclusion from this might be that physics, astronomy, medicine, and all other disciplines which depend on the study of composite things, are doubtful; while arithmetic, geometry and other subjects of this kind, which deal only with the simplest and most general things, regardless of whether they really exist in nature or not, contain something certain and indubitable. For whether I am awake or asleep, two and three added together are five, and a square has no more than four sides. It seems impossible that such transparent truths should incur any suspicion of being false.

And yet firmly rooted in my mind is the long-standing belief that there is an omnipotent God who made me the kind of creature that I am. How do I know that he has not brought it about that there is no earth, no sky, no extended thing, no shape, no size, no place, while at the same time ensuring that all these things appear to me to exist just as they do now? Moreover, since I sometimes consider that others go astray in cases where they think they have the most perfect knowledge, may I not similarly go wrong every time I add two and three or count the sides of a square, or in some even simpler matter, if that is imaginable? But perhaps God would not have wished me to be deceived in this way, since he is said to be supremely good. But if it were inconsistent with his goodness to have created me such that I am deceived all the time, it would seem equally foreign to his goodness to allow me to be deceived even occasionally; yet this last assertion cannot be made. 21

Perhaps there may be some who would prefer to deny the existence of so powerful a God rather than believe that everything else is uncertain. Let us not argue with them, but grant them that everything said about God is a fiction. According to their supposition, then, I have arrived at my present state by fate or chance or a continuous chain of events, or by some other means; yet since deception and error seem to be imperfections, the less powerful they make my original cause, the more likely it is that I am so imperfect as to be deceived all the time. I have no answer to these arguments, but am finally compelled to admit that there is not one of my former beliefs about which a doubt may not properly be raised; and this is not a flippant or ill-considered conclusion, but is based on powerful and well thought-out reasons. So in future I must withhold my assent from these former beliefs just as carefully as I would from obvious falsehoods, if I want to discover any certainty. 22

But it is not enough merely to have noticed this; I must make an effort to remember it. My habitual opinions keep coming back, and, despite my wishes, they capture my belief, which is as it were bound over to them as a result of long occupation and the law of custom. I shall never get out of the habit of confidently assenting to these opinions, so long as I suppose them to be what in fact they are, namely highly probable opinions – opinions which, despite the fact that they are in a sense doubtful, as has just been shown, it is still much more reasonable to believe than to deny. In view of this, I think it will be a good plan to turn my will in completely the opposite direction and deceive myself, by pretending for a time that these former opinions are utterly false and imaginary. I shall do this until the weight of preconceived opinion is counter-balanced and the distorting influence of habit no longer prevents my judgement from perceiving things correctly. In the meantime, I know that no danger or error will result from my plan, and that I cannot possibly go too far in my distrustful attitude. This is because the task now in hand does not involve action but merely the acquisition of knowledge.

I will suppose therefore that not God, who is supremely good and the source of truth, but rather some malicious demon of the utmost power and cunning has employed all his energies in order to deceive me. I shall think that the sky, the air, the earth, colours, shapes, sounds and all external things are merely the delusions of dreams which he has devised to ensnare my judgement. I shall consider myself as not having hands or eyes, or flesh, or blood or senses, but as falsely believing that I have all these things. I shall stubbornly and firmly persist in this meditation; and, even if it is not in my power to know any truth, I shall at least do what is in my power, that is, resolutely guard against assenting to any falsehoods, so that the deceiver, however powerful and cunning he may be, will be unable to impose on me in the slightest degree. But this is an arduous undertaking, and a kind of laziness brings me back to normal life. I am like a prisoner who is enjoying an imaginary freedom while asleep; as he begins to suspect that he is asleep, he dreads being woken up, and goes along with the pleasant illusion as long as he can. In the same way, I happily slide back into my old opinions and dread being shaken out of them, for fear that my peaceful sleep may be followed by hard labour when I wake, and that I shall have to toil not in the light, but amid the inextricable darkness of the problems I have now raised.

Second Meditation: The Nature of the Human Mind, and How It Is Better Known Than the Body

So serious are the doubts into which I have been thrown as a result of yesterday's meditation that I can neither put them out of my mind nor see

any way of resolving them. It feels as if I have fallen unexpectedly into a   24
deep whirlpool which tumbles me around so that I can neither stand on
the bottom nor swim up to the top. Nevertheless I will make an effort and
once more attempt the same path which I started on yesterday. Anything
which admits of the slightest doubt I will set aside just as if I had found it
to be wholly false; and I will proceed in this way until I recognize something certain, or, if nothing else, until I at least recognize for certain that
there is no certainty. Archimedes used to demand just one firm and immovable point in order to shift the entire earth; so I too can hope for great
things if I manage to find just one thing, however slight, that is certain and
unshakeable.

I will suppose then, that everything I see is spurious. I will believe that
my memory tells me lies, and that none of the things that it reports ever
happened. I have no senses. Body, shape, extension, movement and place
are chimeras. So what remains true? Perhaps just the one fact that nothing
is certain.

Yet apart from everything I have just listed, how do I know that there is
not something else which does not allow even the slightest occasion for
doubt? Is there not a God, or whatever I may call him, who puts into me
the thoughts I am now having? But why do I think this, since I myself may
perhaps be the author of these thoughts? In that case am not I, at least,
something? But I have just said that I have no senses and no body. This is
the sticking point: what follows from this? Am I not so bound up with a   25
body and with senses that I cannot exist without them? But I have convinced myself that there is absolutely nothing in the world, no sky, no
earth, no minds, no bodies. Does it now follow that I too do not exist? No:
if I convinced myself of something then I certainly existed. But there is a
deceiver of supreme power and cunning who is deliberately and constantly
deceiving me. In that case I too undoubtedly exist, if he is deceiving me;
and let him deceive me as much as he can, he will never bring it about that
I am nothing so long as I think that I am something. So after considering
everything every thoroughly, I must finally conclude that this proposition,
I am, I exist, is necessarily true whenever it is put forward by me or conceived in my mind.[1]

But I do not yet have a sufficient understanding of what this 'I' is, that
now necessarily exists. So I must be on my guard against carelessly taking
something else to be this 'I', and so making a mistake in the very item of
knowledge that I maintain is the most certain and evident of all. I will
therefore go back and meditate on what I originally believed myself to be,
before I embarked on this present train of thought. I will then subtract
anything capable of being weakened, even minimally, by the arguments

now introduced, so that what is left at the end may be exactly and only what is certain and unshakeable.

What then did I formerly think I was? A man. But what is a man? Shall I say 'a rational animal'? No; for then I should have to inquire what an animal is, what rationality is, and in this way one question would lead me down the slope to other harder ones, and I do not now have the time to waste on subtleties of this kind. Instead I propose to concentrate on what came into my thoughts spontaneously and quite naturally whenever I used to consider what I was. Well, the first thought to come to mind was that I had a face, hands, arms and the whole mechanical structure of limbs which can be seen in a corpse, and which I called the body. The next thought was that I was nourished, that I moved about, and that I engaged in sense-perception and thinking; and these actions I attributed to the soul. But as to the nature of this soul, either I did not think about this or else I imagined it to be something tenuous, like a wind or fire or ether, which permeated my more solid parts. As to the body, however, I had no doubts about it, but thought I knew its nature distinctly. If I had tried to describe the mental conception I had of it, I would have expressed it as follows: by a body I understand whatever has a determinable shape and a definable location and can occupy a space in such a way as to exclude any other body; it can be perceived by touch, sight, hearing, taste or smell, and can be moved in various ways, not by itself but by whatever else comes into contact with it. For, according to my judgement, the power of self-movement, like the power of sensation or of thought, was quite foreign to the nature of a body; indeed, it was a source of wonder to me that certain bodies were found to contain faculties of this kind.

But what shall I now say that I am, when I am supposing that there is some supremely powerful and, if it is permissible to say so, malicious deceiver, who is deliberately trying to trick me in every way he can? Can I now assert that I possess even the most insignificant of all the attributes which I have just said belong to the nature of a body? I scrutinize them, think about them, go over them again, but nothing suggests itself; it is tiresome and pointless to go through the list once more. But what about the attributes I assigned to the soul? Nutrition or movement? Since now I do not have a body, these are mere fabrications. Sense-perception? This surely does not occur without a body, and besides, when asleep I have appeared to perceive through the senses many things which I afterwards realized I did not perceive through the senses at all. Thinking? At last I have discovered it – thought; this alone is inseparable from me. I am, I exist – that is certain. But for how long? For as long as I am thinking. For it could be that were I totally to cease from thinking, I should totally cease to exist. At present I am not admitting anything except what is necessarily true. I am, then, in the strict sense only a thing that thinks; that is, I am a mind, or intelligence, or intellect, or reason – words whose meaning I have been ignorant of until now. But for all that I am a thing which is real and which truly exists. But what kind of a thing? As I have just said – a thinking thing.

What else am I? I will use my imagination. I am not that structure of limbs which is called a human body. I am not even some thin vapour which permeates the limbs – a wind, fire, air, breath, or whatever I depict in my imagination; for these are things which I have supposed to be nothing. Let this supposition stand; for all that I am still something. And yet may it not perhaps be the case that these very things which I am supposing to be nothing, because they are unknown to me, are in reality identical with the 'I' of which I am aware? I do not know, and for the moment I shall not argue the point, since I can make judgements only about things which are known to me. I know that I exist; the question is, what is this 'I' that I know? If the 'I' is understood strictly as we have been taking it, then it is quite certain that knowledge of it does not depend on things of whose existence I am as yet unaware; so it cannot depend on any of the things which I invent in my imagination. And this very word 'invent' shows me my mistake. It would indeed be a case of fictitious invention if I used my imagination to establish that I was something or other; for imagining is simply contemplating the shape or image of a corporeal thing. Yet now I know for certain both that I exist and at the same time that all such images and, in general, everything relating to the nature of body, could be mere dreams <and chimeras>. Once this point has been grasped, to say 'I will use my imagination to get to know more distinctly what I am' would seem to be as silly as saying 'I am now awake, and see some truth; but since my vision is not yet clear enough, I will deliberately fall asleep so that my dreams may provide a truer and clearer representation.' I thus realize that none of the things that the imagination enables me to grasp is at all relevant to this knowledge of myself which I possess, and that the mind must therefore be most carefully diverted from such things if it is to perceive its own nature as distinctly as possible.

But what then am I? A thing that thinks. What is that? A thing that doubts, understands, affirms, denies, is willing, is unwilling, and also imagines and has sensory perceptions.

This is a considerable list, if everything on it belongs to me. But does it? Is it not one and the same 'I' who is now doubting almost everything, who nonetheless understands some things, who affirms that this one thing is true, denies everything else, desires to know more, is unwilling to be

28

deceived, imagines many things even involuntarily, and is aware of many things which apparently come from the senses? Are not all these things just as true as the fact that I exist, even if I am asleep all the time, and even if he who created me is doing all he can to deceive me? Which of all these activities is distinct from my thinking? Which of them can be said to be separate from myself? The fact that it is I who am doubting and understanding and willing is so evident that I see no way of making it any clearer. But it is also the case that the 'I' who imagines is the same 'I'. For even if, as I have supposed, none of the objects of imagination are real, the power of imagination is something which really exists and is part of my thinking. Lastly, it is also the same 'I' who has sensory perceptions, or is aware of bodily things as it were through the senses. For example, I am now seeing light, hearing a noise, feeling heat. But I am asleep, so all this is false. Yet I certainly *seem* to see, to hear, and to be warmed. This cannot be false; what is called 'having a sensory perception' is strictly just this, and in this restricted sense of the term it is simply thinking.

From all this I am beginning to have a rather better understanding of what I am. But it still appears – and I cannot stop thinking this – that the corporeal things of which images are formed in my thought, and which the senses investigate, are known with much more distinctness than this puzzling 'I' which cannot be pictured in the imagination. And yet it is surely surprising that I should have a more distinct grasp of things which I realize are doubtful, unknown and foreign to me, than I have of that which is true and known – my own self. But I see what it is: my mind enjoys wandering off and will not yet submit to being restrained within the bounds of truth. Very well then; just this once let us give it a completely free rein, so that after a while, when it is time to tighten the reins, it may more readily submit to being curbed.

Let us consider the things which people commonly think they understand most distinctly of all; that is, the bodies which we touch and see. I do not mean bodies in general – for general perceptions are apt to be somewhat more confused – but one particular body. Let us take, for example, this piece of wax. It has just been taken from the honeycomb; it has not yet quite lost the taste of the honey; it retains some of the scent of the flowers from which it was gathered; its colour, shape and size are plain to see; it is hard, cold and can be handled without difficulty; if you rap it with your knuckle it makes a sound. In short, it has everything which appears necessary to enable a body to be known as distinctly as possible. But even as I speak, I put the wax by the fire, and look: the residual taste is eliminated, the smell goes away, the colour changes, the shape is lost, the size increases; it becomes liquid and hot; you can hardly touch it, and if you strike it, it no longer makes a sound. But does the same wax remain? It must be admitted that it does; no one denies it, no one thinks otherwise. So what was it in the wax that I understood with such distinctness? Evidently none of the features which I arrived at by means of the senses; for whatever came under taste, smell, sight, touch or hearing has now altered – yet the wax remains.

Perhaps the answer lies in the thought which now comes to my mind; namely, the wax was not after all the sweetness of the honey, or the fragrance of the flowers, or the whiteness, or the shape, or the sound, but was rather a body which presented itself to me in these various forms a little while ago, but which now exhibits different ones. But what exactly is it that I am now imagining? Let us concentrate, take away everything which does   31
not belong to the wax, and see what is left: merely something extended, flexible and changeable. But what is meant here by 'flexible' and 'changeable'? Is it what I picture in my imagination: that this piece of wax is capable of changing from a round shape to a square shape, or from a square shape to a triangular shape? Not at all; for I can grasp that the wax is capable of countless changes of this kind, yet I am unable to run through this immeasurable number of changes in my imagination, from which it follows that it is not the faculty of imagination that gives me my grasp of the wax as flexible and changeable. And what is meant by 'extended'? Is the extension of the wax also unknown? For it increases if the wax melts, increases again if it boils, and is greater still if the heat is increased. I would not be making a correct judgement about the nature of wax unless I believed it capable of being extended in many more different ways than I will ever encompass in my imagination. I must therefore admit that the nature of this piece of wax is in no way revealed by my imagination, but is perceived by the mind alone. (I am speaking of this particular piece of wax; the point is even clearer with regard to wax in general.) But what is this wax which is perceived by the mind alone? It is of course the same wax which I see, which I touch, which I picture in my imagination, in short the same wax which I thought it to be from the start. And yet, and here is the point, the perception I have of it is a case not of vision or touch or imagination – nor has it ever been, despite previous appearances – but of purely mental scrutiny; and this can be imperfect and confused, as it was before, or clear and distinct as it is now, depending on how carefully I concentrate on what the wax consists in.

But as I reach this conclusion I am amazed at how <weak and> prone to error my mind is. For although I am thinking about these matters within myself, silently and without speaking, nonetheless the actual words bring   32
me up short, and I am almost tricked by ordinary ways of talking. We say

that we see the wax itself, if it is there before us, not that we judge it to be there from its colour or shape; and this might lead me to conclude without more ado that knowledge of the wax comes from what the eye sees, and not from the scrutiny of the mind alone. But then if I look out of the window and see men crossing the square, as I just happen to have done, I normally say that I see the men themselves, just as I say that I see the wax. Yet do I see any more than hats and coats which could conceal automatons? I *judge* that they are men. And so something which I thought I was seeing with my eyes is in fact grasped solely by the faculty of judgement which is in my mind.

However, one who wants to achieve knowledge above the ordinary level should feel ashamed at having taken ordinary ways of talking as a basis for doubt. So let us proceed, and consider on which occasion my perception of the nature of the wax was more perfect and evident. Was it when I first looked at it, and believed I knew it by my external senses, or at least by what they call the 'common' sense – that is, the power of imagination? Or is my knowledge more perfect now, after a more careful investigation of the nature of the wax and of the means by which it is known? Any doubt on this issue would clearly be foolish; for what distinctness was there in my earlier perception? Was there anything in it which an animal could not possess? But when I distinguish the wax from its outward forms – take the clothes off, as it were, and consider it naked – then although my judgement may still contain errors, at least my perception now requires a human mind.

33   But what am I to say about this mind, or about myself? (So far, remember, I am not admitting that there is anything else in me except a mind.) What, I ask, is this 'I' which seems to perceive the wax so distinctly? Surely my awareness of my own self is not merely much truer and more certain than my awareness of the wax, but also much more distinct and evident. For if I judge that the wax exists from the fact that I see it, clearly this same fact entails much more evidently that I myself also exist. It is possible that what I see is not really the wax; it is possible that I do not even have eyes with which to see anything. But when I see, or think I see (I am not here distinguishing the two), it is simply not possible that I who am now thinking am not something. By the same token, if I judge that the wax exists from the fact that I touch it, the same result follows, namely that I exist. If I judge that it exists from the fact that I imagine it, or for any other reason, exactly the same thing follows. And the result that I have grasped in the case of the wax may be applied to everything else located outside me. Moreover, if my perception of the wax seemed more distinct after it was established not just by sight or touch but by many other considerations, it

must be admitted that I now know myself even more distinctly. This is because every consideration whatsoever which contributes to my perception of the wax, or of any other body, cannot but establish even more effectively the nature of my own mind. But besides this, there is so much else in the mind itself which can serve to make my knowledge of it more distinct, that it scarcely seems worth going through the contributions made by considering bodily things.

I see that without any effort I have now finally got back to where I 34 wanted. I now know that even bodies are not strictly perceived by the senses or the faculty of imagination but by the intellect alone, and that this perception derives not from their being touched or seen but from their being understood; and in view of this I know plainly that I can achieve an easier and more evident perception of my own mind than of anything else. But since the habit of holding on to old opinions cannot be set aside so quickly, I should like to stop here and meditate for some time on this new knowledge I have gained, so as to fix it more deeply in my memory.

Third Meditation: The Existence of God

I will now shut my eyes, stop my ears, and withdraw all my senses. I will eliminate from my thoughts all images of bodily things, or rather, since this is hardly possible, I will regard all such images as vacuous, false and worthless. I will converse with myself and scrutinize myself more deeply; and in this way I will attempt to achieve, little by little, a more intimate knowledge of myself. I am a thing that thinks: that is, a thing that doubts, affirms, denies, understands a few things, is ignorant of many things, is willing, is unwilling, and also which imagines and has sensory perceptions; for as I have noted before, even though the objects of my sensory experience and imagination may have no existence outside me, nonetheless the modes of thinking which I refer to as cases of sensory perception and imagination, in so far as they are simply modes of thinking, do exist within me – of that I 35 am certain.

In this brief list I have gone through everything I truly know, or at least everything I have so far discovered that I know. Now I will cast around more carefully to see whether there may be other things within me which I have not yet noticed. I am certain that I am a thinking thing. Do I not therefore also know what is required for my being certain about anything? In this first item of knowledge there is simply a clear and distinct perception of what I am asserting; this would not be enough to make me certain of the truth of the matter if it could ever turn out that something which I perceived with such clarity and distinctness was false. So I now seem to be able to lay it down as a general rule that whatever I perceive very clearly and distinctly is true.

Yet I previously accepted as wholly certain and evident many things which I afterwards realized were doubtful. What were these? The earth, sky, stars, and everything else that I apprehended with the senses. But what was it about them that I perceived clearly? Just that the ideas, or thoughts, of such things appeared before my mind. Yet even now I am not denying that these ideas occur within me. But there was something else which I used to assert, and which through habitual belief I thought I perceived clearly, although I did not in fact do so. This was that there were things outside me which were the sources of my ideas and which resembled them in all respects. Here was my mistake; or at any rate, if my judgement was true, it was not thanks to the strength of my perception.

36   But what about when I was considering something very simple and straightforward in arithmetic or geometry, for example that two and three added together make five, and so on? Did I not see at least these things clearly enough to affirm their truth? Indeed, the only reason for my later judgement that they were open to doubt was that it occurred to me that perhaps some God could have given me a nature such that I was deceived even in matters which seemed most evident. And whenever my preconceived belief in the supreme power of God comes to mind, I cannot but admit that it would be easy for him, if he so desired, to bring it about that I go wrong even in those matters which I think I see utterly clearly with my mind's eye. Yet when I turn to the things themselves which I think I perceive very clearly, I am so convinced by them that I spontaneously declare: let whoever can do so deceive me, he will never bring it about that I am nothing, so long as I continue to think I am something; or make it true at some future time that I have never existed, since it is now true that I exist; or bring it about that two and three added together are more or less than five, or anything of this kind in which I see a manifest contradiction. And since I have no cause to think that there is a deceiving God, and I do not yet even know for sure whether there is a God at all, any reason for doubt which depends simply on this belief is a very slight and, so to speak, metaphysical one. But in order to remove even this slight reason for doubt, as soon as the opportunity arises I must examine whether there is a God, and, if there is, whether he can be a deceiver. For if I do not know this, it seems that I can never be quite certain about anything else. . . .[2]

Objections and Replies [Selections]

[On Meditation One]

[The rejection of previous beliefs]

Here I shall employ an everyday example to explain to my critic the ration- 481
ale for my procedure, so as to prevent him misunderstanding it, or having
the gall to pretend he does not understand it, in future. Suppose he had a
basket full of apples and, being worried that some of the apples were rotten, wanted to take out the rotten ones to prevent the rot spreading. How
would he proceed? Would he not begin by tipping the whole lot out of the
basket? And would not the next step be to cast his eye over each apple in
turn, and pick up and put back in the basket only those he saw to be sound,
leaving the others? In just the same way, those who have never philosophized
correctly have various opinions in their minds which they have begun to
store up since childhood, and which they therefore have reason to believe
may in many cases be false. They then attempt to separate the false beliefs
from the others, so as to prevent their contaminating the rest and making
the whole lot uncertain. Now the best way they can accomplish this is to
reject all their beliefs together in one go, as if they were all uncertain and
false. They can then go over each belief in turn and re-adopt only those
which they recognize to be true and indubitable. Thus I was right to begin
by rejecting all my beliefs. [*Seventh Replies*]

*　　*　　*

[The reliability of the senses]

Although there is deception or falsity, it is not to be found in the senses; for (332)
the senses are quite passive and report only appearances, which must appear
in the way they do owing to their causes. The error or falsity is in the judgement or the mind, which is not circumspect enough and does not notice
that things at a distance will for one reason or another appear smaller and
more blurred than when they are nearby, and so on. Nevertheless, when
deception occurs, we must not deny that it exists; the only difficulty is whether
it occurs all the time, thus making it impossible for us ever to be sure of the
truth of anything which we perceive by the senses. [*Fifth Objections*]

Here you show quite clearly that you are relying entirely on a preconceived
opinion which you have never got rid of. You maintain that we never suspect

386   any falsity in situations where we have never detected it, and hence that when we look at a tower from nearby and touch it we are sure that it is square, if it appears square. You also maintain that when we are really awake, we cannot doubt whether we are awake or asleep, and so on. But you have no reason to think that you have previously noticed all the circumstances in which error can occur; moreover, it is easy to prove that you are from time to time mistaken in matters which you accept as certain.   [*Fifth Replies*]

*   *   *

(418) · Our *ninth* and most worrying difficulty is your assertion that we ought to mistrust the operations of the senses and that the reliability of the intellect is much greater than that of the senses. But how can the intellect enjoy any certainty unless it has previously derived it from the senses when they are working as they should? How can it correct a mistake made by one of the senses unless some other sense first corrects the mistake? Owing to refraction, a stick which is in fact straight appears bent in water. What corrects the error? The intellect? Not at all; it is the sense of touch. And the same sort of thing must be taken to occur in other cases. Hence if you have recourse to all your senses when they are in good working order, and they all give the same report, you will achieve the greatest certainty of which man is naturally capable. But you will often fail to achieve it if you trust the operations of the mind; for the mind often goes astray in just those areas where it had previously supposed doubt to be impossible.   [*Sixth Objections*]

When people say that a stick in water 'appears bent because of refraction', this is the same as saying that it appears to us in a way which would lead a child to judge that it was bent – and which may even lead us to make the same judgement, following the preconceived opinions which we have be-
439   come accustomed to accept from our earliest years. But I cannot grant my critics' further comment that this error is corrected 'not by the intellect but by the sense of touch'. As a result of touching it, we may judge that the stick is straight, and the kind of judgement involved may be the kind we have been accustomed to make since childhood, and which is therefore referred to as the 'sense' of touch. But the sense alone does not suffice to correct the visual error: in addition we need to have some degree of reason which tells us that in this case we should believe the judgement based on touch rather than that elicited by vision. And since we did not have this power of reasoning in our infancy, it must be attributed not to the senses but to the intellect. Thus even in the very example my critics produce, it is the intellect alone which corrects the error of the senses; and it is not

possible to produce any case in which error results from our trusting the operation of the mind more than the senses. [*Sixth Replies*]

*　　*　　*

[Certainty in dreams]

Has it never happened to you, as it has to many people, that things seemed clear and certain to you while you were dreaming, but that afterwards you discovered that they were doubtful or false? It is indeed 'prudent never to trust completely those who have deceived you even once'. 'But', you reply, 'matters of the utmost certainty are quite different. They are such that they cannot appear doubtful even to those who are dreaming or mad.' But are you really serious in what you say? Can you pretend that matters of the utmost certainty cannot appear doubtful even to dreamers or madmen? What are these utterly certain matters? If things which are ridiculous or absurd sometimes appear certain, even utterly certain, to people who are asleep or insane, then why should not things which are certain, even utterly certain, appear false and doubtful? I know a man who once, when falling asleep, heard the clock strike four, and counted the strokes as 'one, one, one, one'. It then seemed to him that there was something absurd about this, and he shouted out: 'That clock must be going mad; it has struck one o'clock four times!' Is there really anything so absurd or irrational that it could not come into the mind of someone who is asleep or raving? There are no limits to what a dreamer may not 'prove' or believe, and indeed congratulate himself on, as if he had managed to invent some splendid thought. [*Seventh Objections*]

'But matters of the utmost certainty are quite different. They are such that they cannot appear doubtful even to those who are dreaming or mad.' I do not know what kind of analysis has enabled my supremely subtle critic to deduce this from my writings. Admittedly he might have inferred from what I wrote that everything that anyone clearly and distinctly perceives is true, although the person in question may from time to time doubt whether he is dreaming or awake, and may even, if you like, be dreaming or mad. For no matter who the perceiver is, nothing can be clearly and distinctly perceived without its being just as we perceive it to be, i.e. without being true. But because it requires some care to make a proper distinction between what is clearly and distinctly perceived and what merely seems or appears to be, I am not surprised that my worthy critic should here mistake the one for the other. [*Seventh Replies*]

[On Meditation Two]

[Cogito ergo sum ('I am thinking, therefore I exist')]

259
You conclude that this proposition, *I am, I exist*, is true whenever it is put forward by you or conceived in your mind. But I do not see that you needed all this apparatus, when on other grounds you were certain, and it was true, that you existed. You could have made the same inference from any one of your other actions, since it is known by the natural light that whatever acts exists. [*Fifth Objections*]

(352)
When you say that I 'could have made the same inference from any one of my other actions' you are far from the truth, since I am not wholly certain of any of my actions, with the sole exception of thought (in using the word 'certain' I am referring to metaphysical certainty, which is the sole issue at this point). I may not, for example, make the inference 'I am walking, therefore I exist', except in so far as the awareness of walking is a thought. The inference is certain only if applied to this awareness, and not to the movement of the body which sometimes – in the case of dreams – is not occurring at all, despite the fact that I seem to myself to be walking. Hence from the fact that I think I am walking I can very well infer the existence of a mind which has this thought, but not the existence of a body that walks. And the same applies in other cases. [*Fifth Replies*]

*   *   *

When someone says 'I am thinking, therefore I am, or I exist', he does not deduce existence from thought by means of a syllogism, but recognizes it as something self-evident by a simple intuition of the mind. This is clear from the fact that if he were deducing it by means of a syllogism, he would have to have had previous knowledge of the major premiss 'Everything which thinks is, or exists'; yet in fact he learns it from experiencing in his
141
own case that it is impossible that he should think without existing.[3] It is in the nature of our mind to construct general propositions on the basis of our knowledge of particular ones. [*Second Replies*]

*   *   *

413
From the fact that we are thinking it does not seem to be entirely certain that we exist. For in order to be certain that you are thinking you must know what thought or thinking is, and what your existence is; but since you do not yet

know what these things are, how can you know that you are thinking or that you exist? Thus neither when you say 'I am thinking' nor when you add 'therefore, I exist' do you really know what you are saying. Indeed, you do not even know that you are saying or thinking anything, since this seems to require that you should know that you know what you are saying; and this in turn requires that you be aware of knowing that you know what you are saying, and so on *ad infinitum*. Hence it is clear that you cannot know whether you exist or even whether you are thinking.   [*Sixth Objections*]

It is true that no one can be certain that he is thinking or that he exists unless   422
he knows what thought is and what existence is. But this does not require reflective knowledge, or the kind of knowledge that is acquired by means of demonstrations; still less does it require knowledge of reflective knowledge, i.e. knowing that we know, and knowing that we know that we know, and so on *ad infinitum*. This kind of knowledge cannot possibly be obtained about anything. It is quite sufficient that we should know it by that internal awareness which always precedes reflective knowledge. This inner awareness of one's thought and existence is so innate in all men that, although we may pretend that we do not have it if we are overwhelmed by preconceived opinions and pay more attention to words than to their meanings, we cannot in fact fail to have it. Thus when anyone notices that he is thinking and that it follows from this that he exists, even though he may never before have asked what thought is or what existence is, he still cannot fail to have sufficient knowledge of them both to satisfy himself in this regard.   [*Sixth Replies*]

*   *   *

[Sum res cogitans ('I am a thinking thing')]

Correct. For from the fact that I think, or have an image (whether I am awake or dreaming), it can be inferred that I am thinking; for 'I think' and 'I am thinking' mean the same thing. And from the fact that I am thinking it follows that I exist, since that which thinks is not nothing. But when the author adds 'that is, I am a mind, or intelligence, or intellect or reason', a doubt arises. It does not seem to be a valid argument to say 'I am thinking, therefore I am thought' or 'I am using my intellect, hence I am an intellect.' I might just as well say 'I am walking, therefore I am a walk.' M. Descartes is identifying the thing which understands with intellection, which is an act of that which understands. Or at least he is identifying the thing which understands with the intellect, which is a power of that which understands. Yet all philosophers make a distinction between a subject and its faculties and acts, i.e. between a subject and its properties and its essences: 173 an entity is one thing, its essence is another. Hence it may be that the thing that thinks is the subject to which mind, reason or intellect belong; and this subject may thus be something corporeal. The contrary is assumed, not proved. Yet this inference is the basis of the conclusion which M. Descartes seems to want to establish.[4]   [*Third Objections*]

(174) When I said 'that is, I am a mind, or intelligence, or intellect or reason', what I meant by these terms was not mere faculties, but things endowed with the faculty of thought. This is what the first two terms are commonly taken to mean by everyone; and the second two are often understood in this sense. I stated this point so explicitly, and in so many places, that it seems to me there was no room for doubt.

There is no comparison here between 'a walk' and 'thought'. 'A walk' is usually taken to refer simply to the act of walking, whereas 'thought' is sometimes taken to refer to the act, sometimes to the faculty, and sometimes to the thing which possesses the faculty.

I do not say that the thing which understands is the same as intellection. Nor, indeed, do I identify the thing which understands with the intellect, if 'the intellect' is taken to refer to a faculty; they are identical only if 'the intellect' is taken to refer to the thing which understands. Now I freely admit that I used the most abstract terms I could in order to refer to the thing or substance in question, because I wanted to strip away from it everything that did not belong to it. This philosopher, by contrast, uses absolutely concrete words, namely 'subject', 'matter' and 'body', to refer to this thinking thing, because he wants to prevent its being separated from the body.

[*Third Replies*]

Notes

1 Or '*cogito ergo sum*' – 'I am thinking, therefore I exist' – as Descartes more famously put it in his *Principles of Philosophy* I.7.
2 The previous paragraphs may give the impression that Descartes intends, having established God's existence, to reinstate nearly all our familiar conceptions. In fact, Descartes never fully reverts to 'commonsense'. Notably, he follows Galileo in denying that our perception of colours and other 'secondary qualities' resembles anything in the objective world.
3 This important reply shows that '*cogito ergo sum*' is not to be read as a standard inference. How the *cogito* argument should be interpreted remains a matter of dispute.
4 This crucial objection challenges Descartes' move from 'I am a thing that thinks' to the conclusion that the 'I' is distinct from the body. Readers may feel that Descartes' reply evades the challenge.

(A) John Locke, *An Essay Concerning Human Understanding*, Book I, Chapter 2, Sections 1–24 (B) G. W. Leibniz, *New Essays on the Human Understanding*, Preface

(A) *From* John Locke, *An Essay Concerning Human Understanding*, ed. John W. Yolton, Vol. 1. London: Dent, 1961, pp. 9–22. (B) *From* Gottfried Wilhelm Leibniz, *Philosophical Writings*, ed. G. Parkinson. London: Dent, 1973, pp. 150–4 [some passages omitted]; reprinted by permission of David Campbell Publishers Ltd.

Descartes' argument for the existence of God requires the premise that our idea of God is not an acquired one, but innate – an idea, in fact, which God Himself must have implanted in our minds. In appealing to what we innately know, Descartes was recalling a tradition that goes back to Plato who, in his *Meno*, argued that a boy's recognition of geometrical truths presupposes a pre-natal knowledge of mathematical principles. (Aristotle, we saw in chapter 2 above, allows that we know things innately in *one* sense.) By the time John Locke (1632–1704) launched his famous attack on innate ideas, Cartesians, the Cambridge Platonists and others were busily postulating any number of innate principles – moral and religious ones as well as those of logic and mathematics.[1] Because of this, it was this part of Locke's *Essay* that quickly became the work's most notorious section.

For good or ill, the issue of innate knowledge came to be seen as the pivotal one joined by the empiricists and their rationalist rivals. Certainly it looks to be pivotal when empiricism is characterized, in Locke's words, as the view that 'all our knowledge is founded' in, and 'ultimately derives from', experience (Book II, ch. 1). It might be argued, however, that a characterization of empiricism in terms of a psychological thesis about the origin of knowledge, rather than of

---

[1] See John Yolton, *John Locke and the Way of Ideas*, Oxford: Oxford University Press, 1956.

an epistemological claim about the justification of knowledge-claims, is an unhappy one. Be that as it may, the question of innate knowledge is important, quite apart from its connection with seventeenth–eighteenth-century rivalries.

It is misleading to write that 'Locke plainly treats the question ... as an empirical one, to be settled by evidence' about children and 'savage nations'.[2] More important than his denial that children and savages have the knowledge which Cartesians regard as universally innate are Locke's attempts to identify a version of the innateness doctrine which is neither blatantly false nor a misleading way of stating the obvious (e.g. that we have the capacity to come to know mathematical truths). It is his conclusion that no such version can be found, together with his attempted demonstration in the *Essay* as a whole that experience does suffice to explain our ideas and knowledge, which constitute his real case against his opponents.

When Leibniz (1646–1716) wrote his critique of Locke's *Essay*, it was that conclusion and demonstration which he challenged, arguing for example that experience cannot explain our recognition of the *necessity* of mathematical truths. (The criticism of Locke contained in the Preface to Leibniz's *New Essays* is continued at greater leisure in Book I of the work.)

There is a certain irony in Locke's objection to the innateness doctrine which appeals to the need to have learned a language in order to articulate, and so come to know, any principles. For, in recent years, that doctrine has been revitalized by Noam Chomsky's claim that it is precisely linguistic knowledge, of the principles of 'universal grammar', which must be innate.[3] It is a moot question, however, whether his claim is significantly similar to the seventeenth-century doctrine, and indeed whether his point is best expressed as one about innate *knowledge* at all.

In paying rather scant attention to the notion of knowledge, Chomsky is, unfortunately, emulating those involved in the older debate. Neither Locke nor Leibniz makes clear what he means by knowledge when they respectively deny and affirm the existence of innate knowledge. Surely, though, it does make a difference to the plausibility of the innateness doctrine which concept of knowledge is being employed. If knowing a principle to be true requires an ability to justify and defend one's claim to know this, then it will indeed sound absurd to attribute knowledge to neonates. On a more relaxed understanding of knowledge, that attribution might sound a good deal more acceptable.

[2] J. L. Mackie, *Problems From Locke*, Oxford: Clarendon Press, 1976, p. 215.
[3] See Chomsky, *Cartesian Linguistics*, New York: Harper & Row, 1966, and, for critical discussions of Chomsky, S. P. Stich (ed.), *Innate Ideas*, Berkeley: University of California Press, 1975, and my 'Innateness: old and new', *Philosophical Review*, 81, 1972.

(A) Locke, Book I, Chapter II: No Innate Principles in the Mind

1. It is an established opinion amongst some men that there are in the *understanding* certain *innate principles*, some primary notions, κοιναì ἔννοιαι, characters, as it were, stamped upon the mind of man, which the soul receives in its very first being and brings into the world with it. It would be sufficient to convince unprejudiced readers of the falseness of this supposition, if I should only show (as I hope I shall in the following parts of this discourse) how men, barely by the use of their natural faculties, may attain to all the knowledge they have, without the help of any innate impressions, and may arrive at certainty without any such original notions or principles. For I imagine anyone will easily grant that it would be impertinent to suppose the *ideas* of colours innate in a creature to whom God has given sight, and a power to receive them by the eyes, from external objects; and no less unreasonable would it be to attribute several truths to the impressions of nature and innate characters, when we may observe in ourselves faculties, fit to attain as easy and certain knowledge of them, as if they were originally imprinted on the mind.

But because a man is not permitted without censure to follow his own thoughts in the search of truth, when they lead him ever so little out of the common road, I shall set down the reasons that made me doubt of the truth of that opinion, as an excuse for my mistake, if I be in one; which I leave to be considered by those who, with me, dispose themselves to embrace truth, wherever they find it.

2. There is nothing more commonly taken for granted than that there are certain principles, both *speculative* and *practical* (for they speak of both), universally agreed upon by all mankind: which therefore, they argue, must needs be constant impressions which the souls of men receive in their first beings, and which they bring into the world with them, as necessarily and really as they do any of their inherent faculties.

3. This argument, drawn from *universal consent*, has this misfortune in it, that if it were true in matter of fact that there were certain truths wherein all mankind agreed, it would not prove them innate, if there can be any other way shown how men may come to that universal agreement, in the things they do consent in, which I presume may be done.

4. But, which is worse, this argument of universal consent, which is made use of to prove innate principles, seems to me a demonstration that there are none such: because there are none to which all mankind give an universal assent. I shall begin with the speculative, and instance in those magnified principles of demonstration, *Whatsoever is, is* and *It is impossible for the*

same thing to be and not to be, which of all others I think have the most allowed title to innate. These have so settled a reputation of maxims universally received that it will, no doubt, be thought strange if anyone should seem to question it. But yet I take liberty to say that these propositions are so far from having an universal assent, that there are a great part of mankind to whom they are not so much as known.

5.   For, first, it is evident that all *children* and *idiots* have not the least apprehension or thought of them. And the want of that is enough to destroy that universal assent which must needs be the necessary concomitant of all innate truths: it seeming to me near a contradiction to say that there are truths imprinted on the soul which it perceives or understands not: imprinting, if it signify anything, being nothing else but the making certain truths to be perceived. But to imprint anything on the mind, without the mind's perceiving it, seems to me hardly intelligible. If therefore *children* and *idiots* have souls, have minds, with those impressions upon them, they must unavoidably perceive them, and necessarily know and assent to these truths; which since they do not, it is evident that there are no such impressions. For if they are not notions naturally imprinted, how can they be innate? And if they are notions imprinted, how can they be unknown? To say a notion is imprinted on the mind, and yet at the same time to say that the mind is ignorant of it, and never yet took notice of it, is to make this impression nothing. No proposition can be said to be in the mind, which it never yet knew, which it was never yet conscious of. For if any one may, then by the same reason all propositions that are true and the mind is capable ever of assenting to, may be said to be in the mind and to be imprinted: since, if any one can be said to be in the mind which it never yet knew, it must be only because it is capable of knowing it; and so the mind is of all truths it ever shall know. Nay, thus truths may be imprinted on the mind which it never did nor ever shall know; for a man may live long, and die at last in ignorance of many truths which his mind was capable of knowing, and that with certainty. So that if the capacity of knowing be the natural impression contended for, all the truths a man ever comes to know will, by this account, be every one of them innate; and this great point will amount to no more, but only to a very improper way of speaking; which, whilst it pretends to assert the contrary, says nothing different from those who deny innate principles. For nobody, I think, ever denied that the mind was capable of knowing several truths. The capacity they say is innate, the knowledge acquired. But then to what end such contest for certain innate maxims? If truths can be imprinted on the understanding without being perceived, I can see no difference there can be between any truths the mind is capable of knowing, in respect of their original: they must all be

innate, or all adventitious. In vain shall a man go about to distinguish them. He therefore that talks of innate notions in the understanding, cannot (if he intend thereby any distinct sort of truths) mean such truths to be in the understanding as it never perceived, and is yet wholly ignorant of. For if these words (*to be in the understanding*) have any propriety, they signify to be understood. So that to be in the understanding and not to be understood, to be in the mind and never to be perceived, is all one as to say: anything is and is not in the mind or understanding. If therefore these two propositions, *Whatsoever is, is* and *It is impossible for the same thing to be and not to be*, are by nature imprinted, children cannot be ignorant of them; infants, and all that have souls, must necessarily have them in their understandings, know the truth of them, and assent to it.

6.   To avoid this, it is usually answered that all men know and *assent* to them, *when they come to the use of reason*; and this is enough to prove them innate. I answer:

7.   Doubtful expressions, that have scarce any signification, go for clear reasons to those who, being prepossessed, take not the pains to examine even what they themselves say. For, to apply this answer with any tolerable sense to our present purpose, it must signify one of these two things: either, that as soon as men come to the use of reason these supposed native inscriptions come to be known and observed by them; or else, that the use and exercise of men's reason assists them in the discovery of these principles, and certainly makes them known to them.

·8.   If they mean that by the *use of reason* men may discover these principles, and that this is sufficient to prove them innate, their way of arguing will stand thus: viz. that whatever truths reason can certainly discover to us and make us firmly assent to, those are all naturally imprinted on the mind, since that universal assent, which is made the mark of them, amounts to no more but this: that by the use of reason we are capable to come to a certain knowledge of and assent to them; and, by this means, there will be no difference between the maxims of the mathematicians and theorems they deduce from them: all must be equally allowed innate, they being all discoveries made by the use of reason, and truths that a rational creature may certainly come to know, if he apply his thoughts rightly that way.

9.   But how can these men think the *use of reason* necessary to discover principles that are supposed innate, when reason (if we may believe them) is nothing else but the faculty of deducing unknown truths from principles or propositions that are already known? That certainly can never be thought innate which we have need of reason to discover, unless, as I have said, we will have all the certain truths that reason ever teaches us to be innate. We may as well think the use of reason necessary to make our eyes discover

visible objects, as that there should be need of reason, or the exercise thereof, to make the understanding see what is originally engraven in it, and cannot be in the understanding before it be perceived by it. So that to make reason discover those truths thus imprinted is to say that the use of reason discovers to a man what he knew before; and if men have those innate, impressed truths originally, and before the use of reason, and yet are always ignorant of them till they come to the use of reason, it is in effect to say that men know and know them not at the same time.

10. It will perhaps be said that mathematical demonstrations and other truths that are not innate, are not assented to as soon as proposed, wherein they are distinguished from these maxims and other innate truths. I shall have occasion to speak of assent upon the first proposing, more particularly by and by. I shall here only, and that very readily, allow that these maxims and mathematical demonstrations are in this different: that the one have need of reason, using of proofs, to make them out and to gain our assent; but the other, as soon as understood, are, without any the least reasoning, embraced and assented to. But I withal beg leave to observe that it lays open the weakness of this subterfuge which requires the *use of reason* for the discovery of these general truths, since it must be confessed that in their discovery there is no use made of reasoning at all. And I think those who give this answer will not be forward to affirm that the knowledge of this maxim, *That it is impossible for the same thing to be, and not to be*, is a deduction of our reason. For this would be to destroy that bounty of nature they seem so fond of, whilst they make the knowledge of those principles to depend on the labour of our thoughts. For all reasoning is search and casting about and requires pains and application. And how can it with any tolerable sense be supposed that what was imprinted by nature, as the foundation and guide of our reason, should need the use of reason to discover it?

11. Those who will take the pains to reflect with a little attention on the operations of the understanding will find that this ready assent of the mind to some truths depends not either on native inscription or the *use of reason*, but on a faculty of the mind quite distinct from both of them, as we shall see hereafter. Reason, therefore, having nothing to do in procuring our assent to these maxims, if by saying that *men know and assent to them when they come to the use of reason* be meant that the use of reason assists us in the knowledge of these maxims, it is utterly false; and were it true, would prove them not to be innate.

12. If by knowing and assenting to them *when we come to the use of reason* be meant that this is the time when they come to be taken notice of by the mind; and that as soon as children come to the use of reason, they come

also to know and assent to these maxims: this also is false and frivolous. *First*, it is false. Because it is evident these maxims are not in the mind so early as the use of reason; and therefore the coming to the use of reason is falsely assigned as the time of their discovery. How many instances of the use of reason may we observe in children a long time before they have any knowledge of this maxim, *That it is impossible for the same thing to be, and not to be?* And a great part of illiterate people and savages pass many years, even of their rational age, without ever thinking on this, and the like general propositions. I grant men come not to the knowledge of these general and more abstract truths, which are thought innate, till they come to the use of reason; and I add, nor then neither. Which is so, because, till after they come to the use of reason, those general abstract *ideas* are not framed in the mind, about which those general maxims are which are mistaken for innate principles, but are indeed discoveries made and verities introduced and brought into the mind by the same way and discovered by the same steps as several other propositions, which nobody was ever so extravagant as to suppose innate. This I hope to make plain in the sequel of this discourse. I allow therefore a necessity that men should come to the use of reason before they get the knowledge of those general truths, but deny that men's coming to the use of reason is the time of their discovery.

13.   In the meantime, it is observable that this saying, that men know and assent to these maxims *when they come to the use of reason*, amounts in reality of fact to no more but this, that they are never known nor taken notice of before the use of reason, but may possibly be assented to sometime after, during a man's life; but when, is uncertain. And so may all other knowable truths, as well as these which therefore have no advantage nor distinction from others, by this note of being known when we come to the use of reason; nor are thereby proved to be innate, but quite the contrary.

14.   But, *Secondly*, were it true that the precise time of their being known and assented to were when men come to the *use of reason*, neither would that prove them innate. This way of arguing is so frivolous as the supposition of itself is false. For, by what kind of logic will it appear that any notion is originally by nature imprinted in the mind in its first constitution, because it comes first to be observed and assented to when a faculty of the mind, which has quite a distinct province, begins to exert itself? And therefore the coming to the use of speech, if it were supposed the time that these maxims are first assented to (which it may be with as much truth as the time when men come to the use of reason), would be as good a proof that they were innate, as to say they are innate because men assent to them when they come to the use of reason. I agree then with these men of innate principles that there is no knowledge of these general and self-evident

maxims in the mind till it comes to the exercise of reason; but I deny that the coming to the use of reason is the precise time when they are first taken notice of; and if that were the precise time, I deny that it would prove them innate. All that can with any truth be meant by this proposition, that men *assent to them when they come to the use of reason*, is no more but this: that the making of general abstract *ideas* and the understanding of general names being a concomitant of the rational faculty and growing up with it, children commonly get not those general *ideas* nor learn the names that stand for them, till having for a good while exercised their reason about familiar and more particular *ideas*, they are by their ordinary discourse and actions with others acknowledged to be capable of rational conversation. If assenting to these maxims, when men come to the use of reason, can be true in any other sense, I desire it may be shown; or at least, how in this or any other sense it proves them innate.

15.   The senses at first let in particular *ideas* and furnish the yet empty cabinet; and the mind by degrees growing familiar with some of them, they are lodged in the memory, and names got to them. Afterwards the mind, proceeding further, abstracts them, and by degrees learns the use of general names. In this manner the mind comes to be furnished with *ideas* and language, the materials about which to exercise its discursive faculty. And the use of reason becomes daily more visible, as these materials that give it employment increase. But though the having of general *ideas* and the use of general words and reason usually grow together, yet I see not how this any way proves them innate. The knowledge of some truths, I confess, is very early in the mind, but in a way that shows them not to be innate. For, if we will observe, we shall find it still to be about *ideas*, not innate, but acquired: it being about those first which are imprinted by external things, with which infants have earliest to do, which make the most frequent impressions on their senses. In *ideas* thus got, the mind discovers that some agree and others differ, probably as soon as it has any use of memory, as soon as it is able to retain and receive distinct *ideas*. But whether it be then or no, this is certain: it does so long before it has the use of words, or comes to that which we commonly call the *use of reason*. For a child knows as certainly, before it can speak, the difference between the *ideas* of sweet and bitter (i.e. that sweet is not bitter) as it knows afterwards (when it comes to speak) that wormwood and sugar-plums are not the same thing.

16.   A child knows not that three and four are equal to seven till he comes to be able to count to seven, and has got the name and *idea* of equality; and then upon explaining those words, he presently assents to, or rather perceives the truth of that proposition. But neither does he then readily assent, because it is an innate truth, nor was his assent wanting till then

because he wanted the *use of reason*; but the truth of it appears to him as soon as he has settled in his mind the clear and distinct *ideas* that these names stand for. And then he knows the truth of that proposition upon the same grounds and by the same means that he knew before that a rod and cherry are not the same thing, and upon the same grounds also that he may come to know afterwards that *It is impossible for the same thing to be, and not to be*, as shall be more fully shown hereafter. So that the later it is before anyone comes to have those general *ideas* about which those maxims are, or to know the signification of those general terms that stand for them, or to put together in his mind the *ideas* they stand for, the later also will it be before he comes to assent to those maxims; whose terms, with the *ideas* they stand for, being no more innate than those of a cat or a weasel, he must stay till time and observation have acquainted him with them; and then he will be in a capacity to know the truth of these maxims, upon the first occasion that shall make him put together those *ideas* in his mind and observe whether they agree or disagree, according as is expressed in those propositions. And therefore it is that a man knows that eighteen and nineteen are equal to thirty-seven, by the same self-evidence that he knows one and two to be equal to three; yet a child knows this not so soon as the other, not for want of the use of reason, but because the *ideas* the words eighteen, nineteen, and thirty-seven stand for are not so soon got as those which are signified by one, two, and three.

17. This evasion therefore of general assent when men come to the use of reason failing as it does, and leaving no difference between those supposed innate and other truths that are afterwards acquired and learnt, men have endeavoured to secure an universal assent to those they call maxims by saying they are generally *assented to, as soon as proposed*, and the terms they are proposed in understood; seeing all men, even children, as soon as they hear and understand the terms, assent to these propositions, they think it is sufficient to prove them innate. For since men never fail, after they have once understood the words, to acknowledge them for undoubted truths, they would infer that certainly these propositions were first lodged in the understanding which, without any teaching, the mind at very first proposal immediately closes with and assents to, and after that never doubts again.

18. In answer to this, I demand whether ready *assent* given to a proposition, *upon first hearing* and understanding the terms, be a certain mark of an innate principle? If it be not, such a general assent is in vain urged as a proof of them; if it be said that it is a mark of innate, they must then allow all such propositions to be innate which are generally assented to as soon as heard, whereby they will find themselves plentifully stored with innate

principles. For upon the same ground, viz. of assent at first hearing and understanding the terms, that men would have those maxims pass for innate, they must also admit several propositions about numbers to be innate; and thus, that *One and two are equal to three*, that *Two and two are equal to four*, and a multitude of other the like propositions in numbers that everybody assents to at first hearing and understanding the terms, must have a place amongst these innate axioms. Nor is this the prerogative of numbers alone, and propositions made about several of them; but even natural philosophy and all the other sciences afford propositions which are sure to meet with assent as soon as they are understood. That *Two bodies cannot be in the same place* is a truth that nobody any more sticks at than at these maxims that *It is impossible for the same thing to be and not to be*, that *White is not black*, that *A square is not a circle*, that *Yellowness is not sweetness*. These and a million of other such propositions, as many at least as we have distinct *ideas*, every man in his wits, at first hearing and knowing what the names stand for, must necessarily assent to. If these men will be true to their own rule and have *assent at first hearing and understanding the terms* to be a mark of innate, they must allow not only as many innate propositions as men have distinct *ideas*, but as many as men can make propositions wherein different *ideas* are denied one of another. Since every proposition wherein one different *idea* is denied of another will as certainly find assent at first hearing and understanding the terms as this general one, *It is impossible for the same to be, and not to be*, or that which is the foundation of it and is the easier understood of the two, *The same is not different*: by which account they will have legions of innate propositions of this one sort, without mentioning any other. But since no proposition can be innate unless the *ideas* about which it is be innate, this will be to suppose all our *ideas* of colours, sounds, tastes, figure, etc., innate, than which there cannot be anything more opposite to reason and experience. Universal and ready assent upon hearing and understanding the terms is (I grant) a mark of self-evidence; but self-evidence, depending not on innate impressions but on something else (as we shall show hereafter), belongs to several propositions, which nobody was yet so extravagant as to pretend to be innate.

19.   Nor let it be said that those more particular self-evident propositions which are assented to at first hearing, as that *One and two are equal to three*, that *Green is not red*, etc., are received as the consequences of those more universal propositions which are looked on as innate principles, since anyone who will but take the pains to observe what passes in the understanding will certainly find that these and the like less general propositions are certainly known and firmly assented to by those who are utterly ignorant of those more general maxims, and so, being earlier in the mind than those

(as they are called) first principles, cannot owe to them the assent wherewith they are received at first hearing.

20.   If it be said that these propositions, viz., *Two and two are equal to four, Red is not blue*, etc., are not general maxims nor of any great use, I answer that makes nothing to the argument of universal assent upon hearing and understanding. For, if that be the certain mark of innate, whatever proposition can be found that receives general assent as soon as heard and understood, that must be admitted for an innate proposition, as well as this maxim, that *It is impossible for the same thing to be, and not to be*, they being upon this ground equal. And as to the difference of being more general, that makes this maxim more remote from being innate, those general and abstract *ideas* being more strangers to our first apprehensions than those of more particular self-evident propositions, and therefore it is longer before they are admitted and assented to by the growing understanding. And as to the usefulness of these magnified maxims, that perhaps will not be found so great as is generally conceived when it comes to its due place to be more fully considered.

21.   But we have not yet done with *assenting to propositions at first hearing and understanding their terms*. It is fit we first take notice that this, instead of being a mark that they are innate, is a proof of the contrary, since it supposes that several, who understand and know other things, are ignorant of these principles till they are proposed to them, and that one may be unacquainted with these truths till he hears them from others. For if they were innate, what need they be proposed in order to gaining assent, when, by being in the understanding, by a natural and original impression (if there were any such) they could not but be known before? Or doth the proposing them print them clearer in the mind than nature did? If so, then the consequence will be that a man knows them better after he has been thus taught them than he did before. Whence it will follow that these principles may be made more evident to us by others' teaching than nature has made them by impression: which will ill agree with the opinion of innate principles, and give but little authority to them, but on the contrary makes them unfit to be the foundations of all our other knowledge, as they are pretended to be. This cannot be denied: that men grow first acquainted with many of these self-evident truths upon their being proposed; but it is clear that whosoever does so finds in himself that he then begins to know a proposition which he knew not before, and which from thenceforth he never questions, not because it was innate, but because the consideration of the nature of the things contained in those words would not suffer him to think otherwise, how or whensoever he is brought to reflect on them. And if whatever is

assented to at first hearing and understanding the terms must pass for an innate principle, every well-grounded observation drawn from particulars into a general rule must be innate. When yet it is certain that not all but only sagacious heads light at first on these observations and reduce them into general propositions, not innate but collected from a preceding acquaintance and reflection on particular instances. These, when observing men have made them, unobserving men, when they are proposed to them, cannot refuse their assent to.

22.   If it be said the understanding hath an *implicit knowledge* of these principles, but not an explicit, before this first hearing (as they must who will say that they are in the understanding before they are known), it will be hard to conceive what is meant by a principle imprinted on the understanding implicitly, unless it be this, that the mind is capable of understanding and assenting firmly to such propositions. And thus all mathematical demonstrations, as well as first principles, must be received as native impressions on the mind; which I fear they will scarce allow them to be, who find it harder to demonstrate a proposition than assent to it when demonstrated. And few mathematicians will be forward to believe that all the diagrams they have drawn were but copies of those innate characters which nature had engraven upon their minds.

23.   There is, I fear, this further weakness in the foregoing argument, which would persuade us that therefore those maxims are to be thought innate which men *admit at first hearing*, because they assent to propositions which they are not taught nor do receive from the force of any argument or demonstration, but a bare explication or understanding of the terms. Under which there seems to me to lie this fallacy, that men are supposed not to be *taught* nor to *learn* anything *de novo*, when, in truth, they are taught and do learn something they were ignorant of before. For, first, it is evident they have learned the terms and their signification, neither of which was born with them. But this is not all the acquired knowledge in the case: the *ideas* themselves, about which the proposition is, are not born with them, no more than their names, but got afterwards. So that in all propositions that are assented to at first hearing: the terms of all proposition, their standing for such *ideas*, and the *ideas* themselves that they stand for being neither of them innate, I would fain know what there is remaining in such propositions that is innate. For I would gladly have anyone name that proposition whose terms or *ideas* were either of them innate. We by degrees get *ideas* and names, and learn their appropriated connection one with another; and then to propositions made in such terms, whose signification we have learnt, and wherein the agreement or disagreement we can perceive in our *ideas* when put together is

expressed, we at first hearing assent; though to other propositions, in themselves as certain and evident, but which are concerning *ideas* not so soon or so easily got, we are at the same time no way capable of assenting. For though a child quickly assent to this proposition, that *An apple is not fire*, when by familiar acquaintance he has got the *ideas* of those two different things distinctly imprinted on his mind, and has learnt that the names *apple* and *fire* stand for them: yet it will be some years after, perhaps, before the same child will assent to this proposition, that *It is impossible for the same thing to be, and not to be*. Because, though perhaps the words are as easy to be learnt, yet the signification of them, being more large, comprehensive, and abstract than of the names annexed to those sensible things the child hath to do with, it is longer before he learns their precise meaning, and it requires more time plainly to form in his mind those general *ideas* they stand for. Till that be done, you will in vain endeavour to make any child assent to a proposition made up of such general terms; but as soon as ever he has got those *ideas* and learned their names, he forwardly closes with the one as well as the other of the fore-mentioned propositions, and with both for the same reason, viz. because he finds the *ideas* he has in his mind to agree or disagree, according as the words standing for them are affirmed or denied one of another in the proposition. But if propositions be brought to him in words which stand for *ideas* he has not yet in his mind, to such propositions, however evidently true or false in themselves, he affords neither assent nor dissent but is ignorant. For words being but empty sounds, any further than they are signs of our *ideas* we cannot but assent to them as they correspond to those *ideas* we have, but no further than that. But the showing by what steps and ways knowledge comes into our minds, and the grounds of several degrees of assent, being the business of the following discourse, it may suffice to have only touched on it here, as one reason that made me doubt of those innate principles.

24.   To conclude this argument of *universal consent*, I agree with these defenders of innate principles that if they are *innate* they must needs *have universal assent*. For that a truth should be innate and yet not assented to is to me as unintelligible as for a man to know a truth and be ignorant of it at the same time. But then, by these men's own confession, they cannot be innate, since they are not assented to by those who understand not the terms; nor by a great part of those who do understand them, but have yet never heard nor thought of those propositions; which I think, is at least one-half of mankind. But were the number far less, it would be enough to destroy *universal assent*, and thereby show these propositions not to be innate, if children alone were ignorant of them.

(B)   Leibniz, Preface

. . . The question at issue is whether the soul itself is entirely void, like a tablet whereon nothing has yet been written (*tabula rasa*), as is the view of Aristotle and the author of the essay [i.e. Locke], and everything marked on it comes solely from the senses and from experience, or whether the soul contains originally the principles of various notions and doctrines, which external objects simply recall from time to time, as is my view and that of Plato, and even of the Schoolmen, and of all those who attribute this meaning to the passage from St. Paul (Rom. ii. 15), where he says that the law of God is writ in men's hearts. The Stoics call these principles *prolepses*, that is to say assumptions which are fundamental or taken as agreed in advance. The mathematicians call them *common notions* (κοιναὶ ἔννοιαι). Modern philosophers give them other fine names, and Julius Scaliger in particular called them *semina aeternitatis* ['seeds of eternity'] and again *zopyra*, meaning to say living fires, flashes of light, hidden within us, but caused to appear by the contact of the senses, like the sparks which the shock of the flint strikes from the steel. And it is not an unreasonable belief that these flashes are a sign of something divine and eternal, which makes its appearance above all in necessary truths. From this arises another question, whether all truths depend on experience, that is to say on induction and on instances, or whether there are some which have another basis also. For if certain events can be foreseen before we have made any trial of them, it is clear that we contribute in those cases something of our own. The senses, although they are necessary for all our actual knowledge, are not sufficient to give us the whole of it, since the senses never give anything but instances, that is to say particular or individual truths. Now all the instances which confirm a general truth, however numerous they may be, are not sufficient to establish the universal necessity of this same truth, for it does not follow that what happened before will happen in the same way again. For example, the Greeks and the Romans, and all the other peoples of the earth known to the ancients, always observed that before the passage of twenty-four hours day changes to night and night to day. But they would have been wrong if they had believed that the same rule holds good everywhere, for since that time the contrary has been experienced during a visit to Nova Zembla. And any one who believed that in our zone at least this is a necessary and eternal truth which will last for ever, would likewise be wrong, since we must hold that the earth and even the sun do not exist of necessity, and that there may perhaps come a time when that beautiful star and its whole system will exist no longer, at least in its present form. From which it appears that necessary truths, such as we find in pure mathematics, and particularly in arithmetic and geometry, must have principles whose proof does not depend on instances, nor consequently on the testimony of the senses, although without the senses it would never have occurred to us to think of them. This is a distinction that should be carefully noted; and it is one which Euclid understood so well that he often proves by reason what is evident enough through experience and sensible images. Logic also, together with metaphysics and morals, the one of which forms natural theology and the other natural jurisprudence, are full of such truths; and consequently proof of them can only arise from inner principles, which are called innate. It is true that we must not imagine that we can read in the soul these eternal laws of reason as in an open book, as the edict of the praetor can be read in his *album* without trouble or deep scrutiny. But it is enough that we can find them in ourselves by dint of attention, opportunities for which are afforded by the senses. The success of experiments serves also as a confirmation of reason, more or less as verifications serve in arithmetic to help us to avoid erroneous calculation when the reasoning is long. It is in this also that the knowledge of men differs from that of the brutes: the latter are purely empirical, and guide themselves solely by particular instances; for, as far as we can judge, they never go so far as to form necessary propositions; whereas men are capable of the demonstrative sciences. This also is why the faculty the brutes have of making *sequences* of ideas is something inferior to the reason which is in man. The sequences of the brutes are just like those of the pure empiricists who claim that what has happened sometimes will happen again in a case where what strikes them is similar, without being capable of determining whether the same reasons hold good. It is because of this that it is so easy for men to catch animals, and so easy for pure empiricists to make mistakes. And people whom age and experience has rendered skilful are not exempt from this when they rely too much on their past experience, as some have done in civil and military affairs; they do not pay sufficient attention to the fact that the world changes, and that men become more skilful by discovering countless new contrivances, whereas the stags and hares of today are no more cunning than those of yesterday. The sequences of the brutes are but a shadow of reasoning, that is to say, they are but connexions of imagination, transitions from one image to another; for in a fresh experience, which appears like the preceding one, there is the expectation that what was hitherto joined thereto will occur again, as though the things were connected in fact, because their images are connected in the memory. It is true that reason also teaches us to expect in the ordinary course of events to see occur in the future what conforms to a long experience of the past, but it is not therefore a necessary and infallible truth, and we may cease to be successful when we least expect it, when the reasons which have maintained it change. This is why the wisest people do not rely on it to the extent of not trying to discover, if it is possible, something of the reason of what happens, so as to judge when exceptions must be made. For reason alone is capable of setting up rules which are certain, and of supplying what is lacking to those which are not certain, by inserting the exceptions, and in short of finding connexions which are certain in the force of necessary consequences. This often provides the means of foreseeing the event, without its being necessary to experience the sensible connexions between images which is all that the brutes can do; so that to vindicate the existence within us of the principles of necessary truths is also to distinguish man from the brutes.

Perhaps our gifted author will not entirely dissociate himself from my opinion. For after having devoted the whole of his first book to the rejection of innate ideas, understood in a certain sense, he yet admits in the beginning of the second and in what follows that ideas whose origin is not in sensation arise from reflexion. Now reflexion is nothing but an attention to what is in us, and the senses do not give us what we already bring with us. This being so, can we deny that there is a great deal that is innate in our mind, since we are innate, so to speak, to ourselves, and since there is in ourselves being, unity, substance, duration, change, activity, perception, pleasure, and a thousand other objects of our intellectual ideas? And since these objects are immediate to our understanding and are always present (although they cannot always be apperceived on account of our distractions and our needs),[1] why be surprised that we say that these ideas, and everything which depends on them, are innate in us? This is why I have taken as an illustration a block of veined marble, rather than a wholly uniform block or blank tablets, that is to say what is called *tabula rasa* in the language of the philosophers. For if the soul were like these blank tablets, truths would be in us in the same way as the figure of Hercules is in a block of marble, when the marble is completely indifferent whether it receives this or some other figure. But if there were veins in the stone which marked out the figure of Hercules rather than other figures, this stone would be more determined thereto, and Hercules would be as it were in some manner innate in it, although labour would be needed to uncover those veins, and to clear them by polishing, and by cutting away what prevents them from appearing. It is in this way that ideas and truths are innate in us, like natural inclinations and dispositions, natural habits or potentialities, and not like activities, although these potentialities are always accompanied by some activities which correspond to them, though they are often imperceptible.

It seems that our gifted author claims that there is in us nothing *potential*, nor even anything which we do not always actually apperceive; but he cannot take this quite strictly, otherwise his opinion would be too paradoxical, since acquired habits also and the contents of our memory are not always apperceived, and do not even always come to our aid when needed, although we often easily recall them to mind on some trivial occasion which reminds us of them, in the same way as we only need the beginning of a song to make us remember the rest. Moreover he limits his doctrine in other places by saying that there is nothing in us which we have not at least previously apperceived. But besides the fact that nobody can guarantee by reason alone how far our past apperceptions which may have been forgotten may have gone, especially in view of the Platonic doctrine of reminiscence, which, mythical though it is, is not incompatible, in part at least, with bare reason: besides this, I say, why should it be necessary that everything should be acquired by us by apperceptions of external things, and nothing be able to be unearthed in ourselves? Is our soul of itself alone so empty that apart from images borrowed from without it is nothing? This is not, I am convinced, an opinion that our judicious author could approve. And where are there to be found tablets which have not in themselves a certain amount of variety? We shall never see a perfectly level and uniform surface. Why, therefore, should we not also be able to provide some sort of thought from deep within ourselves, when we are willing to delve there? Thus I am led to believe that fundamentally his opinion on this point does not differ from mine, or rather from the common opinion, inasmuch as he recognises two sources of our knowledge, the senses and reflexion. . . .

Note

1 'Apperception' is Leibniz's term for conscious perception. It is an important part of his philosophy that there are 'at all times an infinite number of *perceptions* in us, though without apperception and without reflexion' (*New Essays on the Human Understanding*, Preface, in *Philosophical Writings*, ed. Parkinson, p. 155).

David Hume, *An Enquiry Concerning Human Understanding*, Section 12

From David Hume, *Enquiries*, 2nd edition, ed. L. A. Selby-Bigge. Oxford: Oxford University Press, 1902, pp. 148–65 [asterisked notes are Hume's own].

'The first thing anyone hears of Hume is that he was a sceptic'.[1] Quite possibly – but this was not a reputation David Hume (1711–76) unambiguously cherished, as we can judge from his testy 'Letter from a gentleman' responding to the Edinburgh clergy's accusations of scepticism and atheism. Indeed, in both *A Treatise of Human Nature* and the later *An Enquiry Concerning Human Understanding*, Hume's attitude towards scepticism vacillates. In the earlier work, especially, he seems to veer from a sustained defence of scepticism to judging it 'strain'd and ridiculous', something to set aside after a good dinner and game of backgammon (I.IV.7). In the final pages of the *Enquiry*, which I have selected, his position is, arguably, a more settled one – that of a 'mitigated' scepticism that steers between 'dogmatism' and the excesses of Pyrrhonian scepticism (see chapter 3 above).

Like many slightly earlier philosophers, such as Pierre Bayle and Bishop Berkeley, Hume was impressed by Descartes' provisional case for scepticism, but markedly unimpressed by the Frenchman's subsequent attempt to overturn that case. Matters were made worse, if anything, by Berkeley's own rebuttal of scepticism: ensuring that our beliefs cannot fail to correspond to material reality by denying the existence of such a reality – by equating *esse* with *percipi* – was, in Hume's view, at once to concede to the sceptics nearly everything they wanted and, through being at once irrefutable yet incredible, to foster the confusion on which scepticism feeds (see Hume's note, p. 140 below).

At first glance, the scepticism Hume is willing to endorse seems severely limited. From the little he offers by way of analysis of the concept of knowl-

[1] Edward Craig, *The Mind of God and the Works of Man*, Oxford: Clarendon Press, 1987, p. 81.

edge, it appears that, for him, we can only have knowledge, strictly speaking, of matters about which we cannot imagine ourselves mistaken – propositions about immediate sense-experience, for example, or ones which are true by definition. To deny that we can know anything else then seems to reduce to the claim that propositions about, say, the external world or moral right and wrong, go beyond what is warranted by immediate sense-experience or definitions. 'Mitigated' scepticism would then amount to little more than a counsel of due modesty and caution when making assertions of such kinds. However, given Hume's view that 'experience is, and must be entirely silent' about the external world – since it is never this world, but only our own 'impressions' we ever experience – it is unclear that Hume can rest here. Like the Pyrrhonian, it seems that he must deny, not merely that we know anything about, but that we have any justification at all for our beliefs about, the external world.[2] Certainly the ringing final lines of the *Enquiry*, committing to the flames what goes beyond mathematical and experimental reasoning, express something more than mere modesty and caution.

Some commentators, however, referring to what is called Hume's 'naturalism', do discern in his writings a genuine and interesting response to 'excessive' scepticism.[3] In both the *Treatise* and the *Enquiry*, Hume stresses that we are compelled, in accordance with our human nature, both to act and think on the basis of 'customary' and ineradicable convictions – to the effect, for instance, that there is an external world, or that there are necessary connections between causes and effects. This is hardly a rebuttal of scepticism if it amounts to no more than the point that, even if scepticism is true, we can only take it seriously during certain contemplative moments, soon to be dispelled by a hearty meal. But perhaps Hume's position is this: the sceptic worries us because he regards nearly all our beliefs as unjustifiable or irrational. Now, whether a belief is rational or not, justifiable or not, presupposes a framework of wider, more basic beliefs and convictions relative to which such judgements can be made. The most basic framework, therefore – that of our 'natural' convictions – cannot itself be judged rational or irrational. It is, one might say, simply *there*. If this is Hume's position, readers will want to compare it with that of Ludwig Wittgenstein (see chapter 17 below).

---

[2] See Richard H. Popkin, 'David Hume: his Pyrrhonism and his critique of Pyrrhonism', in *Hume*, ed. V. Chappell, Indiana: University of Notre Dame Press, 1966.
[3] See especially P. F. Strawson, *Skepticism and Naturalism: Some Varieties*, London: Methuen, 1985.

Section XII: Of the Academical or Sceptical Philosophy

Part I

116   There is not a greater number of philosophical reasonings, displayed upon any subject, than those, which prove the existence of a Deity, and refute the fallacies of *Atheists*; and yet the most religious philosophers still dispute whether any man can be so blinded as to be a speculative atheist. How shall we reconcile these contradictions? The knightserrant, who wandered about to clear the world of dragons and giants, never entertained the least doubt with regard to the existence of these monsters.

The *Sceptic* is another enemy of religion, who naturally provokes the indignation of all divines and graver philosophers; though it is certain, that no man ever met with any such absurd creature, or conversed with a man, who had no opinion or principle concerning any subject, either of action or speculation. This begets a very natural question: What is meant by a sceptic? And how far it is possible to push these philosophical principles of doubt and uncertainty?

There is a species of scepticism, *antecedent* to all study and philosophy, which is much inculcated by Descartes and others, as a sovereign preservative against error and precipitate judgement. It recommends an universal doubt, not only of all our former opinions and principles, but also of our very faculties; of whose veracity, say they, we must assure ourselves, by a chain of reasoning, deduced from some original principle, which cannot possibly be fallacious or deceitful. But neither is there any such original principle, which has a prerogative above others, that are self-evident and convincing: or if there were, could we advance a step beyond it, but by the use of those very faculties, of which we are supposed to be already diffident. The Cartesian doubt, therefore, were it ever possible to be attained by any human creature (as it plainly is not) would be entirely incurable; and no reasoning could ever bring us to a state of assurance and conviction upon any subject.

117   It must, however, be confessed, that this species of scepticism, when more moderate, may be understood in a very reasonable sense, and is a necessary preparative to the study of philosophy, by preserving a proper impartiality in our judgements, and weaning our mind from all those prejudices, which we may have imbibed from education or rash opinion. To begin with clear and self-evident principles, to advance by timorous and sure steps, to review frequently our conclusions, and examine accurately all their consequences; though by these means we shall make both a slow and

a short progress in our systems; are the only methods, by which we can ever hope to reach truth, and attain a proper stability and certainty in our determinations.

There is another species of scepticism, *consequent* to science and enquiry, when men are supposed to have discovered, either the absolute fallaciousness of their mental faculties, or their unfitness to reach any fixed determination in all those curious subjects of speculation, about which they are commonly employed. Even our very senses are brought into dispute, by a certain species of philosophers; and the maxims of common life are subjected to the same doubt as the most profound principles or conclusions of metaphysics and theology. As these paradoxical tenets (if they may be called tenets) are to be met with in some philosophers, and the refutation of them in several, they naturally excite our curiosity, and make us enquire into the arguments, on which they may be founded.

I need not insist upon the more trite topics, employed by the sceptics in all ages, against the evidence of *sense*; such as those which are derived from the imperfection and fallaciousness of our organs, on numberless occasions; the crooked appearance of an oar in water; the various aspects of objects, according to their different distances; the double images which arise from the pressing one eye; with many other appearances of a like nature. These sceptical topics, indeed, are only sufficient to prove, that the senses alone are not implicitly to be depended on; but that we must correct their evidence by reason, and by considerations, derived from the nature of the medium, the distance of the object, and the disposition of the organ, in order to render them, within their sphere, the proper *criteria* of truth and falsehood. There are other more profound arguments against the senses, which admit not of so easy a solution.

118   It seems evident, that men are carried, by a natural instinct or prepossession, to repose faith in their senses; and that, without any reasoning, or even almost before the use of reason, we always suppose an external universe, which depends not on our perception, but would exist, though we and every sensible creature were absent or annihilated. Even the animal creation are governed by a like opinion, and preserve this belief of external objects, in all their thoughts, designs, and actions.

It seems also evident, that, when men follow this blind and powerful instinct of nature, they always suppose the very images, presented by the senses, to be the external objects, and never entertain any suspicion, that the one are nothing but representations of the other. This very table, which we see white, and which we feel hard, is believed to exist, independent of our perception, and to be something external to our mind, which perceives it. Our presence bestows not being on it: our absence does not annihilate it. It preserves its existence uniform and entire, independent of the situation of intelligent beings, who perceive or contemplate it.

But this universal and primary opinion of all men is soon destroyed by the slightest philosophy, which teaches us, that nothing can ever be present to the mind but an image or perception, and that the senses are only the inlets, through which these images are conveyed, without being able to produce any immediate intercourse between the mind and the object. The table, which we see, seems to diminish, as we remove farther from it: but the real table, which exists independent of us, suffers no alteration: it was, therefore, nothing but its image, which was present to the mind. These are the obvious dictates of reason; and no man, who reflects, ever doubted, that the existences, which we consider, when we say, *this house* and *that tree*, are nothing but perceptions in the mind, and fleeting copies or representations of other existences, which remain uniform and independent.

119   So far, then, are we necessitated by reasoning to contradict or depart from the primary instincts of nature, and to embrace a new system with regard to the evidence of our senses. But here philosophy finds herself extremely embarrassed, when she would justify this new system, and obviate the cavils and objections of the sceptics. She can no longer plead the infallible and irresistible instinct of nature: for that led us to a quite different system, which is acknowledged fallible and even erroneous. And to justify this pretended philosophical system, by a chain of clear and convincing argument, or even any appearance of argument, exceeds the power of all human capacity.

By what argument can it be proved, that the perceptions of the mind must be caused by external objects, entirely different from them, though resembling them (if that be possible) and could not arise either from the energy of the mind itself, or from the suggestion of some invisible and unknown spirit, or from some other cause still more unknown to us? It is acknowledged, that, in fact, many of these perceptions arise not from anything external, as in dreams, madness, and other diseases. And nothing can be more inexplicable than the manner, in which body should so operate upon mind as ever to convey an image of itself to a substance, supposed of so different, and even contrary a nature.

It is a question of fact, whether the perceptions of the senses be produced by external objects, resembling them: how shall this question be determined? By experience surely; as all other questions of a like nature. But here experience is, and must be entirely silent. The mind has never anything present to it but the perceptions, and cannot possibly reach any experience of their connexion with objects. The supposition of such a connexion is, therefore, without any foundation in reasoning.

120   To have recourse to the veracity of the supreme Being, in order to prove the veracity of our senses, is surely making a very unexpected circuit. If his veracity were at all concerned in this matter, our senses would be entirely infallible; because it is not possible that he can ever deceive. Not to mention, that, if the external world be once called in question, we shall be at a loss to find arguments, by which we may prove the existence of that Being or any of his attributes.

121   This is a topic, therefore, in which the profounder and more philosophical sceptics will always triumph, when they endeavour to introduce an universal doubt into all subjects of human knowledge and enquiry. Do you follow the instincts and propensities of nature, may they say, in assenting to the veracity of sense? But these lead you to believe that the very perception or sensible image is the external object. Do you disclaim this principle, in order to embrace a more rational opinion, that the perceptions are only representations of something external? You here depart from your natural propensities and more obvious sentiments; and yet are not able to satisfy your reason, which can never find any convincing argument from experience to prove, that the perceptions are connected with any external objects.

122   There is another sceptical topic of a like nature, derived from the most profound philosophy; which might merit our attention, were it requisite to dive so deep, in order to discover arguments and reasonings, which can so little serve to any serious purpose. It is universally allowed by modern enquirers, that all the sensible qualities of objects, such as hard, soft, hot, cold, white, black, &c. are merely secondary, and exist not in the objects themselves, but are perceptions of the mind, without any external archetype or model, which they represent. If this be allowed, with regard to secondary qualities, it must also follow, with regard to the supposed primary qualities of extension and solidity; nor can the latter be any more entitled to that denomination than the former. The idea of extension is entirely acquired from the senses of sight and feeling; and if all the qualities, perceived by the senses, be in the mind, not in the object, the same conclusion must reach the idea of extension, which is wholly dependent on the sensible ideas or the ideas of secondary qualities. Nothing can save us from this conclusion, but the asserting, that the ideas of those primary qualities are attained by *Abstraction*, an opinion, which, if we examine it accurately, we shall find to be unintelligible, and even absurd. An extension, that is neither tangible nor visible, cannot possibly be conceived: and a tangible or visible extension, which is neither hard nor soft, black nor white, is equally beyond the reach of human conception. Let any man try to conceive a triangle in general, which is neither *Isosceles* nor *Scalenum*,

nor has any particular length or proportion of sides; and he will soon perceive the absurdity of all the scholastic notions with regard to abstraction and general ideas.*

123   Thus the first philosophical objection to the evidence of sense or to the opinion of external existence consists in this, that such an opinion, if rested on natural instinct, is contrary to reason, and if referred to reason, is contrary to natural instinct, and at the same time carries no rational evidence with it, to convince an impartial enquirer. The second objection goes farther, and represents this opinion as contrary to reason: at least, if it be a principle of reason, that all sensible qualities are in the mind, not in the object. Bereave matter of all its intelligible qualities, both primary and secondary, you in a manner annihilate it, and leave only a certain unknown, inexplicable *something*, as the cause of our perceptions; a notion so imperfect, that no sceptic will think it worth while to contend against it.

Part II

It may seem a very extravagant attempt of the sceptics to destroy *reason* by argument and ratiocination; yet is this the grand scope of all their enquiries and disputes. They endeavour to find objections, both to our abstract reasonings, and to those which regard matter of fact and existence.

The chief objection against all *abstract* reasonings is derived from the ideas of space and time; ideas, which, in common life and to a careless view, are very clear and intelligible, but when they pass through the scrutiny of the profound sciences (and they are the chief object of these sciences) afford principles, which seem full of absurdity and contradiction. No priestly *dogmas*, invented on purpose to tame and subdue the rebellious reason of mankind, ever shocked commonsense more than the doctrine of the infinite divisibility of extension, with its consequences;[1] as they are pompously displayed by all geometricians and metaphysicians, with a kind of triumph and exultation. A real quantity, infinitely less than any finite quantity, containing quantities infinitely less than itself, and so on *in infinitum*; this is

---

* This argument is drawn from Dr. Berkeley; and indeed most of the writings of that very ingenious author form the best lessons of scepticism, which are to be found either among the ancient or modern philosophers, Bayle not excepted. He professes, however, in his title-page (and undoubtedly with great truth) to have composed his book against the sceptics as well as against the atheists and free-thinkers. But that all his arguments, though otherwise intended, are, in reality, merely sceptical, appears from this, *that they admit of no answer and produce no conviction*. Their only effect is to cause that momentary amazement and irresolution and confusion, which is the result of scepticism.

an edifice so bold and prodigious, that it is too weighty for any pretended demonstration to support, because it shocks the clearest and most natural principles of human reason.* But what renders the matter more extraordinary, is, that these seemingly absurd opinions are supported by a chain of reasoning, the clearest and most natural; nor is it possible for us to allow the premises without admitting the consequences. Nothing can be more convincing and satisfactory than all the conclusions concerning the properties of circles and triangles; and yet, when these are once received, how can we deny, that the angle of contact between a circle and its tangent is infinitely less than any rectilineal angle, that as you may increase the diameter of the circle *in infinitum*, this angle of contact becomes still less, even *in infinitum*, and that the angle of contact between other curves and their tangents may be infinitely less than those between any circle and its tangent, and so on, *in infinitum?* The demonstration of these principles seems as unexceptionable as that which proves the three angles of a triangle to be equal to two right ones, though the latter opinion be natural and easy, and the former big with contradiction and absurdity. Reason here seems to be thrown into a kind of amazement and suspence, which, without the suggestions of any sceptic, gives her a diffidence of herself, and of the ground on which she treads. She sees a full light, which illuminates certain places; but that light borders upon the most profound darkness. And between these she is so dazzled and confounded, that she scarcely can pronounce with certainty and assurance concerning any one object.

125   The absurdity of these bold determinations of the abstract sciences seems to become, if possible, still more palpable with regard to time than extension. An infinite number of real parts of time, passing in succession, and exhausted one after another, appears so evident a contradiction, that no man, one should think, whose judgement is not corrupted, instead of being improved, by the sciences, would ever be able to admit of it.

    Yet still reason must remain restless, and unquiet, even with regard to that scepticism, to which she is driven by these seeming absurdities and contradictions. How any clear, distinct idea can contain circumstances, contradictory to itself, or to any other clear, distinct idea, is absolutely incomprehensible; and is, perhaps, as absurd as any proposition, which can

---

* Whatever disputes there may be about mathematical points, we must allow that there are physical points; that is, parts of extension, which cannot be divided or lessened, either by the eye or imagination. These images, then, which are present to the fancy or senses, are absolutely indivisible, and consequently must be allowed by mathematicians to be infinitely less than any real part of extension; and yet nothing appears more certain to reason, than that an infinite number of them composes an infinite extension. How much more an infinite number of those infinitely small parts of extension, which are still supposed infinitely divisible.

be formed. So that nothing can be more sceptical, or more full of doubt and hesitation, than this scepticism itself, which arises from some of the paradoxical conclusions of geometry or the science of quantity.*

126   The sceptical objections to *moral* evidence, or to the reasonings concerning matter of fact, are either *popular* or *philosophical.* The popular objections are derived from the natural weakness of human understanding; the contradictory opinions, which have been entertained in different ages and nations; the variations of our judgement in sickness and health, youth and old age, prosperity and adversity; the perpetual contradiction of each particular man's opinions and sentiments; with many other topics of that ·kind. It is needless to insist farther on this head. These objections are but weak. For as, in common life, we reason every moment concerning fact and existence, and cannot possibly subsist, without continually employing this species of argument, any popular objections, derived from thence, must be insufficient to destroy that evidence. The great subverter of *Pyrrhonism* or the excessive principles of scepticism is action, and employment, and the occupations of common life. These principles may flourish and triumph in the schools; where it is, indeed, difficult, if not impossible, to refute them. But as soon as they leave the shade, and by the presence of the real objects, which actuate our passions and sentiments, are put in opposition to the more powerful principles of our nature, they vanish like smoke, and leave the most determined sceptic in the same condition as other mortals.

127   The sceptic, therefore, had better keep within his proper sphere, and display those *philosophical* objections, which arise from more profound researches. Here he seems to have ample matter of triumph; while he justly insists, that all our evidence for any matter of fact, which lies beyond the testimony of sense or memory, is derived entirely from the relation of cause and effect; that we have no other idea of this relation than that of two

---

* It seems to me not impossible to avoid these absurdities and contradictions, if it be admitted, that there is no such thing as abstract or general ideas, properly speaking; but that all general ideas are, in reality, particular ones, attached to a general term, which recalls, upon occasion, other particular ones, that resemble, in certain circumstances, the idea, present to the mind.[2] Thus when the term Horse is pronounced, we immediately figure to ourselves the idea of a black or a white animal, of a particular size or figure: But as that term is also usually applied to animals of other colours, figures and sizes, these ideas, though not actually present to the imagination, are easily recalled; and our reasoning and conclusion proceed in the same way, as if they were actually present. If this be admitted (as seems reasonable) it follows that all the ideas of quantity, upon which mathematicians reason, are nothing but particular, and such as are suggested by the senses and imagination, and consequently, cannot be infinitely divisible. It is sufficient to have dropped this hint at present, without prosecuting it any farther. It certainly concerns all lovers of science not to expose themselves to the ridicule and contempt of the ignorant by their conclusions; and this seems the readiest solution of these difficulties.

objects, which have been frequently *conjoined* together; that we have no argument to convince us, that objects, which have, in our experience, been frequently conjoined, will likewise, in other instances, be conjoined in the same manner; and that nothing leads us to this inference but custom or a certain instinct of our nature; which it is indeed difficult to resist, but which, like other instincts, may be fallacious and deceitful. While the sceptic insists upon these topics, he shows his force, or rather, indeed, his own and our weakness; and seems, for the time at least, to destroy all assurance and conviction. These arguments might be displayed at greater length, if any durable good or benefit to society could ever be expected to result from them.

128   For here is the chief and most confounding objection to *excessive* scepticism, that no durable good can ever result from it; while it remains in its full force and vigour. We need only ask such a sceptic, *What his meaning is? And what he proposes by all these curious researches?* He is immediately at a loss, and knows not what to answer. A Copernican or Ptolemaic, who supports each his different system of astronomy, may hope to produce a conviction, which will remain constant and durable, with his audience. A Stoic or Epicurean displays principles, which may not only be durable, but which have an effect on conduct and behaviour. But a Pyrrhonian cannot expect, that his philosophy will have any constant influence on the mind: or if it had, that its influence would be beneficial to society. On the contrary, he must acknowledge, if he will acknowledge anything, that all human life must perish, were his principles universally and steadily to prevail. All discourse, all action would immediately cease; and men remain in a total lethargy, till the necessities of nature, unsatisfied, put an end to their miserable existence. It is true; so fatal an event is very little to be dreaded. Nature is always too strong for principle. And though a Pyrrhonian may throw himself or others into a momentary amazement and confusion by his profound reasonings; the first and most trivial event in life will put to flight all his doubts and scruples, and leave him the same, in every point of action and speculation, with the philosophers of every other sect, or with those who never concerned themselves in any philosophical researches. When he awakes from his dream, he will be the first to join in the laugh against himself, and to confess, that all his objections are mere amusement, and can have no other tendency than to show the whimsical condition of mankind, who must act and reason and believe; though they are not able, by their most diligent enquiry, to satisfy themselves concerning the foundation of these operations, or to remove the objections, which may be raised against them.

Part III

129   There is, indeed, a more *mitigated* scepticism or *academical* philosophy,[3] which may be both durable and useful, and which may, in part, be the result of this Pyrrhonism, or *excessive* scepticism, when its undistinguished doubts are, in some measure, corrected by commonsense and reflection. The greater part of mankind are naturally apt to be affirmative and dogmatical in their opinions; and while they see objects only on one side, and have no idea of any counter-poising argument, they throw themselves precipitately into the principles, to which they are inclined; nor have they any indulgence for those who entertain opposite sentiments. To hesitate or balance perplexes their understanding, checks their passion, and suspends their action. They are, therefore, impatient till they escape from a state, which to them is so uneasy: and they think, that they can never remove themselves far enough from it, by the violence of their affirmations and obstinacy of their belief. But could such dogmatical reasoners become sensible of the strange infirmities of human understanding, even in its most perfect state, and when most accurate and cautious in its determinations; such a reflection would naturally inspire them with more modesty and reserve, and diminish their fond opinion of themselves, and their prejudice against antagonists. The illiterate may reflect on the disposition of the learned, who, amidst all the advantages of study and reflection, are commonly still diffident in their determinations: and if any of the learned be inclined, from their natural temper, to haughtiness and obstinacy, a small tincture of Pyrrhonism might abate their pride, by showing them, that the few advantages, which they may have attained over their fellows, are but inconsiderable, if compared with the universal perplexity and confusion, which is inherent in human nature. In general, there is a degree of doubt, and caution, and modesty, which, in all kinds of scrutiny and decision, ought for ever to accompany a just reasoner.

130   Another species of *mitigated* scepticism which may be of advantage to mankind, and which may be the natural result of the Pyrrhonian doubts and scruples, is the limitation of our enquiries to such subjects as are best adapted to the narrow capacity of human understanding. The *imagination* of man is naturally sublime, delighted with whatever is remote and extraordinary, and running, without control, into the most distant parts of space and time in order to avoid the objects, which custom has rendered too familiar to it. A correct *Judgement* observes a contrary method, and avoiding all distant and high enquiries, confines itself to common life, and to such subjects as fall under daily practice and experience; leaving the more sublime topics to the embellishment of poets and orators, or to the arts of

priests and politicians. To bring us to so salutary a determination, nothing can be more serviceable, than to be once thoroughly convinced of the force of the Pyrrhonian doubt, and of the impossibility, that anything, but the strong power of natural instinct, could free us from it. Those who have a propensity to philosophy, will still continue their researches; because they reflect, that, besides the immediate pleasure, attending such an occupation, philosophical decisions are nothing but the reflections of common life, methodized and corrected. But they will never be tempted to go beyond common life, so long as they consider the imperfection of those faculties which they employ, their narrow reach, and their inaccurate operations. While we cannot give a satisfactory reason, why we believe, after a thousand experiments, that a stone will fall, or fire burn; can we ever satisfy ourselves concerning any determination, which we may form, with regard to the origin of worlds, and the situation of nature, from, and to eternity?

This narrow limitation, indeed, of our enquiries, is, in every respect, so reasonable, that it suffices to make the slightest examination into the natural powers of the human mind and to compare them with their objects, in order to recommend it to us. We shall then find what are the proper subjects of science and enquiry.

131   It seems to me, that the only objects of the abstract sciences or of demonstration are quantity and number, and that all attempts to extend this more perfect species of knowledge beyond these bounds are mere sophistry and illusion. As the component parts of quantity and number are entirely similar, their relations become intricate and involved; and nothing can be more curious, as well as useful, than to trace, by a variety of mediums, their equality or inequality, through their different appearances. But as all other ideas are clearly distinct and different from each other, we can never advance farther, by our utmost scrutiny, than to observe this diversity, and, by an obvious reflection, pronounce one thing not to be another. Or if there be any difficulty in these decisions, it proceeds entirely from the undeterminate meaning of words, which is corrected by juster definitions. That *the square of the hypothenuse is equal to the squares of the other two sides,* cannot be known, let the terms be ever so exactly defined, without a train of reasoning and enquiry. But to convince us of this proposition, *that where there is no property, there can be no injustice,* it is only necessary to define the terms, and explain injustice to be a violation of property. This proposition is, indeed, nothing but a more imperfect definition. It is the same case with all those pretended syllogistical reasonings, which may be found in every other branch of learning, except the sciences of quantity and number; and these may safely, I think, be pronounced the only proper objects of knowledge and demonstration.

132   All other enquiries of men regard only matter of fact and existence; and these are evidently incapable of demonstration. Whatever *is* may *not be*. No negation of a fact can involve a contradiction. The non-existence of any being, without exception, is as clear and distinct an idea as its existence. The proposition, which affirms it not to be, however false, is no less conceivable and intelligible, than that which affirms it to be. The case is different with the sciences, properly so called. Every proposition, which is not true, is there confused and unintelligible. That the cube root of 64 is equal to the half of 10, is a false proposition, and can never be distinctly conceived. But that Cæsar, or the angel Gabriel, or any being never existed, ·may be a false proposition, but still is perfectly conceivable, and implies no contradiction.

The existence, therefore, of any being can only be proved by arguments from its cause or its effect; and these arguments are founded entirely on experience. If we reason *a priori*, anything may appear able to produce anything. The falling of a pebble may, for aught we know, extinguish the sun; or the wish of a man control the planets in their orbits. It is only experience, which teaches us the nature and bounds of cause and effect, and enables us to infer the existence of one object from that of another.* Such is the foundation of moral reasoning, which forms the greater part of human knowledge, and is the source of all human action and behaviour.

Moral reasonings are either concerning particular or general facts. All deliberations in life regard the former; as also all disquisitions in history, chronology, geography, and astronomy.

The sciences, which treat of general facts, are politics, natural philosophy, physic, chemistry, where the qualities, causes and effects of a whole species of objects are enquired into.

Divinity or Theology, as it proves the existence of a Deity, and the immortality of souls, is composed partly of reasonings concerning particular, partly concerning general facts. It has a foundation in *reason*, so far as it is supported by experience. But its best and most solid foundation is *faith* and divine revelation.

Morals and criticism are not so properly objects of the understanding as of taste and sentiment. Beauty, whether moral or natural, is felt, more properly than perceived. Or if we reason concerning it, and endeavour to fix its

---

* That impious maxim of the ancient philosophy, *Ex nihilo, nihil fit*, by which the creation of matter was excluded, ceases to be a maxim, according to this philosophy. Not only the will of the supreme Being may create matter; but, for aught we know *a priori*, the will of any other being might create it, or any other cause, that the most whimsical imagination can assign.

standard, we regard a new fact, to wit, the general taste of mankind, or some such fact, which may be the object of reasoning and enquiry.

When we run over libraries, persuaded of these principles, what havoc must we make? If we take in our hand any volume; of divinity or school metaphysics, for instance; let us ask, *Does it contain any abstract reasoning concerning quantity or number?* No. *Does it contain any experimental reasoning concerning matter of fact and existence?* No. Commit it then to the flames: for it can contain nothing but sophistry and illusion.

Notes

1 Consequences such as the paradoxical ones drawn by Zeno concerning motion.
2 Here Hume is siding with Berkeley, and against Locke, on the issue of whether we can form abstract general ideas.
3 'Academical philosophy' here refers to the brand of scepticism advanced by Carneades (second century BCE) and other teachers at the Academy in Athens founded by Plato.

Thomas Reid, *Essays on the Intellectual Powers of Man*, Essay 6, Chapter 5

From Thomas Reid, *Essays on the Intellectual Powers of Man*, ed. A.D. Woozley. London: Macmillan, 1941, pp. 372–91 [notes and one passage omitted].

Rightly or not, Hume was perceived by his contemporaries as a radical sceptic whose powerful case needed to be answered if the possibility of knowledge was to be restored. In the following chapter, we shall encounter the most famous of these responses, Kant's. But important, too – and in the English-language tradition, arguably, of more enduring influence – was the response of Hume's fellow Scot, and Adam Smith's successor in the Chair of Moral Philosophy at Glasgow, Thomas Reid (1710–96), the preeminent member of the 'Commonsense School' of Scottish philosophy.

Reid's refutation of scepticism was of an entirely different kind from that of Descartes and his rationalist followers, who are indeed as much a target of his criticisms as the sceptics are. Their arguments, for example, to 'support the authority of our senses' – by, say, appealing to a non-deceiving God – are 'very weak' and 'easily refuted'. But nor was Reid an empiricist of the seventeenth- or eighteenth-century ilk. For him, both schools of thought share the mistaken assumption that our commonsense beliefs must either be suspended (rejected even) or justified by something more foundational – rational deduction either from a handful of self-evident axioms (like the *cogito*) or from 'immediate' experience of our own 'ideas' or 'impressions'. In Reid's view, there are a large number of commonsense 'first principles' – including the twelve 'factual' or 'contingent' ones discussed in the pages I have selected – which are themselves certainly true and which allow us to arrive at countless other, more particular truths. Reid's list is not intended to be exhaustive, but it does not contain most of the general claims argued about by epistemologists – for example, that we have knowledge of other minds and of the similarity of the future to the past.

By 'commonsense', he means 'that degree of judgement which is common to men with whom we can converse and transact business', and by 'first principles' those 'propositions which are no sooner understood than they are believed'.[1] Since these principles, once understood, cannot but be believed true, they deserve to be called items of knowledge. Reid is therefore using the term 'knowledge' rather more generously, and surely more in accordance with standard usage, than the philosophers he discusses. For even those, like Locke, who would not normally be regarded as sceptics tend to confine the term to judgements about the relations among ideas, in effect restricting knowledge, 'truly' or 'strictly' so-called, to the necessary truths of mathematics and logic and to minimal statements about immediate sense-experience (about, say, differences in colour between two 'impressions').

Reid is not a 'commonsense philosopher' simply because he defends the pronouncements of commonsense, such as that there exists an external world or that we can know about the past. After all, Descartes *eventually* came to endorse many of the ordinary beliefs he originally determined to doubt. What invites that label is Reid's insistence, first, that commonsense neither needs, nor can be given, the kind of rational foundation which Descartes tries to provide; and, second, that one is perfectly entitled to accept commonsense beliefs despite being unable to specify why or how they belong to commonsense.[2]

Although *we* do not have to justify our commonsense principles in order to count as possessors of knowledge, Reid himself does offer some general reasons why they should not be called into question. For one thing, as his seventh principle (really a metaprinciple) proclaims, 'the natural faculties', such as memory and reason, 'by which we distinguish truth from error, are not fallacious' – or, at least, cannot be regarded as fallacious since, providing us with 'evidence', they 'force' us to accept certain things as true.[3] For another thing, the first principles should be thought of less as 'general propositions' to be mulled over by philosophers than as practical principles implicitly governing everyday discourse, belief and behaviour – those of would-be sceptics as much as everyone else. Hence, to question the reliability of our 'natural faculties' would not only render us 'absolute sceptics', but render unintelligible our capacity to 'converse and transact business' with one another.

As earlier remarked, Reid has been an important influence on English-language, especially British, philosophy. Indeed, it is something of an injustice in the history of ideas that 'a defense of commonsense' should be so closely associated with G. E. Moore's article of that name, given that, as Reid's editor puts it, 'there is scarcely a thought' in that article 'which we would be surprised to find in the *Intellectual Powers*'.[4]

---

[1] *Essays on the Intellectual Powers of Man*, ed. Woozley, pp. 331, 358.

[2] See Noah Lemos, 'Commonsensism and Critical Cognitivism', in *A Companion to Epistemology*, ed. J. Dancy and E. Sosa, Oxford: Blackwell, 1992, p. 72.

[3] On this metaprinciple and Reid's philosophy as a whole, see Keith Lehrer, *Thomas Reid*, London: Routledge, 1989.

[4] *Essays on the Intellectual Powers of Man*, ed. Woozley, p. xxxviii.

Chapter 5: The First Principles of Contingent Truths

"Surely", says Bishop Berkeley, "it is a work well deserving our pains to make a strict inquiry concerning the first principles of knowledge; to sift and examine them on all sides" [*Principles*, Introd. 4]. . . .

But in order that such an inquiry may be actually made, it is necessary that the first principles of knowledge be distinguished from other truths, and presented to view, that they may be sifted and examined on all sides. In order to this end I shall attempt a detail of those I take to be such, and of the reasons why I think them entitled to that character.

The truths that fall within the compass of human knowledge, whether they be self-evident or deduced from those that are self-evident, may be reduced to two classes. They are either necessary and immutable truths whose contrary is impossible, or they are contingent and mutable, depending upon some effect of will and power which had a beginning, and may have an end.

That a cone is the third part of a cylinder of the same base and the same altitude is a necessary truth. It depends not upon the will and power of any being. It is immutably true, and the contrary impossible. That the sun is the centre about which the earth and the other planets of our system perform their revolutions, is a truth; but it is not a necessary truth. It depends upon the power and will of that Being who made the sun and all the planets, and who gave them those motions that seemed best to him.

If all truths were necessary truths there would be no occasion for different tenses in the verbs by which they are expressed. What is true in the present time would be true in the past and future, and there would be no change or variation of anything in nature.

We use the present tense in expressing necessary truths, but it is only because there is no flexion of the verb which includes all times. When I say that three is the half of six, I use the present tense only; but I mean to express not only what now is, but what always was, and always will be; and so every proposition is to be understood by which we mean to express a necessary truth. Contingent truths are of another nature. As they are mutable, they may be true at one time and not at another, and, therefore, the expression of them must include some point or period of time.

The distinction commonly made between abstract truths and those that express matters of fact, or real existences, coincides in a great measure, but not altogether, with that between necessary and contingent truths. The necessary truths that fall within our knowledge are for the most part abstract truths. We must except the existence and nature of the Supreme Being, which is necessary. Other existence are the effects of will and power.

They had a beginning, and are mutable. Their nature is such as the Supreme Being was pleased to give them. Their attributes and relations must depend upon the nature God has given them, the powers with which he has endowed them, and the situation in which he hath placed them.

The conclusions deduced by reasoning from first principles will commonly be necessary or contingent, according as the principles are from which they are drawn. On the one hand, I take it to be certain that whatever can, by just reasoning, be inferred from a principle that is necessary must be a necessary truth, and that no contingent truth can be inferred from principles that are necessary.

Thus, as the axioms in mathematics are all necessary truths, so are all the conclusions drawn from them; that is, the whole body of that science. But from no mathematical truth can we deduce the existence of anything, not even of the objects of the science.

On the other hand, I apprehend there are very few cases in which we can, from principles that are contingent, deduce truths that are necessary. I can only recollect one instance of this kind – namely, that from the existence of things contingent and mutable we can infer the existence of an immutable and eternal cause of them.

As the minds of men are occupied much more about truths that are contingent than about those that are necessary, I shall first endeavour to point out the principles of the former kind.

1. *First*, then, I hold, as a first principle, the existence of everything of which I am conscious.

Consciousness is an operation of the understanding of its own kind and cannot be logically defined. The objects of it are our present pains, our pleasures, our hopes, our fears, our desires, our doubts, our thoughts of every kind; in a word, all the passions and all the actions and operations of our own minds while they are present. We may remember them when they are past, but we are conscious of them only while they are present.

When a man is conscious of pain he is certain of its existence; when he is conscious that he doubts or believes, he is certain of the existence of those operations.

But the irresistible conviction he has of the reality of those operations is not the effect of reasoning; it is immediate and intuitive. The existence therefore of those passions and operations of our minds of which we are conscious is a first principle which nature requires us to believe upon her authority.

If I am asked to prove that I cannot be deceived by consciousness – to prove that it is not a fallacious sense – I can find no proof. I cannot find any antecedent truth from which it is deduced or upon which its evidence depends. It seems to disdain any such derived authority and to claim my assent in its own right.

If any man could be found so frantic as to deny that he thinks, while he is conscious of it, I may wonder, I may laugh, or I may pity him, but I cannot reason the matter with him. We have no common principles from which we may reason, and therefore can never join issue in an argument.

I cannot reconcile this immediate knowledge of the operations of our own minds with Mr. Locke's theory that all knowledge consists in perceiving the agreement and disagreement of ideas. What are the ideas from whose comparison the knowledge of our own thoughts results? Or what are the agreements or disagreements which convince a man that he is in pain when he feels it?

Neither can I reconcile it with Mr. Hume's theory that to believe the existence of anything is nothing else than to have a strong and lively conception of it, or, at most, that belief is only some modification of the idea which is the object of belief. For, not to mention that propositions, not ideas, are the object of belief, in all that variety of thoughts and passions of which we are conscious we believe the existence of the weak as well as of the strong the faint as well as the lively. No modification of the operations of our minds disposes us to the least doubt of their real existence.

As, therefore, the real existence of our thoughts, and of all the operations and feelings of our own minds, is believed by all men – as we find ourselves incapable of doubting it, and as incapable of offering any proof of it – it may justly be considered as a first principle, or dictate of commonsense.

But although this principle rests upon no other, a very considerable and important branch of human knowledge rests upon it.

For from this source of consciousness is derived all that we know, and indeed all that we can know, of the structure and of the powers of our own minds; from which we may conclude that there is no branch of knowledge that stands upon a firmer foundation, for surely no kind of evidence can go beyond that of consciousness.

How does it come to pass, then, that in this branch of knowledge there are so many and so contrary systems? so many subtle controversies that are never brought to an issue? and so little fixed and determined? Is it possible that philosophers should differ most where they have the surest means of agreement – where everything is built upon a species of evidence which all men acquiesce in and hold to be the most certain?

This strange phenomenon may, I think, be accounted for if we distinguish between consciousness and reflection, which are often improperly confounded.

The first is common to all men at all times, but is insufficient of itself to give us clear and distinct notions of the operations of which we are conscious, and of their mutual relations and minute distinctions. The second – to wit, attentive reflection upon those operations, making them objects of thought, surveying them attentively, and examining them on all sides – is so far from being common to all men that it is the lot of very few. The greatest part of men, either through want of capacity or from other causes, never reflect attentively upon the operations of their own minds. The habit of this reflection, even in those whom nature has fitted for it, is not to be attained without much pains and practice.

2.   Another first principle, I think, is, That the thoughts of which I am conscious are the thoughts of a being which I call *myself*, my *mind*, my *person*.

The thoughts and feelings of which we are conscious are continually changing, and the thought of this moment is not the thought of the last; but something which I call myself remains under this change of thought. This self has the same relation to all the successive thoughts I am conscious of – they are all my thoughts; and every thought which is not my thought must be the thought of some other person.

If any man asks a proof of this, I confess I can give none; there is an evidence in the proposition itself which I am unable to resist. Shall I think that thought can stand by itself without a thinking being? or that ideas can feel pleasure or pain? My nature dictates to me that it is impossible.

Here we must leave Mr. Hume, who conceives it to be a vulgar error that, besides the thoughts we are conscious of, there is a mind which is the subject of those thoughts. If the mind be anything else than impressions and ideas, it must be a word without a meaning. The mind therefore, according to this philosopher, is a word which signifies a bundle of perceptions; or, when he defines it more accurately – "It is that succession of related ideas and impressions of which we have an intimate memory and consciousness" [*Treatise*, II.1.2].

I am therefore that succession of related ideas and impressions of which I have the intimate memory and consciousness.

But who is the *I* that has this memory and consciousness of a succession of ideas and impressions? Why, it is nothing but that succession itself.

Hence, I learn that this succession of ideas and impressions intimately remembers and is conscious of itself. I would wish to be further instructed whether the impressions remember and are conscious of the ideas, or the ideas remember and are conscious of the impressions, or if both remember and are conscious of both, and whether the ideas remember those that come after them as well as those that were before them. These are questions naturally arising from this system that have not yet been explained.

This, however, is clear, that this succession of ideas and impressions not only remembers and is conscious, but that it judges, reasons, affirms, denies – nay, that it eats and drinks and is sometimes merry and sometimes sad.

If these things can be ascribed to a succession of ideas and impressions, in a consistency with commonsense, I should be very glad to know what is nonsense.

3.   Another first principle I take to be – That those things did really happen which I distinctly remember.

This has one of the surest marks of a first principle, for no man ever pretended to prove it, and yet no man in his wits calls it in question: the testimony of memory, like that of consciousness, is immediate; it claims our assent upon its own authority.

Mr. Hume has not, as far as I remember, directly called in question the testimony of memory, but he has laid down the premises by which its authority is overturned, leaving it to his reader to draw the conclusion.

Indeed the theory concerning ideas, so generally received by philosophers, destroys all the authority of memory as well as the authority of the senses. Descartes, Malebranche, and Locke were aware that this theory made it necessary for them to find out arguments to prove the existence of external objects which the vulgar believe upon the bare authority of their senses; but those philosophers were not aware that this theory made it equally necessary for them to find arguments to prove the existence of things past which we remember, and to support the authority of memory.

All the arguments they advanced to support the authority of our senses were easily refuted by Bishop Berkeley and Mr. Hume, being indeed very weak and inconclusive. And it would have been as easy to answer every argument they could have brought, consistent with their theory, to support the authority of memory.

For according to that theory the immediate object of memory, as well as of every other operation of the understanding, is an idea present in the mind. And from the present existence of this idea of memory I am left to infer, by reasoning, that six months or six years ago there did exist an object similar to this idea.

But what is there in the idea that can lead me to this conclusion? What mark does it bear of the date of its archetype? Or what evidence have I that it had an archetype and that it is not the first of its kind?

Perhaps it will be said that this idea or image in the mind must have had a cause.

I admit that if there is such an image in the mind, it must have had a cause, and a cause able to produce the effect; but what can we infer from its having a cause? Does it follow that the effect is a type, an image, a copy of its cause? Then it will follow that a picture is an image of the painter, and a coach of the coachmaker.

A past event may be known by reasoning; but that is not remembering it. When I remember a thing distinctly, I disdain equally to hear reasons for it or against it. And so I think does every man in his senses.

4. Another first principle is, Our own personal identity and continued existence, as far back as we remember anything distinctly.

This we know immediately, and not by reasoning. It seems, indeed, to be a part of the testimony of memory. Everything we remember has such a relation to ourselves as to imply necessarily our existence at the time remembered. And there cannot be a more palpable absurdity than that a man should remember what happened before he existed. He must therefore have existed as far back as he remembers anything distinctly, if his memory be not fallacious. This principle, therefore, is so connected with the last mentioned that it may be doubtful whether both ought not to be included in one. Let everyone judge of this as he sees reason. The proper notion of identity, and the sentiments of Mr. Locke on this subject, have been considered before under the head of Memory [see *Essay* 3].

5. Another first principle is, That those things do really exist which we distinctly perceive by our senses, and are what we perceive them to be.

It is too evident to need proof that all men are by nature led to give implicit faith to the distinct testimony of their senses, long before they are capable of any bias from prejudices of education or of philosophy.

How came we at first to know that there are certain beings about us whom we call father, and mother, and sisters, and brothers, and nurse? Was it not by the testimony of our senses? How did these persons convey to us any information or instruction? Was it not by means of our senses?

It is evident we can have no communication, no correspondence or society with any created being but by means of our senses. And until we rely upon their testimony, we must consider ourselves as being alone in the universe, without any fellow-creature, living or inanimate, and be left to converse with our own thoughts.

Bishop Berkeley surely, did not duly consider that it is by means of the material world that we have any correspondence with thinking beings, or any knowledge of their existence; and that, by depriving us of the material world, he deprived us at the same time of family, friends, country, and every human creature; of every object of affection, esteem, or concern, except ourselves.

When I consider myself as speaking to men who hear me, and can judge of what I say, I feel that respect which is due to such an audience. I feel an enjoyment in a reciprocal communication of sentiments with candid and ingenious friends, and my soul blesses the Author of my being, who has made me capable of this manly and rational entertainment.

But the Bishop shows me that this is all a dream; that I see not a human face; that all the objects I see, and hear, and handle, are only the ideas of my own mind; ideas are my only companions. Cold company indeed! Every social affection freezes at the thought!

This dismal system, which, if it could be believed, would deprive men of every social comfort, a very good Bishop, by strict and accurate reasoning, deduced from the principles commonly received by philosophers concerning ideas. The fault is not in the reasoning, but in the principles from which it is drawn.

All the arguments urged by Berkeley and Hume against the existence of a material world are grounded upon this principle – that we do not perceive external objects themselves, but certain images or ideas in our own minds. But this is no dictate of commonsense, but directly contrary to the sense of all who have not been taught it by philosophy.

We have before examined the reasons given by philosophers to prove that ideas, and not external objects, are the immediate objects of perception, and the instances given to prove the senses fallacious.[1] Without repeating what has before been said upon those points, we shall only here observe that, if external objects be perceived immediately, we have the same reason to believe their existence as philosophers have to believe the existence of ideas, while they hold them to be the immediate objects of perception.

6.   Another first principle, I think, is, That we have some degree of power over our actions, and the determinations of our will.

All power must be derived from the fountain of power and of every good gift. Upon his good pleasure its continuance depends, and it is always subject to his control.

Beings to whom God has given any degree of power and understanding to direct them to the proper use of it must be accountable to their Maker. But those who are entrusted with no power can have no account to make; for all good conduct consists in the right use of power, all bad conduct in the abuse of it.

It is not easy to say in what way we first get the notion or idea of *power*. It is neither an object of sense nor of consciousness. We see events, one succeeding another; but we see not the power by which they are produced. We are conscious of the operations of our minds; but power is not an operation of mind. If we had no notions but such as are furnished by the external senses and by consciousness, it seems to be impossible that we should ever have any conception of power. Accordingly Mr. Hume, who has reasoned the most accurately upon this hypothesis, denies that we have any idea of power, and clearly refutes the account given by Mr. Locke of the origin of this idea.

But it is in vain to reason from a hypothesis against a fact the truth of which every man may see by attending to his own thoughts. It is evident that all men, very early in life, not only have an idea of power, but a conviction that they have some degree of it in themselves; for this conviction is necessarily implied in many operations of mind which are familiar to every man, and without which no man can act the part of a reasonable being.

First, It is implied in every act of volition. "Volition, it is plain," says Mr. Locke, "is an act of the mind, knowingly exerting that dominion which it takes itself to have over any part of the man, by employing it in, or withholding it from, any particular action" [*Essay Concerning Human Understanding*, II. 21.15]. Every volition, therefore, implies a conviction of power to do the action willed. A man may desire to make a visit to the moon, or to the planet Jupiter, but nothing but insanity could make him will to do so. And if even insanity produced this effect, it must be by making him think it to be in his power.

Secondly, This conviction is implied in all deliberation, for no man in his wits deliberates whether he shall do what he believes not to be in his power. *Thirdly*, The same conviction is implied in every resolution or purpose formed in consequence of deliberation. A man may as well form a resolution to pull the moon out of her sphere as to do the most insignificant action which he believes not to be in his power. The same thing may be said of every promise or contract wherein a man plights his faith, for he is not an honest man who promises what he does not believe he has power to perform.

As these operations imply a belief of some degree of power in ourselves, so there are others equally common and familiar which imply a like belief with regard to others.

When we impute to a man any action or omission as a ground of approbation or of blame, we must believe he had power to do otherwise. The same is implied in all advice, exhortation, command, and rebuke, and in every case in which we rely upon his fidelity in performing any engagement of executing any trust.

7. Another first principle is, That the natural faculties, by which we distinguish truth from error, are not fallacious.[2] If any man should demand a proof of this, it is impossible to satisfy him. For suppose it should be mathematically demonstrated, this would signify nothing in this case, because, to judge of a demonstration, a man must trust his faculties, and take

for granted the very thing in question.

If a man's honesty were called in question, it would be ridiculous to refer it to the man's own word whether he be honest or not. The same absurdity there is in attempting to prove by any kind of reasoning, probable or demonstrative, that our reason is not fallacious, since the very point in question is whether reasoning may be trusted.

How then come we to be assured of this fundamental truth on which all others rest? Perhaps evidence, as in many other respects it resembles light, so in this also – that, as light, which is the discoverer of all visible objects, discovers itself at the same time, so evidence, which is the voucher for all truth, vouches for itself at the same time.

This, however, is certain, that such is the constitution of the human mind that evidence discerned by us forces a corresponding degree of assent. And a man who perfectly understood a just syllogism, without believing that the conclusion follows from the premises, would be a greater monster than a man born without hands or feet.

We may here take notice of a property of the principle under consideration that seems to be common to it with many other first principles, and which can hardly be found in any principle that is built solely upon reasoning; and that is, that in most men it produces its effect without ever being attended to, or made an object of thought. No man ever thinks of this principle unless when he considers the grounds of scepticism; yet it invariably governs his opinions. When a man in the common course of life gives credit to the testimony of his senses, his memory, or his reason, he does not put the question to himself whether these faculties may deceive him, yet the trust he reposes in them supposes an inward conviction that, in that instance at least, they do not deceive him.

It is another property of this and of many first principles, that they force assent in particular instances more powerfully than when they are turned into a general proposition. Many sceptics have denied every general principle of science, excepting perhaps the existence of our present thoughts; yet these men reason, and refute, and prove, they assent and dissent in particular cases. They use reasoning to overturn all reasoning, and judge that they ought to have no judgment, and see clearly that they are blind. Many have in general maintained that the senses are fallacious, yet there never was found a man so sceptical as not to trust his senses in particular instances when his safety required it; and it may be observed of those who have professed scepticism that their scepticism lies in generals, while in particulars they are no less dogmatical than others.

8.   Another first principle relating to existence is, That there is life and intelligence in our fellow-men with whom we converse.

As soon as children are capable of asking a question or of answering a question, as soon as they show the signs of love, of resentment, or of any other affection, they must be convinced that those with whom they have this intercourse are intelligent beings.

It is evident they are capable of such intercourse long before they can reason. Everyone knows that there is a social intercourse between the nurse and the child before it is a year old. It can at that age understand many things that are said to it.

It can by signs ask and refuse, threaten and supplicate. It clings to its nurse in danger, enters into her grief and joy, is happy in her soothing and caresses, and unhappy in her displeasure. That these things cannot be without a conviction in the child that the nurse is an intelligent being, I think must be granted.

Now I would ask how a child of a year old comes by this conviction? Not by reasoning surely, for children do not reason at that age. Nor is it by external senses, for life and intelligence are not objects of the external senses.

By what means, or upon what occasions, nature first gives this information to the infant mind is not easy to determine. We are not capable of reflecting upon our own thoughts at that period of life, and before we attain this capacity we have quite forgot how or on what occasion we first had this belief; we perceive it in those who are born blind and in others who are born deaf; and therefore nature has not connected it solely either with any object of sight or with any object of hearing. When we grow up to the years of reason and reflection, this belief remains. No man thinks of asking himself what reason he has to believe that his neighbour is a living creature. He would be not a little surprised if another person should ask him so absurd a question, and perhaps could not give any reason which would not equally prove a watch or a puppet to be a living creature.

But though you should satisfy him of the weakness of the reasons he gives for his belief, you cannot make him in the least doubtful. This belief stands upon another foundation than that of reasoning, and therefore, whether a man can give good reasons for it or not, it is not in his power to shake it off.

Setting aside this natural conviction, I believe the best reason we can give to prove that other men are living and intelligent is that their words and actions indicate like powers of understanding as we are conscious of in ourselves. The very same argument applied to the works of nature leads us to conclude that there is an intelligent Author of nature, and appears equally strong and obvious in the last case as in the first; so that it may be doubted whether men, by the mere exercise of reasoning, might not as soon discover the existence of a Deity as that other men have life and intelligence.

9.   Another first principle I take to be, That certain features of the countenance, sounds of the voice, and gestures of the body, indicate certain thoughts and dispositions of mind.

That many operations of the mind have their natural signs in the countenance, voice, and gesture, I suppose every man will admit. The only question is whether we understand the signification of those signs by the constitution of our nature, by a kind of natural perception similar to the perceptions of sense; or whether we gradually learn the signification of such signs from experience, as we learn that smoke is a sign of fire or that freezing of water is a sign of cold. I take the first to be the truth.

It seems to me incredible that the notions men have of the expression of features, voice, and gesture are entirely the fruit of experience. Children, almost as soon as born, may be frighted and thrown into fits by a threatening or angry tone of voice.

The countenance and gesture have an expression no less strong and natural than the voice. The first time one sees a stern and fierce look, a contracted brow, and a menacing posture, he concludes that the person is inflamed with anger. Shall we say that, previous to experience, the most hostile countenance has as agreeable an appearance as the most gentle and benign? This surely would contradict all experience, for we know that an angry countenance will fright a child in the cradle. Who has not observed that children, very early, are able to distinguish what is said to them in jest from what is said in earnest, by the tone of the voice and the features of the face? They judge by these natural signs, even when they seem to contradict the artificial.

If it were by experience that we learn the meaning of features, and sound, and gesture, it might be expected that we should recollect the time when we first learned those lessons, or at least some of such a multitude.

Those who give attention to the operations of children can easily discover the time when they have their earliest notices from experience – such as that flame will burn or that knives will cut. But no man is able to recollect in himself, or to observe in others, the time when the expression of the face, voice, and gesture were learned.

Nay, I apprehend that it is impossible that this should be learned from experience.

When we see the sign, and see the thing signified always conjoined with it, experience may be the instructor and teach us how that sign is to be interpreted. But how shall experience instruct us when we see the sign only, when the thing signified is invisible? Now, this is the case here: the thoughts and passions of the mind, as well as the mind itself, are invisible, and therefore their connection with any sensible sign cannot be first discovered by experience; there must be some earlier source of this knowledge.

Nature seems to have given to men a faculty or sense by which this connection is perceived. And the operation of this sense is very analogous to that of the external senses.

When I grasp an ivory ball in my hand, I feel a certain sensation of touch. In the sensation there is nothing external, nothing corporeal. The sensation is neither round nor hard; it is an act of feeling of the mind from which I cannot, by reasoning, infer the existence of any body. But by the constitution of my nature, the sensation carries along with it the conception and belief of a round hard body really existing in my hand.

In like manner when I see the features of an expressive face, I see only figure and colour variously modified. But by the constitution of my nature the visible object brings along with it the conception and belief of a certain passion or sentiment in the mind of the person.

In the former case a sensation of touch is the sign, and the hardness and roundness of the body I grasp is signified by that sensation. In the latter case the features of the person is the sign, and the passion or sentiment is signified by it.

10. Another first principle appears to me to be, That there is a certain regard due to human testimony in matters of fact, and even to human authority in matters of opinion.

11. There are many events depending upon the will of man in which there is a self-evident probability, greater or less, according to circumstances.

There may be in some individuals such a degree of frenzy and madness that no man can say what they may or may not do. Such persons we find it necessary to put under restraint, that as far as possible they may be kept from doing harm to themselves or to others. They are not considered as reasonable creatures or members of society. But as to men who have a sound mind, we depend upon a certain degree of regularity in their conduct, and could put a thousand different cases wherein we could venture ten to one that they will act in such a way and not in the contrary.

If we had no confidence in our fellow-men that they will act such a part in such circumstances, it would be impossible to live in society with them. For that which makes men capable of living in society, and uniting in a political body under government, is that their actions will always be regulated, in a great measure, by the common principles of human nature.

It may always be expected that they will regard their own interest and reputation, and that of their families and friends; that they will repel injuries, and have some sense of good offices; and that they will have some regard to truth and justice, so far at least as not to swerve from them without temptation.

It is upon such principles as these that all political reasoning is grounded. Such reasoning is never demonstrative, but it may have a very great degree of probability, especially when applied to great bodies of men.

12.   The last principle of contingent truths I mention is, That, in the phenomena of nature, what is to be will probably be like to what has been in similar circumstances.

We must have this conviction as soon as we are capable of learning anything from experience, for all experience is grounded upon a belief that the future will be like the past. Take away this principle and the experience of a hundred years makes us no wiser with regard to what is to come.

This is one of those principles which, when we grow up and observe the course of nature, we can confirm by reasoning. We perceive that nature is governed by fixed laws, and that, if it were not so, there could be no such thing as prudence in human conduct; there would be no fitness in any means to promote an end, and what on one occasion promoted it might as probably on another occasion obstruct it.

But the principle is necessary for us before we are able to discover it by reasoning, and therefore is made a part of our constitution and produces its effects before the use of reason.

This principle remains in all its force when we come to the use of reason, but we learn to be more cautious in the application of it. We observe more carefully the circumstances on which the past event depended, and learn to distinguish them from those which were accidentally conjoined with it.

In order to this, a number of experiments, varied in their circumstances, is often necessary. Sometimes a single experiment is thought sufficient to establish a general conclusion. Thus, when it was once found that, in a certain degree of cold, quicksilver became a hard and malleable metal, there was good reason to think that the same degree of cold will always produce this effect to the end of the world.

I need hardly mention that the whole fabric of natural philosophy is built upon this principle, and if it be taken away, must tumble down to the foundation.

Therefore the great Newton lays it down as an axiom, or as one of his laws of philosophising, in these words, *Effectuum naturalium ejusdem generis easdem esse causas* [Similar effects have similar causes]. This is what every man assents to, as soon as he understands it, and no man asks a reason for it. It has, therefore, the most genuine marks of a first principle.

It is very remarkable that, although all our expectation of what is to happen in the course of nature is derived from the belief of this principle, yet no man thinks of asking what is the ground of this belief.

Mr. Hume, I think, was the first who put this question; and he has shown clearly and invincibly that it is neither grounded upon reasoning nor has that kind of intuitive evidence which mathematical axioms have. It is not a necessary truth [*Treatise*, I.3.6].

He has endeavoured to account for it upon his own principles. It is not my business, at present, to examine the account he has given of this universal belief of mankind; because, whether his account of it be just or not (and I think it is not), yet as this belief is universal among mankind, and is not grounded upon any antecedent reasoning but upon the constitution of the mind itself, it must be acknowledged to be a first principle in the sense in which I use that word.

I do not at all affirm that those I have mentioned are all the first principles from which we may reason concerning contingent truths. Such enumerations, even when made after much reflection, are seldom perfect.

Notes

1 See Essay 2, ch. 7. Reid was one of the first to argue against the *idée fixe* of seventeenth–eighteenth-century philosophers that what we immediately perceive can only be our own 'ideas' or 'impressions'.
2 This principle might seem redundant, a mere summary of other principles which assert the reliability of such faculties as memory and perception. But, as Reid soon explains, this principle in fact supports the others, the point being that any *natural* faculty must, for the reasons he gives, be deemed reliable. That memory, etc. are indeed *natural* faculties therefore provides a consideration in favour of trusting their pronouncements.

Immanuel Kant, *Critique of Pure Reason*, Introduction (2nd Edition), Sections I–VI

Excerpt *from Critique of Pure Reason*, by Immanuel Kant, tr. Werner S. Pluhar. Indianapolis: Hackett, 1996, pp. 43–63 [some notes omitted; asterisked notes are the translator's]; reprinted by permission of Hackett Publishing Company. Copyright © 1996 by Hackett Publishing Company, Inc. All rights reserved.

Critique of Pure Reason, Immanuel Kant's (1724–1804) greatest work – the greatest, arguably, in modern philosophy – ranges over metaphysical, ethical, religious and other issues, not just those of epistemology. Its fundamental concern, however, is with the possibility and nature of our knowledge of objective reality. Central to Kant's enterprise, a distinguished commentator writes, is the notion of the 'epistemic condition(s) . . . necessary for the representation of . . . an objective state of affairs'.[1] Kant's revolutionary thesis in the book, which he compares to Copernicus' revolution in astronomy, is that such representations and knowledge are possible, not through our 'conforming' our 'intuitions' to mind-independent objects, but because any objects we can experience must 'conform' to what we contribute to experience through our cognitive powers (Preface, B xvi–xviii). (NB Page numbers in the margins prefixed by B refer to material added or changed in the Second Edition; those prefixed by A to material in the First Edition, much of which is retained in the later edition.)

In the Introduction to the Second (1787) Edition, Kant does not attempt to defend that thesis, but he prepares the ground for it and, in doing so, makes a number of distinctions which, ever since, have been staple topics of discussion in epistemology. These distinctions are crucial to draw if, as he sees it, the sorry state of philosophy in his time is to be reformed. Both major trends of eighteenth-century philosophy – empiricism as represented, especially, by Hume, and the 'dogmatic', rationalist metaphysics of Leibniz and others – result in scepticism towards our capacity for objective knowledge, though for contrasting reasons.

Humean empiricism, by resting knowledge on immediate experience of

---

[1] Henry E. Allison, *Kant's Transcendental Idealism: An Interpretation and Defense*, New Haven: Yale University Press, 1983, p. 10.

'impressions' and 'ideas', directly results in scepticism concerning the external world, the course of future experience and so on. However, it was Hume who, as Kant elsewhere wrote, 'interrupted my dogmatic slumber',[2] and did so by anticipating Kant's own appreciation that 'dogmatic' metaphysical speculation, unhinged from ordinary experience, leads to irresolvable 'stand-offs' or 'antinomies' over such questions as whether the universe had a beginning and whether there exists a necessary being (God). That it does so only serves to discredit reason, and hence to foster a sceptical attitude towards philosophical claims to knowledge (B 23).

If progress is to be made, and the central question about knowledge properly posed, we need, first, clearly to distinguish between 'intuitions' (including perceptions) and concepts, and between the respective faculties – 'sensibility' and 'understanding' – to which they belong. Empiricists are wrong to treat concepts as pale copies of perceptions, just as Leibniz et al. are wrong to regard the latter as confused forms of understanding. With that distinction firmly in place, we can ask about the respective contributions to knowledge of the two faculties. In particular, we will distinguish the correct claim that 'all our cognition starts *with* experience' from the false (empiricist) one that it all arises *from* experience, for the latter ignores what our understanding 'supplies from itself'. Equally, by keeping the former, correct claim in mind, we shall not be seduced by a 'dogmatic' rationalism which ignores the requirement for metaphysical assertions to retain application to 'possible objects of experience'.

Once the grip of the idea that all knowledge arises from experience, in the sense of having to be legitimated by it, has been loosened, it should be obvious, Kant thinks – invoking another distinction – that we have *a priori*, as well as *a posteriori*, knowledge: knowledge whose 'ground' is different from experience, as well as knowledge whose 'ground' is experience. Indeed, all necessary and strictly universal truths, such as those of mathematics, will be *a priori*, for experience can only vindicate contingent and particular truths. Previous philosophers have not, of course, denied the existence of *a priori* truths, but they have generally treated them all, in the terms of Kant's next distinction, as 'analytic' ones, not 'synthetic'. The former, roughly, are those recognized to be true solely in virtue of our understanding of the concepts involved. It is Kant's most important epistemological claim that, while many *a priori* truths are analytic (e.g. 'All bachelors are unmarried'), many are not. '7 + 5 = 12', 'The quantity of matter in the universe is constant' and 'Every event has a cause' – to take examples from mathematics, natural science and metaphysics – are all synthetic *a priori* truths. Hence the ground of their truth is a different and more puzzling thing than the relations between concepts or meanings of words.

Kant, we know, will argue that this ground is our own cognitive powers

---

[2] *Prolegomena to any Future Metaphysics*, tr. P. G. Lucas, Manchester: Manchester University Press, 1962, p. 9.

which, so to speak, 'give the orders' to how things must be if they are to be objects of our experience.[3] In the Introduction, however, Kant contents himself with formulating, in the light of the above distinctions, the fundamental question which philosophy has to address, 'How are synthetic judgements possible *a priori*?' As later chapters in this volume will show, this is indeed the question which most later philosophers have felt obliged either to answer or to reject.

[3] Gilles Deleuze, *Kant's Critical Philosophy: The Doctrine of the Faculties*, tr. H. Tomlinson and B. Habberjam, London: Athlone, 1984, p. 14.

Introduction [Second Edition]

I.* On the Distinction Between Pure and Empirical Cognition

There can be no doubt that all our cognition begins with experience. For what else might rouse our cognitive power to its operation if objects stir-

INTRODUCTION [FIRST EDITION]

A1   I. The Idea of Transcendental Philosophy

Experience is, without doubt, the first product to which our understanding gives rise, by working on the raw material of sense impressions. That is precisely why experience is our first instruction, and why, as it progresses, it is so inexhaustible in new information – so much so that if the lives of all future generations are strung together, they will never be lacking in new knowledge that can be gathered on that soil. Yet experience is far from being our understanding's only realm, and our understanding cannot be confined to it. Experience does indeed tell us what is, but not that it must necessarily be so and not otherwise. And that is precisely why experience gives us no true universality; and reason, which is so eager for that [universal] kind of cognitions, is more stimulated by experience than satisfied. Now, such universal cognitions, which are at the same time characterized by intrinsic necessity, must be independent of experience, clear and certain by themselves. Hence they are called a priori cognitions; by contrast, what is borrowed solely from experience is, as we put it, cognized only a posteriori, or empirically.

A2

Now, it turns out – what is extremely remarkable – that even among our experiences there is an admixture of cognitions that must originate a priori, and that serve perhaps only to give coherence to our presentations of the senses. For even if we remove from our experiences everything belonging to the senses, there still remain certain original concepts, and judgments generated from these, that must have arisen entirely a priori, independently of experience. These concepts and judgments must have arisen in this way because through them we can – or at least we believe that we can – say more about the objects that appear to the senses than mere experience would teach us; and through them do assertions involve true universality and strict necessity, such as merely empirical cognition cannot supply.

* [Sections I and II in B replace the first two paragraphs (and section heading) from Section I in A. The Introduction in A starts as follows:]

ring our senses did not do so? In part these objects by themselves bring about presentations. In part they set in motion our understanding's activity, by which it compares these presentations, connects or separates them, and thus processes the raw material of sense impressions into a cognition of objects that is called experience. *In terms of time*, therefore, no cognition in us precedes experience, and all our cognition begins with experience.

But even though all our cognition starts **with** experience, that does not mean that all of it arises **from** experience. For it might well be that even our experiential cognition is composite, consisting of what we receive through impressions and what our own cognitive power supplies from itself (sense impressions merely prompting it to do so). If our cognitive power does make such an addition, we may not be able to distinguish it from that basic material until long practice has made us attentive to it and skilled in separating it from the basic material.   B2

This question, then, whether there is such a cognition that is independent of experience and even of all impressions of the senses, is one that cannot be disposed of as soon as it comes to light, but that at least still needs closer investigation. Such cognitions are called *a priori cognitions;* they are distinguished from empirical cognitions, whose sources are a posteriori, namely, in experience.

But that expression, [viz., *a priori,*] is not yet determinate enough to indicate adequately the full meaning of the question just posed. For it is customary, I suppose, to say of much cognition derived from experiential sources that we can or do partake of it a priori. We say this because we derive the cognition not directly from experience but from a universal rule, even though that rule itself was indeed borrowed by us from experience. Thus if someone has undermined the foundation of his house, we say that he could have known a priori that the house would cave in, i.e., he did not have to wait for the experience of its actually caving in. And yet he could not have known this completely a priori. For he did first have to find out through experience that bodies have weight and hence fall when their support is withdrawn.

In what follows, therefore, we shall mean by a priori cognitions not those that occur independently of this or that experience, but those that occur *absolutely* independently of all experience. They contrast with empirical   B3 cognitions, which are those that are possible only a posteriori, i.e., through experience. But we call a priori cognitions *pure* if nothing empirical whatsoever is mixed in with them. Thus, e.g., the proposition, Every change has its cause, is an a priori proposition; yet it is not pure, because change is a concept that can be obtained only from experience.

II. We are in Possession of Certain A Priori Cognitions, and Even Common Understanding Is Never without Them

What matters here is that we find a characteristic by which we can safely distinguish a pure cognition from empirical ones. Now, experience does indeed teach us that something is thus or thus, but not that it cannot be otherwise. **First**, then, if we find a proposition such that in thinking it we think at the same time its *necessity*, then it is an a priori judgment; and if, in addition, it is not derived from any proposition except one that itself has the validity of a necessary proposition, then it is absolutely a priori. **Second**, experience never provides its judgments with true or strict *universality*, but only (through induction) with assumed and comparative universality; hence [there] we should, properly speaking, say [merely] that as far as we

B4   have observed until now, no exception is to be found to this or that rule. If, therefore, a judgment is thought with strict universality, i.e., thought in such a way that no exception whatever is allowed as possible, then the judgment is not derived from experience, but is valid absolutely a priori. Hence empirical universality is only [the result of] our choosing to upgrade validity from one that holds in most cases to one that holds in all, as, e.g., in the proposition, All bodies have weight. But when universality is strict and belongs to a judgment essentially, then it points to a special cognitive source for the judgment, viz., a power of a priori cognition. Hence necessity and strict universality are safe indicators of a priori cognition, and they do moreover belong together inseparably. It is nevertheless advisable to make separate use of the two criteria, even though each is infallible by itself. For, in using them, there are times when showing the empirical limitedness of a cognition is easier than showing the contingency of the judgments based on it; and there are times when showing the unlimited universality that we attribute to a judgment is more convincing than is showing the judgment's necessity.

Now, it is easy to show that in human cognition there actually are such judgments [as we are looking for, viz.], judgments that are necessary and in the strictest sense universal, and hence are pure a priori judgments. If we want an example from the sciences, we need only look to all the proposi

B5   tions of mathematics; if we want one from the most ordinary use of understanding, then we can use the proposition that all change must have a cause. Indeed, in this latter proposition the very concept of a cause so manifestly contains the concept of a necessity in [the cause's] connection with an effect, and of a strict universality of the rule [governing that connection], that the concept of a cause would get lost entirely if we derived it as *Hume* did: viz., from a repeated association of what happens with what precedes, and from our resulting habit* of connecting presentations (hence from a merely subjective necessity). But we do not need such examples in order to prove that pure a priori principles actual[ly exist] in our cognition. We could, alternatively, establish that these principles are indispensable for the possibility of experience as such, and hence establish [their existence] a priori. For where might even experience get its certainty if all the rules by which it proceeds were always in turn empirical and hence contingent, so that they could hardly be considered first principles? But here we may settle for having established as a matter of fact [that there is a] pure use of our cognitive power, and to have established what its indicators, are. However, we can see such an a priori origin not merely in judgments, but even in some concepts. If from your experiential concept of a *body* you gradually omit everything that is empirical in a body – the color, the hardness or softness, the weight, even the impenetrability – there yet remains the *space* that was occupied by the body (which has now entirely vanished), and this   B6 space you cannot omit [from the concept]. Similarly, if from your empirical concept of any object whatever, corporeal or incorporeal, you omit all properties that experience has taught you, you still cannot take away from the concept the property through which you think the object either as a *substance* or as *attaching* to a substance (even though this concept of substance is more determinate than that of an object as such). Hence you must, won over by the necessity with which this concept of substance forces itself upon you, admit that this concept resides a priori in your cognitive power.

III. Philosophy Needs a Science¹ That Will Determine the Possibility, the Principles, and the Range of All A Priori Cognitions†

Much more significant yet than all the preceding is the fact that there are certain cognitions that [not only extend to but] even leave the realm of all possible experiences. These cognitions, by means of concepts to which no   A3 corresponding object can be given in experience at all, appear to expand the range of our judgments beyond all bounds of experience.

---

* [Or 'custom': *Enquiry Concerning Human Understanding*, V, Pt. I, and cf. VII, Pt. II. Cf. also below, B 19–20, 127.]

† [The text of A continues, together with that of B, just below. The section number and heading were added in B.]

And precisely in these latter cognitions, which go beyond the world of sense, where experience cannot provide us with any guide or correction, reside our reason's inquiries. We regard these inquiries as far superior in importance, and their final aim as much more sublime, than anything that our understanding can learn in the realm of appearances. Indeed, we would sooner dare anything, even at the risk of error, than give up such treasured inquiries [into the unavoidable problems of reason], whether on the ground that they are precarious somehow, or from disdain and indifference. These unavoidable problems of reason themselves are *God, freedom, and immortality*. But the science whose final aim, involving the science's entire apparatus, is in fact directed solely at solving these problems is called *metaphysics*. Initially, the procedure of metaphysics is *dogmatic*; i.e., [metaphysics], without first examining whether reason is capable or incapable of so great an enterprise, confidently undertakes to carry it out.[2]

Now, suppose that we had just left the terrain of experience. Would we immediately erect an edifice by means of what cognitions we have, though we do not know from where? Would we erect it on credit, i.e., on principles whose origin is unfamiliar to us? It does seem natural that we would not, but that we would first seek assurance through careful inquiries that the foundation had been laid. In other words, it does seem natural that we would, rather, long since have raised the question as to just how our understanding could arrive at all these a priori cognitions, and what might be their range, validity, and value. And in fact nothing would be more natural, if by the term *natural* we mean what properly and reasonably ought to happen. If, on the other hand, we mean by this term what usually happens, then nothing is more natural and comprehensible than the fact that for a long time this inquiry had to remain unperformed. For, one part of these [a priori] cognitions, viz., the mathematical ones, possess long-standing reliability, and thereby raise favorable expectations concerning other [a priori] cognitions as well, even though these may be of a quite different nature. Moreover, once we are beyond the sphere of experience, we are assured of not being refuted by experience. The appeal of expanding our cognitions is so great that nothing but hitting upon a clear contradiction can stop our progress. On the other hand, we can avoid such contradiction by merely being cautious in our inventions – even though they remain nonetheless inventions. Mathematics provides us with a splendid example of how much we can achieve, independently of experience, in a priori cognition. Now, it is true that mathematics deals with objects and cognitions only to the extent that they can be exhibited in intuition. But this detail is easily overlooked because that intuition can itself be given a priori and hence is rarely distinguished from a mere pure concept. Captivated by such a proof of reason's might, our urge to expand [our cognitions] sees no boundaries. When the light dove parts the air in free flight and feels the air's resistance, it might come to think that it would do much better still in space devoid of air. In the same way *Plato* left the world of sense because it sets such narrow limits to our understanding; on the wings of the ideas, he ventured beyond that world and into the empty space of pure understanding. He did not notice that with all his efforts he made no headway. He failed to make headway because he had no resting point against which – as a foothold, as it were – he might brace himself and apply his forces in order to set the understanding in motion. But [Plato is no exception]: it is human reason's usual fate, in speculation, to finish its edifice as soon as possible, and not to inquire until afterwards whether a good foundation has in fact been laid for it. Then all sorts of rationalizations are hunted up in order to reassure us that the edifice is sturdy, or, preferably, even to reject altogether so late and risky an examination of it. But what keeps us, while we are building, free from all anxiety and suspicion, and flatters us with a seeming thoroughness, is the following. A large part – perhaps the largest – of our reason's business consists in dissecting what concepts of objects we already have. This [procedure] supplies us with a multitude of cognitions. And although these cognitions are nothing more than clarifications or elucidations of what has already been thought in our concepts (although thought as yet in a confused way), they are yet rated equal to new insights at least in form, even though in matter or content they do not expand the concepts we have but only spell them out. Now since this procedure yields actual a priori cognitions that progresses in a safe and useful way, reason uses this pretense, though without itself noticing this, to lay claim surreptitiously to assertions of a quite different kind. In these assertions, reason adds to given concepts others quite foreign to them, doing so moreover a priori. Yet how reason arrived at these concepts is not known; indeed, such a question is not even thought of. Hence I shall deal at the very outset with the distinction between these two kinds of cognition.

B9

A6

B10

IV. On the Distinction between Analytic and Synthetic Judgments

In all judgments in which we think the relation of a subject to the predicate (I here consider affirmative judgments only, because the application to negative judgments is easy afterwards), this relation is possible in two ways. Either the predicate B belongs to the subject A as something that is (covertly) contained in this concept A; or B, though connected with concept A, lies quite outside it. In the first case I call the judgment *analytic*, in the second, *synthetic*. Hence (affirmative) analytic judgments are those in which the predicate's connection with the subject is thought by [thinking] identity, whereas those judgments in which this connection is thought without [thinking] identity are to be called synthetic. Analytic judgments could also be called *elucidatory*. For they do not through the predicate add anything to the concept of the subject; rather, they only dissect the concept, breaking it up into its component concepts which had already been thought in it (although thought confusedly). Synthetic judgments, on the other hand, could also be called *expansive*. For they do add to the concept of the subject a predicate that had not been thought in that concept at all and could not have been extracted from it by any dissection. For example, if I say: All bodies are extended – then this is an analytic judgment. For I do not need to go beyond the concept that I link with the word body in order to find that extension is connected with it. All I need to do in order to find this predicate in the concept is to dissect the concept, i.e., become conscious of the manifold that I always think in it. Hence the judgment is analytic. By contrast, if I say: All bodies are heavy – then the predicate is something quite different from what I think in the mere concept of a body as such. Hence adding such a predicate yields a synthetic judgment.[3]

* *Experiential judgments, as such, are one and all synthetic.* For to base an analytic judgment on experience would be absurd, because in its case I can formulate my judgment without going outside my concept, and hence do not need for it any testimony of experience. Thus the [analytic] proposition that bodies are extended is one that holds a priori and is not an expe-

---

* [This paragraph in B replaces the following two in A:]

Now, this shows clearly: (1) that analytic judgments do not at all expand our cognition, but spell out and make understandable to myself the concept that I already have; (2) that in synthetic judgments, where the predicate does not lie within the concept of the subject, I must have besides this concept something else (X) on which the understanding relies in order to cognize nonetheless that the predicate belongs to that concept.

In empirical judgments, or in judgments of experience, it is not difficult at all to find this X. For here this X is the complete experience of the object that I think by means of a concept A, the concept amounting only to part of the experience. For although in the concept of a body as such I do not at all include the predicate of heaviness, yet the concept designates the complete experience [of a body] by means of part of it; hence I can add to this part, as belonging to it, further parts of the same experience. I can begin by cognizing the concept of a body analytically through the characteristics of extension, impenetrability, shape, etc., all of which are thought in this concept. But then I expand my cognition: by looking back to the experience from which I have abstracted this concept of body, I also find heaviness to be always connected with the above characteristics. Hence experience is the X that lies outside the concept A and makes possible the synthesis of the predicate B of heaviness with the concept A.

riential judgment. For before I turn to experience, I already have in the　B12
concept [of body] all the conditions required for my judgment. I have only
to extract from it, in accordance with the principle of contradiction, the
predicate [of extension]; in doing so, I can at the same time become conscious of the judgment's necessity, of which experience would not even
inform me. On the other hand, though in the concept of a body as such I
do not at all include the predicate of heaviness, yet the concept designates
an object of experience by means of part of this experience; hence I can
[synthetically] add to this part further parts, of the same experience, in
addition to those that belonged to the concept of a body as such. I can
begin by cognizing the concept of a body *analytically* through the characteristics of extension, impenetrability, shape, etc., all of which are thought
in this concept. But then I expand my cognition: by looking back to the
experience from which I have abstracted this concept of body, I also find
heaviness to be always connected with the above characteristics; and so I
add it, as a predicate, to that concept *synthetically*. Hence experience is
what makes possible the synthesis of the predicate of heaviness with the
concept of body. For although neither of the two concepts is contained in
the other, yet they belong to each other, though only contingently, as parts
of a whole; that whole is experience, which is itself a synthetic combination
of intuitions.

In synthetic judgments that are a priori, however, this remedy is entirely　A9
lacking. If I am to go beyond the concept A in order to cognize another　B13
concept B as combined with it, I rely on something that makes the synthesis possible: what is that something, considering that here I do not have the
advantage of looking around for it in the realm of experience? Take the
proposition: Everything that happens has its cause. – In the concept of
something that happens I do indeed think an existence preceded by a time,
etc., and from this one can obtain analytic judgments. But the concept of a
cause lies quite outside that earlier concept and indicates something different from what happens; hence it is not part of what is contained in this
latter presentation. In speaking generally of what happens, how can I say
about it something quite different from it, and cognize as belonging to it –
indeed, belonging to it necessarily – the concept of cause, even though this
concept is not contained in the concept of what happens? What is here the
unknown = X on which the understanding relies when it believes that it
discovers, outside the concept A, a predicate B that is foreign to concept A
but that the understanding considers nonetheless to be connected with
that concept? This unknown cannot be experience. For in adding the presentation of cause to the presentation of what happens, the above principle
does so not only with greater universality than experience can provide, but

also with the necessity's being expressed; hence it does so entirely a priori and on the basis of mere concepts. Now, on such synthetic, i.e., expansive, principles depends the whole final aim of our speculative a priori cognition.

A10
B14

For, analytic principles are indeed exceedingly important and needed, but only for attaining that distinctness in concepts which is required for a secure and extensive synthesis that, as such, will actually be a new acquisition [of cognition].

V. All Theoretical Sciences of Reason Contain Synthetic A Priori Judgments as Principles

1. *Mathematical judgments are one and all synthetic.* Although this proposition is incontestably certain and has very important consequences, it seems thus far to have escaped the notice of those who have analyzed human reason; indeed, it seems to be directly opposed to all their conjectures. For they found that all the inferences made by mathematicians proceed (as the nature of all apodeictic certainty requires) according to the principle of contradiction; and thus they came to be persuaded that the principle of contradiction is also the basis on which we cognize the principles [of mathematics]. In this they were mistaken. For though we can indeed gain insight into a synthetic proposition according to the principle of contradiction, we can never do so [by considering] that proposition by itself, but can do so only by presupposing another synthetic proposition from which it can be deduced.

We must note, first of all, that mathematical propositions, properly so called, are always a priori judgments rather than empirical ones; for they carry with them necessity, which we could never glean from experience.

B15

But if anyone refuses to grant that all such propositions are a priori – all right: then I restrict my assertion to *pure mathematics*, in the very concept of which is implied that it contains not empirical but only pure a priori cognition.

It is true that one might at first think that the proposition 7 + 5 = 12 is a merely analytic one that follows, by the principle of contradiction, from the concept of a sum of seven and five. Yet if we look more closely, we find that the concept of the sum of 7 and 5 contains nothing more than the union of the two numbers into one; but in [thinking] that union we are not thinking in any way at all what that single number is that unites the two. In thinking merely that union of seven and five, I have by no means already thought the concept of twelve; and no matter how long I dissect my concept of such a possible sum, still I shall never find in it that twelve.

We must go beyond these concepts and avail ourselves of the intuition corresponding to one of the two: e.g., our five fingers, or (as *Segner* does in his *Arithmetic*) five dots. In this way we must gradually add, to the concept of seven, the units of the five given in intuition. For I start by taking the number 7. Then, for the concept of the 5, I avail myself of the fingers of my hand as intuition. Thus, in that image of mine, I gradually add to the number 7 the units that I previously gathered together in order to make up   B16
the number 5. In this way I see the number 12 arise. That 5 *were to be added* to 7, this I had indeed already thought in the concept of a sum = 7 + 5, but not that this sum is equal to the number 12. Arithmetic propositions are therefore always synthetic. We become aware of this all the more distinctly if we take larger numbers. For then it is very evident that, no matter how much we twist and turn our concepts, we can never find the [number of the] sum by merely dissecting our concepts, i.e., without availing ourselves of intuition.

Just as little are any principles of pure geometry analytic. That the straight line between two points is the shortest is a synthetic proposition. For my concept of *straight* contains nothing about magnitude, but contains only a quality. Therefore the concept of shortest is entirely added to the concept of a straight line and cannot be extracted from it by any dissection. Hence we must here avail ourselves of intuition; only by means of it is the synthesis possible.

It is true that a few propositions presupposed by geometricians are actually analytic and based on the principle of contradiction. But, like identical propositions, they serve not as principles but only [as links in] the chain of   B17
method. Examples are a = a; the whole is equal to itself; or (a + b) > a, i.e., the whole is greater than its part. And yet even these principles, although they hold according to mere concepts, are admitted in mathematics only because they can be exhibited in intuition. [As for mathematics generally,] what commonly leads us to believe that the predicate of its apodeictic judgments is contained in our very concept, and that the judgment is therefore analytic, is merely the ambiguity with which we express ourselves. For we say that we *are to* add in thought a certain predicate to a given concept, and this necessity adheres indeed to the very concepts. But here the question is not what we *are to* add in thought to the given concept, but what we *actually* think in the concept, even if only obscurely; and there we find that, although the predicate does indeed adhere necessarily to such concepts, yet it does so not as something thought in the concept itself, but by means of an intuition that must be added to the concept.

   2. *Natural science (physica) contains synthetic a priori judgments as principles.* Let me cite as examples just a few propositions: e.g., the proposition

that in all changes in the corporeal world the quantity of matter remains unchanged; or the proposition that in all communication of motion, action and reaction must always be equal to each other. Both propositions are clearly not only necessary, and hence of a priori origin, but also synthetic. For in the concept of matter I do not think permanence, but think merely the matter's being present in space insofar as it occupies space. Hence I do actually go beyond the concept of matter, in order to add to it a priori in thought something that I have not thought *in it*. Hence the proposition is thought not analytically but synthetically and yet a priori, and the same occurs in the remaining propositions of the pure part of natural science.

3. *Metaphysics* is to *contain synthetic a priori cognitions*. This holds even if metaphysics is viewed as a science that thus far has merely been attempted, but that because of the nature of human reason is nonetheless indispensable. Metaphysics is not at all concerned merely to dissect concepts of things that we frame a priori, and thereby to elucidate them analytically. Rather, in metaphysics we want to expand our a priori cognition. In order to do this, we must use principles which go beyond the given concept and which add to it something that was not contained in it; and, by means of such synthetic a priori judgments, we must presumably go so far beyond such concepts that even experience can no longer follow us; as in the proposition: The world must have a first beginning – and others like that. And hence metaphysics consists, at least *in terms of its purpose*, of nothing but synthetic a priori propositions.

VI. The General Problem of Pure Reason

Much is gained already when we can bring a multitude of inquiries under the formula of a single problem. For we thereby facilitate not only our own business by defining it precisely, but also – for anyone else who wants to examine it – the judgment as to whether or not we have carried out our project adequately. Now the proper problem of pure reason is contained in this question:

How are synthetic judgments possible a priori?

That metaphysics has thus far remained in such a shaky state of uncertainty and contradictions is attributable to a sole cause: the fact that this problem, and perhaps even the distinction between *analytic* and *synthetic* judgments, has not previously occurred to anyone. Whether metaphysics stands or falls depends on the solution of this problem, or on an adequate proof that the possibility which metaphysics demands to see explained does not exist at all. *David Hume* at least came closer to this problem than any other philosopher. Yet he did not think of it nearly determinately enough and in its universality, but merely remained with the synthetic proposition about the connection of an effect with its causes (*principium causalitatis*). He believed he had discovered that such a proposition is quite impossible a priori. Thus, according to his conclusions, everything that we call metaphysics would amount to no more than the delusion of a supposed rational insight into what in fact is merely borrowed from experience and has, through habit, acquired a seeming necessity. This assertion, which destroys all pure philosophy, would never have entered Hume's mind if he had envisaged our problem in its universality. For he would then have seen that by his argument there could be no pure mathematics either, since it certainly does contain synthetic a priori propositions; and from such an assertion his good sense would surely have saved him.

B20

In solving the above problem we solve at the same time another one, concerning the possibility of the pure use of reason in establishing and carrying out all sciences that contain theoretical a priori cognition of objects; i.e., we also answer these questions:

How is pure mathematics possible?

How is pure natural science possible?

Since these sciences are actually given [as existent], it is surely proper for us to ask **how** they are possible; for that they must be possible is proved by their being actual.* As regards *metaphysics*, however, there are grounds on which everyone must doubt its possibility: its progress thus far has been poor; and thus far not a single metaphysics has been put forth of which we can say, as far as the essential purpose of metaphysics is concerned, that it is actually at hand.

Yet in a certain sense this *kind of cognition* must likewise be regarded as given; and although metaphysics is not actual as a science, yet it is actual as a natural predisposition (i.e., as a *metaphysica naturalis*). For human reason, impelled by its own need rather than moved by the mere vanity of gaining a lot of knowledge, proceeds irresistibly to such questions as cannot be answered by any experiential use of reason and any principles taken from such use. And thus all human beings, once their reason has expanded

---

* This actuality may still be doubted by some in the case of pure natural science. Yet we need only examine the propositions that are to be found at the beginning of physics proper (empirical physics), such as those about the permanence of the quantity of matter, about inertia, about the equality of action and reaction, etc., in order to soon be convinced that these propositions themselves amount to a *physica pura* (or *physica rationalis*). Such a physics, as a science in its own right, surely deserves to be put forth separately and in its whole range, whether this range be narrow or broad.

to [the point where it can] speculate, actually have always had in them, and always will have in them, some metaphysics. Now concerning it, too, there is this question:

B22   **How is metaphysics as a natural predisposition possible?** i.e., how, from the nature of universal human reason, do the questions arise that pure reason poses to itself and is impelled, by its own need, to answer as best it can?

Thus far, however, all attempts to answer these natural questions – e.g., whether the world has a beginning or has been there from eternity, etc. – have met with unavoidable contradictions. Hence we cannot settle for our mere natural predisposition for metaphysics, i.e., our pure power of reason itself, even though some metaphysics or other (whichever it might be) always arises from it. Rather, it must be possible, by means of this predisposition, to attain certainty either concerning our knowledge or lack of knowledge of the objects [of metaphysics], i.e., either concerning a decision about the objects that its questions deal with, or certainty concerning the ability or inability of reason to make judgments about these objects. In other words, it must be possible to expand our pure reason in a reliable way, or to set for it limits that are determinate and safe. This last question, which flows from the general problem above, may rightly be stated thus:

How is metaphysics as science possible?

Ultimately, therefore, critique of pure reason leads necessarily to science; the dogmatic use of pure reason without critique, on the other hand, to

B23   baseless assertions that can always be opposed by others that seem equally plausible, and hence to *skepticism*.

This science, moreover, cannot be overly, forbiddingly voluminous. For it deals not with objects of reason, which are infinitely diverse, but merely with [reason] itself. [Here reason] deals with problems that issue entirely from its own womb; they are posed to it not by the nature of things distinct from it, but by its own nature. And thus, once it has become completely acquainted with its own ability regarding the objects that it may encounter in experience, reason must find it easy to determine, completely and safely, the range and the bounds of its use [when] attempted beyond all bounds of experience.

Hence all attempts that have been made thus far to bring a metaphysics about *dogmatically* can and must be regarded as if they had never occurred. For whatever is analytic in one metaphysics or another, i.e., is mere dissection of the concepts residing a priori in our reason, is only a prearrangement for metaphysics proper, and is not yet its purpose at all. That purpose is to expand our a priori cognition synthetically, and for this purpose the dissection of reason's a priori concepts is useless. For it shows merely what is contained in these concepts; it does not show how we arrive at such concepts a priori, so that we could then also determine the valid use of such concepts in regard to the objects of all cognition generally. Nor do we need much self-denial to give up all these claim; for every metaphysics put forth thus far has long since been deprived of its reputation by the fact that it gave rise to undeniable, and in the dogmatic procedure indeed unavoidable, contradictions of reason with itself. A different treatment, completely opposite to the one used thus far, must be given to metaphysics – a science, indispensable to human reason, whose every new shoot can indeed be lopped off but whose root cannot be eradicated. We shall need more perseverance in order to keep from being deterred – either from within by the difficulty of this science or from without by people's resistance to it – from thus finally bringing it to a prosperous and fruitful growth.

B24

Notes

1 The German word *Wissenschaft* is wider in application than our word 'science', and applies to philosophy and history as much as to physics. When he has science in the contemporary English sense in mind, Kant writes of 'natural science'.
2 Here we get a foretaste of Kant's discussion in Division II of the book, 'Transcendental Dialectic', of such 'ideas of reason' as God and freedom which, while beyond the reach of our understanding, have a 'regulative' use and are essential to morality.
3 Most later philosophers, even those who accept an analytic/synthetic distinction, question Kant's ways of making that distinction. The tendency has been to express it in linguistic terms: for example, an analytic truth is one true in virtue, simply, of the meanings of the component terms – any other truth being a synthetic one.

Friedrich Nietzsche, 'On Truth and Lies in a Nonmoral Sense'

From Friedrich Nietzsche, *Philosophy and Truth: Selections from Nietzsche's Notebooks of the Early 1870s*, ed. and tr. Daniel Breazeale. New Jersey: Humanities Library, 1990, pp. 79–91, 93–4, 97 [some notes and passages omitted; asterisked notes are the translator's]; reprinted by permission of Humanities Press International, Inc., Atlantic Highlands, NJ.

Kant, we saw in chapter 11, regarded himself as securing the possibility of objective knowledge in arguing that certain things must be true of objects of experience in order for them to *be* experienced. Many of his contemporaries and successors, however, were more impressed – and sometimes depressed – by his admission that this knowledge only encompasses objects as experienced – 'appearances' or 'phenomena' – and not 'things in themselves' or 'noumena' (things considered apart from the epistemic conditions under which alone we can encounter them). This was the attitude, for example, of Arthur Schopenhauer and of a young German Professor of Philology at Basel whom he had profoundly influenced, Friedrich Nietzsche (1844–1900).

In the remarkable essay of 1873 which follows – one whose importance has only been recently appreciated – Nietzsche subscribes to Kant's distinction between appearances and things in themselves and to his insistence on the unknowability of the latter. Nietzsche concludes, however, that there can therefore be *no* truth and knowledge as these are standardly understood – namely, in terms of agreement or correspondence with how things really are 'apart from man'. As he succinctly put it in an earlier note, 'if Kant is right, then the sciences are wrong',[1] since scientific claims purport to be true of an independent reality, not a merely 'anthropomorphic' world. Since we are condemned to scepticism towards claims about that independent reality, there is no reason, Nietzsche holds, to regard these as anything but 'lies' (in a 'nonmoral' sense). Where Kant, then, accentuates the positive (our knowledge of appearances), Nietzsche accentuates the negative (the gap between this and 'real' knowledge).

[1] The Philosopher', in *Philosophy and Truth*, ed. and tr. Breazeale, p. 32.

There are two further, and perhaps more substantial, differences between the two philosophers. First, whereas for Kant the synthetic *a priori* principles presupposed by experience are fixed, universal principles of cognition, for Nietzsche the explanation of our compulsion to accept, say, the laws of logic or physics is a 'naturalistic' one, in terms of our specifically human drives, interests and 'welfare'. Creatures with different drives, etc. would be under no similar compulsion to accept those laws.

Secondly and relatedly, Nietzsche emphasizes, in a manner Kant never did, the pivotal role of *language* in shaping our concepts and beliefs. 'Logic', he writes, 'is merely slavery within the fetters of language' (p. 194 below). Had we developed a very different language, we would have arrived at a correspondingly different logic. And we might very well have developed a very different language, for there is arbitrariness and contingency in our linguistic, and hence conceptual, categorizations. In the most famous part of the essay, Nietzsche argues that language is essentially *metaphorical* – the result, in one case after another, of applying a single word to things which may be quite unalike. So-called truths, therefore, are themselves metaphors, but ones so well established that we have forgotten this fact. (Quotation of the description of truth as 'a movable host of metaphors' (p. 186 below) is almost *de rigueur* for the postmodernists Nietzsche has so decisively influenced.)[2]

Language plays a further important role in Nietzsche's essay. Although, in a sense, all our statements may be 'lies', Nietzsche allows – indeed, stresses – a workaday distinction between truth and falsity, between knowledge and error. It is crucial, if human beings are to 'exist socially' and so satisfy various needs, that they *agree* with one another on many matters, including especially the 'designations' they give to things for purposes of communication and cooperation. In the workaday sense, a man speaks truthfully when he gives to a thing its agreed, conventional designation. Here we find a very early version of that understanding of truth and knowledge as products of public agreement or consensus which was to become familiar in the twentieth century.

Commentators differ as to how much of Nietzsche's position in this early essay remains in his later writings. Certainly he was to give up the Kantian distinction between appearances and things in themselves, and hence the kind of scepticism which assumes that distinction. But, in my judgement, the ideas surely remain that workable notions of truth and knowledge must be understood in terms of our species-specific needs and drives (both biological and social), that language decisively shapes our concepts and beliefs, and that

[2] See, e.g., Paul de Man, *Allegories of Reading*, New Haven: Yale University Press, 1979, pp. 103ff. For a contrasting interpretation, see Maudemarie Clark, *Nietzsche on Truth and Philosophy*, Cambridge: Cambridge University Press, 1990, pp. 63ff.

allegedly *a priori* principles of judgement are simply ones 'which must be *believed* to be true, for the sake of the preservation of creatures like ourselves'.[3]

(NB The passages following the essay proper are from Nietzsche's sketch of proposed additions to it)

On Truth and Lies in a Nonmoral Sense

1

Once upon a time, in some out of the way corner of that universe which is dispersed into numberless twinkling solar systems, there was a star upon which clever beasts invented knowing. That was the most arrogant and mendacious minute of "world history," but nevertheless, it was only a minute. After nature had drawn a few breaths, the star cooled and congealed, and the clever beasts had to die. – One might invent such a fable, and yet he still would not have adequately illustrated how miserable, how shadowy and transient, how aimless and arbitrary the human intellect looks within nature. There were eternities during which it did not exist. And when it is all over with the human intellect, nothing will have happened. For this intellect has no additional mission which would lead it beyond human life. Rather, it is human, and only its possessor and begetter takes it so solemnly – as though the world's axis turned within it. But if we could communicate with the gnat, we would learn that he likewise flies through the air with the same solemnity, that he feels the flying center of the universe within himself. There is nothing so reprehensible and unimportant in nature that it would not immediately swell up like a balloon at the slightest puff of this power of knowing. And just as every porter wants to have an admirer, so even the proudest of men, the philosopher, supposes that he sees on all sides the eyes of the universe telescopically focused upon his action and thought.

It is remarkable that this was brought about by the intellect, which was certainly allotted to these most unfortunate, delicate, and ephemeral beings merely as a device for detaining them a minute within existence. For without this addition they would have every reason to flee this existence as quickly as Lessing's son [who died on the day of his birth]. The pride

---

[3] *Beyond Good and Evil*, §11, in *Basic Writings of Nietzsche*, tr. W. Kaufmann, New York: Modern Library, 1968, p. 209. For different accounts of the relation of 'On Truth and Lies' to Nietzsche's later work, see Clark, *Nietzsche on Truth and Philosophy*, and Peter Poellner, *Nietzsche and Metaphysics*, Oxford: Clarendon Press, 1995.

connected with knowing and sensing lies like a blinding fog over the eyes and senses of men, thus deceiving them concerning the value of existence. For this pride contains within itself the most flattering estimation of the value of knowing. Deception is the most general effect of such pride, but even its most particular effects contain within themselves something of the same deceitful character.

As a means for the preserving of the individual, the intellect unfolds its principal powers in dissimulation, which is the means by which weaker, less robust individuals preserve themselves – since they have been denied the chance to wage the battle for existence with horns or with the sharp teeth of beasts of prey. This art of dissimulation reaches its peak in man. Deception, flattering, lying, deluding, talking behind the back, putting up a false front, living in borrowed splendor, wearing a mask, hiding behind convention, playing a role for others and for oneself – in short, a continuous fluttering around the *solitary* flame of vanity – is so much the rule and the law among men that there is almost nothing which is less comprehensible than how an honest and pure drive for truth could have arisen among them. They are deeply immersed in illusions and in dream images; their eyes merely glide over the surface of things and see "forms." Their senses nowhere lead to truth; on the contrary, they are content to receive stimuli and, as it were, to engage in a groping game on the backs of things. Moreover, man permits himself be deceived in his dreams every night of his life. His moral sentiment does not even make an attempt to prevent this, whereas there are supposed to be men who have stopped snoring through sheer will power. What does man actually know about himself? Is he, indeed, ever able to perceive himself completely, as if laid out in a lighted display case? Does nature not conceal most things from him – even concerning his own body – in order to confine and lock him within a proud, deceptive consciousness, aloof from the coils of the bowels, the rapid flow of the blood stream, and the intricate quivering of the fibers! She threw away the key. And woe to that fatal curiosity which might one day have the power to peer out and down through a crack in the chamber of consciousness and then suspect that man is sustained in the indifference of his ignorance by that which is pitiless, greedy, insatiable, and murderous – as if hanging in dreams on the back of a tiger. Given this situation, where in the world could the drive for truth have come from?

Insofar as the individual wants to maintain himself against other individuals, he will under natural circumstances employ the intellect mainly for dissimulation. But at the same time, from boredom and necessity, man wishes to exist socially and with the herd; therefore, he needs to make peace and strives accordingly to banish from his world at least the most flagrant *bellum omni contra omnes.* This peace treaty brings in its wake something which appears to be the first step toward acquiring that puzzling truth drive: to wit, *that* which shall count as 'truth' from now on is established. That is to say, a uniformly valid and binding designation is invented for things, and this legislation of language likewise establishes the first laws of truth. For the contrast between truth and lie arises here for the first time. The liar is a person who uses the valid designations, the words, in order to make something which is unreal appear to be real. He says, for example, "I am rich," when the proper designation for his condition would be "poor." He misuses fixed conventions by means of arbitrary substitutions or even reversals of names. If he does this in a selfish and moreover harmful manner, society will cease to trust him and will thereby exclude him. What men avoid by excluding the liar is not so much being defrauded as it is being harmed by means of fraud. Thus, even at this stage, what they hate is basically not deception itself, but rather the unpleasant, hated consequences of certain sorts of deception. It is in a similarly restricted sense that man now wants nothing but truth: he desires the pleasant, life-preserving consequences of truth. He is indifferent toward pure knowledge which has no consequences; toward those truths which are possibly harmful and destructive he is even hostilely inclined. And besides, what about these linguistic conventions themselves? Are they perhaps products of knowledge, that is, of the sense of truth? Are designations congruent with things? Is language the adequate expression of all realities?

It is only by means of forgetfulness that man can ever reach the point of fancying himself to possess a "truth" of the grade just indicated. If he will not be satisfied with truth in the form of tautology, that is to say, if he will not be content with empty husks, then he will always exchange truths for illusions. What is a word? It is the copy in sound of a nerve stimulus. But the further inference from the nerve stimulus to a cause outside of us is already the result of a false and unjustifiable application of the principle of sufficient reason. If truth alone had been the deciding factor in the genesis of language, and if the standpoint of certainty had been decisive for designations, then how could we still dare to say "the stone is hard," as if "hard" were something otherwise familiar to us, and not merely a totally subjective stimulation! We separate things according to gender [in German], designating the tree as masculine and the plant as feminine. What arbitrary assignments! How far this oversteps the canons of certainty! We speak of a "snake": this designation touches only upon its ability to twist itself and could therefore also fit a worm. What arbitrary differentiations! What one-sided preferences, first for this, then for that property of a thing! The various languages placed side by side show that with words it is never a question of truth, never a question of adequate expression; otherwise, there would not be so many languages. The "thing in itself" (which is precisely what the pure truth, apart from any of its consequences, would be) is likewise something quite incomprehensible to the creator of language and something not in the least worth striving for. This creator only designates the relations of things to men, and for expressing these relations he lays hold of the boldest metaphors. To begin with, a nerve stimulus is transferred into an image:[1] first metaphor. The image, in turn, is imitated in a sound: second metaphor. And each time there is a complete overleaping of one sphere, right into the middle of an entirely new and different one. One can imagine a man who is totally deaf and has never had a sensation of sound and music. Perhaps such a person will gaze with astonishment at Chladni's sound figures;[2] perhaps he will discover their causes in the vibrations of the string and will now swear that he must know what men mean by "sound." It is this way with all of us concerning language: we believe that we know something about the things themselves when we speak of trees, colors, snow, and flowers; and yet we possess nothing but metaphors for things – metaphors which correspond in no way to the original entities. In the same way that the sound appears as a sand figure, so the mysterious X of the thing in itself first appears as a nerve stimulus, then as an image, and finally as a sound. Thus the genesis of language does not proceed logically in any case, and all the material within and with which the man of truth, the scientist, and the philosopher later work and build, if not derived from never-never land, is at least not derived from the essence of things.

In particular, let us further consider the formation of concepts. Every word instantly becomes a concept precisely insofar as it is not supposed to serve as a reminder of the unique and entirely individual original experience to which it owes its origin; but rather, a word becomes a concept insofar as it simultaneously has to fit countless more or less similar cases – which means, purely and simply, cases which are never equal and thus altogether unequal. Every concept arises from the equation of unequal things. Just as it is certain that one leaf is never totally the same as another, so it is certain that the concept "leaf" is formed by arbitrarily discarding these individual differences and by forgetting the distinguishing aspects. This awakens the idea that, in addition to the leaves, there exists in nature the "leaf": the original model according to which all the leaves were perhaps woven, sketched, measured, colored, curled, and painted – but by incompetent hands, so that no specimen has turned out to be a correct, trustworthy, and faithful likeness of the original model. We call a person "honest," and then we ask "why has he behaved so honestly today?" Our usual answer is, "on account of his honesty." Honesty! This in turn means that the leaf is the cause of the leaves. We know nothing whatsoever about an essential quality called "honesty"; but we do know of countless individualized and consequently unequal actions which we equate by omitting the aspects in which they are unequal and which we now designate as "honest" actions. Finally we formulate from them a *qualitas occulta* which has the name "honesty." We obtain the concept, as we do the form, by overlooking what is individual and actual; whereas nature is acquainted with no forms and no concepts, and likewise with no species, but only with an X which remains inaccessible and undefinable for us. For even our contrast between individual and species is something anthropomorphic and does not originate in the essence of things; although we should not presume to claim that this contrast does not correspond to the essence of things: that would of course be a dogmatic assertion and, as such, would be just as indemonstrable as its opposite.[3]

What then is truth? A movable host of metaphors, metonymies, and anthropomorphisms: in short, a sum of human relations which have been poetically and rhetorically intensified, transferred, and embellished, and which, after long usage, seem to a people to be fixed, canonical, and binding. Truths are illusions which we have forgotten are illusions; they are metaphors that have become worn out and have been drained of sensuous force, coins which have lost their embossing and are now considered as metal and no longer as coins.

We still do not yet know where the drive for truth comes from. For so far we have heard only of the duty which society imposes in order to exist: to be truthful means to employ the usual metaphors. Thus, to express it morally, this is the duty to lie according to a fixed convention, to lie with the herd and in a manner binding upon everyone. Now man of course forgets that this is the way things stand for him. Thus he lies in the manner indicated, unconsciously and in accordance with habits which are centuries old; and precisely *by means of this unconsciousness* and forgetfulness he arrives at his sense of truth. From the sense that one is obliged to designate one thing as "red," another as "cold," and a third as "mute," there arises a moral impulse in regard to truth. The venerability, reliability, and utility of truth is something which a person demonstrates for himself from the contrast with the liar, whom no one trusts and everyone excludes. As a "*rational*" being, he now places his behavior under the control of abstractions. He will no longer tolerate being carried away by sudden impressions, by intuitions. First he universalizes all these impressions into less colorful, cooler concepts, so that he can entrust the guidance of his life and conduct to them. Everything which distinguishes man from the animals depends upon this ability to volatilize perceptual metaphors in a schema, and thus to dissolve an image into a concept. For something is possible in the realm of these schemata which could never be achieved with the vivid first impressions: the construction of a pyramidal order according to castes and degrees, the creation of a new world of laws, privileges, subordinations, and clearly marked boundaries – a new world, one which now confronts that other vivid world of first impressions as more solid, more universal, better known, and more human than the immediately perceived world, and thus as the regulative and imperative world. Whereas each perceptual metaphor is individual and without equals and is therefore able to elude all classification, the great edifice of concepts displays the rigid regularity of a Roman columbarium* and exhales in logic that strength and coolness which is characteristic of mathematics. Anyone who has felt this cool breath [of logic] will hardly believe that even the concept – which is as bony, four-square, and transposable as a die – is nevertheless merely the *residue of a metaphor*, and that the illusion which is involved in the artistic transference of a nerve stimulus into images is, if not the mother, then the grandmother of every single concept. But in this conceptual crap game "truth" means using every die in the designated manner, counting its spots accurately, fashioning the right categories, and never violating the order of caste and class rank. Just as the Romans and Etruscans cut up the heavens with rigid mathematical lines and confined a god within each of the spaces thereby delimited, as within a *templum*,† so every people has a similarly mathematically divided conceptual heaven above themselves and henceforth thinks that truth demands that each conceptual god be sought only within *his own* sphere. Here one may certainly admire man as a mighty genius of construction, who succeeds in piling up an infinitely complicated dome of concepts upon an unstable foundation, and, as it were, on running water. Of course, in order to be supported by such a foundation, his construction must be like one constructed of spiders' webs: delicate enough to be carried along by the waves, strong enough not to be blown apart by every wind. As a genius of construction man raises himself far above the bee in the following way: whereas the bee builds with wax that he gathers from nature, man builds with the far more delicate conceptual material which he first has to manufacture from himself. In this he is greatly to be admired, but not on account of his drive for truth or for pure knowledge of things. When someone hides something behind a bush and looks for it again in the same place and finds it there as well, there is not much to praise in such seeking and finding. Yet this is how matters stand regarding seeking and

---

* A columbarium is a vault with niches for funeral urns containing the ashes of cremated bodies.
† A delimited space restricted to a particular purpose, especially a religiously sanctified area.

finding "truth" within the realm of reason. If I make up the definition of a mammal, and then, after inspecting a camel, declare "look, a mammal," I have indeed brought a truth to light in this way, but it is a truth of limited value. That is to say, it is a thoroughly anthropomorphic truth which contains not a single point which would be "true in itself" or really and universally valid apart from man. At bottom, what the investigator of such truths is seeking is only the metamorphosis of the world into man. He strives to understand the world as something analogous to man, and at best he achieves by his struggles the feeling of assimilation. Similar to the way in which astrologers considered the stars to be in man's service and connected with his happiness and sorrow, such an investigator considers the entire universe in connection with man: the entire universe as the infinitely fractured echo of one original sound – man; the entire universe as the infinitely multiplied copy of one original picture – man. His method is to treat man as the measure of all things, but in doing so he again proceeds from the error of believing that he has these things [which he intends to measure] immediately before him as mere objects. He forgets that the original perceptual metaphors are metaphors and takes them to be the things themselves.

Only by forgetting this primitive world of metaphor can one live with any repose, security, and consistency: only by means of the petrification and coagulation of a mass of images which originally streamed from the primal faculty of human imagination like a fiery liquid, only in the invincible faith that *this* sun, *this* window, *this* table is a truth in itself, in short, only by forgetting that he himself is an *artistically creating* subject, does man live with any repose, security, and consistency. If but for an instant he could escape from the prison walls of this faith, his "self consciousness" would be immediately destroyed. It is even a difficult thing for him to admit to himself that the insect or the bird perceives an entirely different world from the one that man does, and that the question of which of these perceptions of the world is the more correct one is quite meaningless, for this would have to have been decided previously in accordance with the criterion of the *correct perception*, which means, in accordance with a criterion which is *not available*. But in any case it seems to me that "the correct perception" – which would mean "the adequate expression of an object in the subject" – is a contradictory impossibility. For between two absolutely different spheres, as between subject and object, there is no causality, no correctness, and no expression; there is, at most, an *aesthetic* relation: I mean, a suggestive transference, a stammering translation into a completely foreign tongue – for which there is required, in any case, a freely inventive intermediate sphere and mediating force. "Appearance" is a word that contains many temptations, which is why I avoid it as much as possible. For it is not true that the essence of things "appears" in the empirical world. A painter without hands who wished to express in song the picture before his mind would, by means of this substitution of spheres, still reveal more about the essence of things than does the empirical world. Even the relationship of a nerve stimulus to the generated image is not a necessary one. But when the same image has been generated millions of times and has been handed down for many generations and finally appears on the same occasion every time for all mankind, then it acquires at last the same meaning for men it would have if it were the sole necessary image and if the relationship of the original nerve stimulus to the generated image were a strictly causal one. In the same manner, an eternally repeated dream would certainly be felt and judged to be reality. But the hardening and congealing of a metaphor guarantees absolutely nothing concerning its necessity and exclusive justification.

Every person who is familiar with such considerations has no doubt felt a deep mistrust of all idealism of this sort: just as often as he has quite clearly convinced himself of the eternal consistency, omnipresence, and infallibility of the laws of nature. He has concluded that so far as we can penetrate here – from the telescopic heights to the microscopic depths – everything is secure, complete, infinite, regular, and without any gaps. Science will be able to dig successfully in this shaft forever, and all the things that are discovered will harmonize with and not contradict each other. How little does this resemble a product of the imagination, for if it were such, there should be some place where the illusion and unreality can be divined. Against this, the following must be said: if each of us had a different kind of sense perception – if we could only perceive things now as a bird, now as a worm, now as a plant, or if one of us saw a stimulus as red, another as blue, while a third even heard the same stimulus as a sound – then no one would speak of such a regularity of nature, rather, nature would be grasped only as a creation which is subjective in the highest degree. After all, what is a law of nature as such for us? We are not acquainted with it in itself, but only with its effects, which means in its relation to other laws of nature – which, in turn, are known to us only as sums of relations. Therefore all these relations always refer again to others and are thoroughly incomprehensible to us in their essence. All that we actually know about these laws of nature is what we ourselves bring to them – time and space, and therefore relationships of succession and number. But everything marvelous about the laws of nature, everything that quite astonishes us therein and seems to demand our explanation, everything that might lead us to distrust idealism: all this is completely and solely contained within the mathematical strictness and inviolability of our representations of time and space. But we produce these representations in and from ourselves with the same necessity with which the spider spins.[4] If we are forced to comprehend all things only under these forms, then it ceases to be amazing that in all things we actually comprehend nothing but these forms. For they must all bear within themselves the laws of number, and it is precisely number which is most astonishing in things. All that conformity to law, which impresses us so much in the movement of the stars and in chemical processes, coincides at bottom with those properties which we bring to things. Thus it is we who impress ourselves in this way. In conjunction with this, it of course follows that the artistic process of metaphor formation with which every sensation begins in us already presupposes these forms and thus occurs within them. The only way in which the possibility of subsequently constructing a new conceptual edifice from metaphors themselves can be explained is by the firm persistence of these original forms. That is to say, this conceptual edifice is an imitation of temporal, spatial, and numerical relationships in the domain of metaphor.

2

We have seen how it is originally *language* which works on the construction of concepts, a labor taken over in later ages by *science*. Just as the bee simultaneously constructs cells and fills them with honey, so science works unceasingly on this great columbarium of concepts, the graveyard of perceptions. It is always building new, higher stories and shoring up, cleaning, and renovating the old cells; above all, it takes pains to fill up this monstrously towering framework and to arrange therein the entire empirical world, which is to say, the anthropomorphic world. Whereas the man of action binds his life to reason and its concepts so that he will not be swept away and lost, the scientific investigator builds his hut right next to the tower of science so that he will be able to work on it and to find shelter for himself beneath those bulwarks which presently exist. And he requires shelter, for there are frightful powers which continuously break in upon him, powers which oppose scientific "truth" with completely different kinds of "truths" which bear on their shields the most varied sorts of emblems.

The drive toward the formation of metaphors is the fundamental human drive, which one cannot for a single instant dispense with in thought, for one would thereby dispense with man himself. This drive is not truly vanquished and scarcely subdued by the fact that a regular and rigid new world is constructed as its prison from its own ephemeral products, the concepts. It seeks a new realm and another channel for its activity, and it finds this in *myth* and in *art* generally. This drive continually confuses the conceptual categories and cells by bringing forward new transferences, metaphors, and metonymies. It continually manifests an ardent desire to refashion the world which presents itself to waking man, so that it will be as colorful, irregular, lacking in results and coherence, charming, and eternally new as the world of dreams. Indeed, it is only by means of the rigid and regular web of concepts that the waking man clearly sees that he is awake; and it is precisely because of this that he sometimes thinks that he must be dreaming when this web of concepts is torn by art. Pascal is right in maintaining that if the same dream came to us every night we would be just as occupied with it as we are with the things that we see every day. "If a workman were sure to dream for twelve straight hours every night that he was king," said Pascal, "I believe that he would be just as happy as a king who dreamt for twelve hours every night that he was a workman."* In fact, because of the way that myth takes it for granted that miracles are always happening, the waking life of a mythically inspired people – the Ancient Greeks, for instance – more closely resembles a dream than it does the waking world of a scientifically disenchanted thinker. When every tree can suddenly speak as a nymph, when a god in the shape of a bull can drag away maidens, when even the goddess Athena herself is suddenly seen in the company of Peisastratus driving through the market place of Athens with a beautiful team of horses – and this is what the honest Athenian believed – then, as in a dream, anything is possible at each moment, and all of nature swarms around man as if it were nothing but a masquerade of the gods, who were merely amusing themselves by deceiving men in all these shapes.

But man has an invincible inclination to allow himself to be deceived and is, as it were, enchanted with happiness when the rhapsodist tells him epic fables as if they were true, or when the actor in the theater acts more royally than any real king. So long as it is able to deceive without *injuring*, that master of deception, the intellect, is free; it is released from its former slavery and celebrates its Saturnalia. It is never more luxuriant, richer, prouder, more clever and more daring. With creative pleasure it throws metaphors into confusion and displaces the boundary stones of abstractions, so that, for example, it designates the stream as "the moving path which carries man where he would otherwise walk." The intellect has now thrown the token of bondage from itself. At other times it endeavors, with gloomy officiousness, to show the way and to demonstrate the tools to a poor individual who covets existence; it is like a serv-

---

* *Pensées*, number 386. Actually, Pascal says that the workman would be "almost as happy" as the king in this case!

ant who goes in search of booty and prey for his master. But now it has become the master and it dares to wipe from its face the expression of indigence. In comparison with its previous conduct, everything that it now does bears the mark of dissimulation, just as that previous conduct did of distortion. The free intellect copies human life, but it considers this life to be something good and seems to be quite satisfied with it. That immense framework and planking of concepts to which the needy man clings his whole life long in order to preserve himself is nothing but a scaffolding and toy for the most audacious feats of the liberated intellect. And when it smashes this framework to pieces, throws it into confusion, and puts it back together in an ironic fashion, pairing the most alien things and separating the closest, it is demonstrating that it has no need of these makeshifts of indigence and that it will now be guided by intuitions rather than by concepts. There is no regular path which leads from these intuitions into the land of ghostly schemata, the land of abstractions. There exists no word for these intuitions; when man sees them he grows dumb, or else he speaks only in forbidden metaphors and in unheard-of combinations of concepts. He does this so that by shattering and mocking the old conceptual barriers he may at least correspond creatively to the impression of the powerful present intuition.

There are ages in which the rational man and the intuitive man stand side by side, the one in fear of intuition, the other with scorn for abstraction. The latter is just as irrational as the former is inartistic. They both desire to rule over life: the former, by knowing how to meet his principle needs by means of foresight, prudence, and regularity; the latter, by disregarding these needs and, as an "overjoyed hero," counting as real only that life which has been disguised as illusion and beauty. Whenever, as was perhaps the case in Ancient Greece, the intuitive man handles his weapons more authoritatively and victoriously than his opponent, then, under favorable circumstances, a culture can take shape and art's mastery over life can be established. All the manifestations of such a life will be accompanied by this dissimulation, this disavowal of indigence, this glitter of metaphorical intuitions, and, in general, this immediacy of deception: neither the house, nor the gait, nor the clothes, nor the clay jugs give evidence of having been invented because of a pressing need. It seems as if they were all intended to express an exalted happiness, an Olympian cloudlessness, and, as it were, a playing with seriousness. The man who is guided by concepts and abstractions only succeeds by such means in warding off misfortune, without ever gaining any happiness for himself from these abstractions. And while he aims for the greatest possible freedom from pain, the intuitive man, standing in the midst of a culture, already reaps from his intuition a harvest of continually inflowing illumination, cheer, and redemption – in addition to obtaining a defense against misfortune. To be sure, he suffers more intensely, *when* he suffers; he even suffers more frequently, since he does not understand how to learn from experience and keeps falling over and over again into the same ditch. He is then just as irrational in sorrow as he is in happiness: he cries aloud and will not be consoled. How differently the stoical man who learns from experience and governs himself by concepts is affected by the same misfortunes! This man, who at other times seeks nothing but sincerity, truth, freedom from deception, and protection against ensnaring surprise attacks, now executes a masterpiece of deception: he executes his masterpiece of deception in misfortune, as the other type of man executes his in times of happiness. He wears no quivering and changeable human face, but, as it were, a mask with dignified, symmetrical features. He does not cry; he does not even alter his voice. When a real storm cloud thunders above him, he wraps himself in his cloak, and with slow steps he walks from beneath it.

Drafts

177

. . . Truthfulness, considered as the foundation of all utterances and the presupposition for the maintenance of the human species, is a eudaemonic demand,* a demand which is opposed by the knowledge that the supreme welfare of men depends to a far greater extent upon *illusions.* Consequently, according to the eudaemonean principle, both truth *and lies* must be utilized – which is also the way it happens. . . .

. . . Analysis of the *belief in truth*: for all possession of truth is at bottom nothing but a belief that one possesses truth. The pathos, the feeling of duty, proceeds from *this belief*, not from the alleged truth. This belief in truth presupposes that the individual has an unconditional *power of knowledge*, as well as the conviction that no knowing being will ever have a greater power of knowledge; hence the belief in truth presupposes that the duty to speak the truth is binding upon all other knowing beings. The *relation* suspends the pathos of belief, that is to say, the human limitation, with the skeptical supposition that we are perhaps all in error.

But how is *skepticism* possible? It appears to be the truly *ascetic* stand-

* I.e. a demand connected with the desire for human happiness.

point of thought. For it does not believe in belief and thereby destroys everything that prospers by means of belief.

But even skepticism contains a belief: the belief in logic. Therefore what is most extreme is the surrender of logic, the *credo quia absurdum est*.* doubt concerning reason and thereby its negation. How this occurs as a consequence of asceticism. No one can *live* within such a denial of reason, no more than within pure asceticism. This demonstrates that belief in logic and belief as such is necessary for life, and consequently, that the realm of thinking is eudaemonic. But of course when life and eudaemonia are counted as arguments, then the demand for lies stands out in bold relief. Skepticism turns against the forbidden truth. There then remains no foundation for pure truth in itself; the drive thereto is merely a disguised eudaemonistic drive.

Every natural process is fundamentally inexplicable to us. All we do in each case is to identify the setting in which the actual drama unfolds. Thus we speak of causality when we really see nothing but a succession of events. That this succession must always occur in a particular setting is a belief which is refuted with endless frequency.

Logic is merely slavery within the fetters of language. But language includes within itself an illogical element: metaphor, etc. The initial power produces an equation between things that are unequal, and is thus an operation of the imagination. The existence of concepts, forms, etc. is based upon this.

184

. . . Pure disinterested contemplation is possible only in regard to illusions which have been recognized as illusions, illusions which have no desire to entice us into belief and to this extent do not stimulate our wills at all.

Only a person who could contemplate the entire world *as an illusion* would be in a position to view it apart from desires and drives: the artist and the philosopher. Here instinctive drive comes to an end.

So long as one seeks the *truth* about the world he remains under the control of the drives. But he who desires *pleasure* rather than truth will desire the belief in truth, and consequently the pleasurable effects of this belief.

The world as an illusion: saint, artist, philosopher.

---

* "I believe it because it is absurd": a famous saying attributed to Tertullian (c. 160–220).

185

All eudaemonic drives awaken belief in the truth of things, in the truth of the world. Thus science in its entirety is directed toward becoming and not toward being.

187

I.   Truth as a cloak for quite different impulses and drives.
II.   The pathos of truth is based upon belief.
III.   The drive to lie is fundamental.
IV.   Truth cannot be recognized. Everything which is knowable is illusion. The significance of art as truthful illusion.

Notes

1 Nietzsche's employment of the term 'metaphor' takes seriously its original Greek sense of 'transference'. His general point is that, in the process which leads from things' impact upon our sensory organs to the formation of concepts, a number of 'transfers' or transpositions – physiological, perceptual, linguistic – take place.
2 These are patterns in sand caused by sound vibrations.
3 Here Nietzsche is disagreeing with Kant, who *did* deny that our 'anthropomorphic' conceptions can correspond to 'the essence of things' in themselves.
4 Here Nietzsche follows Kant and Schopenhauer in holding that space and time are forms of perception, not features of reality in itself.

Charles S. Peirce, 'Some Consequences of Four Incapacities' (Excerpt) and 'The Fixation of Belief'

From Charles S. Peirce, *Selected Writings*, ed. P. Wiener. New York: Dover, 1966, pp. 39–41, 92–112 [some notes and passages omitted; asterisked notes are the editor's].

For much of our century, the reputation and importance of the American philosopher Charles Sanders Peirce (1839–1914) were rather eclipsed by that of his younger pragmatist followers, William James and John Dewey. Recently, however, and especially among epistemologists, Peirce is increasingly recognized as an original and radical critic of traditional approaches and a main inspiration for ideas, like that of 'fallibilism', which loom large in contemporary discussion.[1]

Although he is generally referred to as 'the founder of pragmatism', Peirce's position is far removed from the brand of humanistic anti-realism associated with that label by, for example, Richard Rorty.[2] Indeed, Peirce himself was so dismayed by James' deviation from the realist principle that the nature of things is 'entirely independent of our opinions about them' that he disowned the 'pragmatist' tag for fear of being associated with James. The issue of realism apart, however, it is clear even from the early piece on the 'Four incapacities' (1868) why Peirce is standardly classed as a pragmatist. For here, in the opening pages I have selected, we find, in brisk order, some characteristically 'practical' objections to Cartesian epistemology. The Cartesian merely pretends to cast doubt on all our beliefs; he ignores the social character of knowledge, within communities of enquirers; and he fails to recognize that science's success depends, not on the certainty of its component claims and arguments, but

[1] For an excellent discussion of Peirce's general philosophy and his influence, see Christopher Hookway, *Peirce*, London: Routledge & Kegan Paul, 1985.

[2] For a defense of Peircean pragmatism against such later interpretations of pragmatism, see Susan Haack, *Evidence and Inquiry: Towards Reconstruction in Epistemology*, Oxford: Blackwell, 1993, ch. 9.

on their holding together like the intertwined fibres in a strong cable.

In the later essay, 'The fixation of belief' (1877), Peirce's pragmatism is on view in the attention which he, like Nietzsche at the same time (chapter 12 above), pays to the practical role which beliefs play in life. A belief is a guide to actions performed in order to 'satisfy our desires', and something we are impelled to 'fix' so as to escape from 'irritating' and stultifying states of doubt. With belief understood in these terms, however, a serious question is raised (§ V) which it is the main aim of the essay to address. Surely there are plenty of ways, other than rational scientific enquiry, whereby we can 'fix' our beliefs – by letting political or divine authority decide for us, for example, or by indulging in metaphysical tastes. If these alternatives were equally effective in terms of enabling the satisfaction of desires, how could we prefer to engage in scientific enquiry?

Peirce cannot, without qualification, reply that only scientific method reliably leads to *true* beliefs, since he characterizes truth, as much as belief, in terms of 'tend[ing] to satisfy desires'. Perhaps the most interesting answers Peirce offers to his own question are the following. First, only by 'fixing' beliefs according to scientific enquiry is justice done to the *public* character of belief. A person does not hold beliefs in isolation, but as a member of a community or, at any rate, of the human race. He will, therefore, be aware of conflicts between his own beliefs and those of other people: and, unless he is entirely ostrich-like, these conflicts will make him question his own beliefs and seek for consensus. It is Peirce's view that scientific enquiry has already proven itself by far the most effective procedure for approximating to relatively stable consensus. Second, Peirce contends, only scientific enquiry among the alternative ways of 'fixing' beliefs is inspired by, and faithful to, a conviction that surely everyone at least implicitly feels. This is the realist conviction that there is a way 'things really are', one which obtains quite independently of our opinions and to which we should seek to make our beliefs conform.

Both of these Peircean answers to his own question are contentious. Maybe scientific enquiry is not the most effective route towards stable consensus, and maybe it does not presuppose any realist commitment. But they are answers which no contemporary epistemologist could, or would want to, ignore.

Some Consequences of Four Incapacities

Descartes is the father of modern philosophy, and the spirit of Cartesianism – that which principally distinguishes it from the scholasticism which it displaced – may be compendiously stated as follows:

1.   It teaches that philosophy must begin with universal doubt; whereas scholasticism had never questioned fundamentals.

2.   It teaches that the ultimate test of certainty is to be found in the individual consciousness; whereas scholasticism had rested on the testimony of sages and of the Catholic Church.

3.   The multiform argumentation of the Middle Ages is replaced by a single thread of inference depending often upon inconspicuous premises.

4.   Scholasticism had its mysteries of faith, but undertook to explain all created things. But there are many facts which Cartesianism not only does not explain but renders absolutely inexplicable, unless to say that "God makes them so" is to be regarded as an explanation.

In some, or all of these respects, most modern philosophers have been, in effect, Cartesians. Now without wishing to return to scholasticism, it seems to me that modern science and modern logic require us to stand upon a very different platform from this.

1.   We cannot begin with complete doubt. We must begin with all the prejudices which we actually have when we enter upon the study of philosophy. These prejudices are not to be dispelled by a maxim, for they are things which it does not occur to us *can* be questioned. Hence this initial skepticism will be a mere self-deception, and not real doubt; and no one who follows the Cartesian method will ever be satisfied until he has formally recovered all those beliefs which in form he has given up. It is, therefore, as useless a preliminary as going to the North Pole would be in order to get to Constantinople by coming down regularly upon a meridian. A person may, it is true, in the course of his studies, find reason to doubt what he began by believing; but in that case he doubts because he has a positive reason for it, and not on account of the Cartesian maxim. Let us not pretend to doubt in philosophy what we do not doubt in our hearts.

2.   The same formalism appears in the Cartesian criterion, which amounts to this: "Whatever I am clearly convinced of, is true." If I were really convinced, I should have done with reasoning and should require no test of certainty. But thus to make single individuals absolute judges of truth is most pernicious. The result is that metaphysicians will all agree that metaphysics has reached a pitch of certainty far beyond that of the physical sciences – only they can agree upon nothing else. In sciences in which men come to agreement, when a theory has been broached it is considered to be on probation until this agreement is reached. After it is reached, the question of certainty becomes an idle one, because there is no one left who doubts it. We individually cannot reasonably hope to attain the ultimate philosophy which we pursue; we can only seek it, therefore, for the *community* of philosophers. Hence, if disciplined and candid minds carefully examine a theory and refuse to accept it, this ought to create doubts in the mind of the author of the theory himself.

3. Philosophy ought to imitate the successful sciences in its methods, so far as to proceed only from tangible premises which can be subjected to careful scrutiny, and to trust rather to the multitude and variety of its arguments than to the conclusiveness of any one. Its reasoning should not form a chain which is no stronger than its weakest link, but a cable whose fibers may be ever so slender, provided they are sufficiently numerous and intimately connected.

4. Every unidealistic philosophy supposes some absolutely inexplicable, unanalyzable ultimate; in short, something resulting from mediation itself not susceptible of mediation. Now that anything *is* thus inexplicable can only be known by reasoning from signs. But the only justification of an inference from signs is that the conclusion explains the fact. To suppose the fact absolutely inexplicable is not to explain it, and hence this supposition is never allowable. . . .

The Fixation of Belief

I

Few persons care to study logic, because everybody conceives himself to be proficient enough in the art of reasoning already. But I observe that this satisfaction is limited to one's own ratiocination, and does not extend to that of other men.

We come to the full possession of our power of drawing inferences the last of all our faculties, for it is not so much a natural gift as a long and difficult art. The history of its practice would make a grand subject for a book. The mediæval schoolman, following the Romans, made logic the earliest of a boy's studies after grammar, as being very easy. So it was as they understood it. Its fundamental principle, according to them, was that all knowledge rests on either authority or reason; but that whatever is deduced by reason depends ultimately on a premise derived from authority. Accordingly, as soon as a boy was perfect in the syllogistic procedure, his intellectual kit of tools was held to be complete.

To Roger Bacon, that remarkable mind who in the middle of the thirteenth century was almost a scientific man, the schoolmen's conception of reasoning appeared only an obstacle to truth. He saw that experience alone teaches anything – a proposition which to us seems easy to understand, because a distinct conception of experience has been handed down to us from former generations; which to him also seemed perfectly clear, because its difficulties had not yet unfolded themselves. Of all kinds of experience, the best, he thought, was interior illumination, which teaches many things about nature which the external senses could never discover, such as the transubstantiation of bread.

Four centuries later, the more celebrated [Francis] Bacon, in the first book of his *Novum Organum*, gave his clear account of experience as something which must be opened to verification and re-examination. But, superior as Lord Bacon's conception is to earlier notions, a modern reader who is not in awe of his grandiloquence is chiefly struck by the inadequacy of his view of scientific procedure. That we have only to make some crude experiments, to draw up briefs of the results in certain blank forms, to go through these by rule, checking off everything disproved and setting down the alternatives, and that thus in a few years physical science would be finished up – what an idea! "He wrote on science like a Lord Chancellor,"* indeed, as Harvey, a genuine man of science, said.

The early scientists, Copernicus, Tycho Brahe, Kepler, Galileo, Harvey, and Gilbert, had methods more like those of their modern brethren. Kepler undertook to draw a curve through the places of Mars; and his greatest service to science was in impressing on men's minds that this was the thing to be done if they wished to improve astronomy; that they were not to content themselves with inquiring whether one system of epicycles was better than another but that they were to sit down by the figures and find out what the curve, in truth, was. He accomplished this by his incomparable energy and courage, blundering along in the most inconceivable way (to us), from one irrational hypothesis to another, until, after trying twenty-two of these, he fell, by the mere exhaustion of his invention, upon the orbit which a mind well furnished with the weapons of modern logic would have tried almost at the outset.

In the same way, every work of science great enough to be remembered for a few generations affords some exemplification of the defective state of the art of reasoning of the time when it was written; and each chief step in science has been a lesson in logic. It was so when Lavoisier and his contemporaries took up the study of Chemistry. The old chemist's maxim had been *Lege, lege, lege, labora, ora, et relege*. Lavoisier's method was not to read and pray, not to dream that some long and complicated chemical process would have a certain effect, to put it into practice with dull patience, after its inevitable failure to dream that with some modification it would have another result, and to end by publishing the last dream as a fact: his way was to carry his mind into his laboratory, and to make of his alembics and cucurbits instruments of thought, giving a new conception of

* Cf. J. Aubrey's *Brief Lives* (Oxford, ed. 1898), I, 299.

reasoning as something which was to be done with one's eyes open, by manipulating real things instead of words and fancies.

The Darwinian controversy is, in large part, a question of logic. Mr. Darwin proposed to apply the statistical method to biology. The same thing has been done in a widely different branch of science, the theory of gases. Though unable to say what the movement of any particular molecule of gas would be on a certain hypothesis regarding the constitution of this class of bodies, Clausius and Maxwell were yet able, by the application of the doctrine of probabilities, to predict that in the long run such and such a proportion of the molecules would, under given circumstances, acquire such and such velocities; that there would take place, every second, such and such a number of collisions, etc.; and from these propositions they were able to deduce certain properties of gases, especially in regard to their heat-relations. In like manner, Darwin, while unable to say what the operation of variation and natural selection in every individual case will be, demonstrates that in the long run they will adapt animals to their circumstances. Whether or not existing animal forms are due to such action, or what position the theory ought to take, forms the subject of a discussion in which questions of fact and questions of logic are curiously interlaced.

II

The object of reasoning is to find out, from the consideration of what we already know, something else which we do not know. Consequently, reasoning is good if it be such as to give a true conclusion from true premises, and not otherwise. Thus, the question of validity is purely one of fact and not of thinking. A being the premises and B being the conclusion, the question is, whether these facts are really so related that if A is B is. If so, the inference is valid; if not, not. It is not in the least the question whether, when the premises are accepted by the mind, we feel an impulse to accept the conclusion also. It is true that we do generally reason correctly by nature. But that is an accident; the true conclusion would remain true if we had no impulse to accept it; and the false one would remain false, though we could not resist the tendency to believe in it.

We are, doubtless, in the main logical animals, but we are not perfectly so. Most of us, for example, are naturally more sanguine and hopeful than logic would justify. We seem to be so constituted that in the absence of any facts to go upon we are happy and self-satisfied; so that the effect of experience is continually to counteract our hopes and aspirations. Yet a lifetime of the application of this corrective does not usually eradicate our sanguine disposition. Where hope is unchecked by any experience, it is likely that our optimism is extravagant. Logicality in regard to practical matters is the most useful quality an animal can possess, and might, therefore, result from the action of natural selection; but outside of these it is probably of more advantage to the animal to have his mind filled with pleasing and encouraging visions, independently of their truth; and thus, upon unpractical subjects, natural selection might occasion a fallacious tendency of thought.

That which determines us, from given premises, to draw one inference rather than another is some habit of mind, whether it be constitutional or acquired. The habit is good or otherwise, according as it produces true conclusions from true premises or not; and an inference is regarded as valid or not, without reference to the truth or falsity of its conclusion specially, but according as the habit which determines it is such as to produce true conclusions in general or not. The particular habit of mind which governs this or that inference may be formulated in a proposition whose truth depends on the validity of the inferences which the habit determines; and such a formula is called a *guiding principle* of inference. Suppose, for example, that we observe that a rotating disk of copper quickly comes to rest when placed between the poles of a magnet, and we infer that this will happen with every disk of copper. The guiding principle is that what is true of one piece of copper is true of another. Such a guiding principle with regard to copper would be much safer than with regard to many other substances – brass, for example.

A book might be written to signalize all the most important of these guiding principles of reasoning. It would probably be, we must confess, of no service to a person whose thought is directed wholly to practical subjects, and whose activity moves along thoroughly beaten paths. The problems which present themselves to such a mind are matters of routine which he has learned once for all to handle in learning his business. But let a man venture into an unfamiliar field, or where his results are not continually checked by experience, and all history shows that the most masculine intellect will ofttimes lose his orientation and waste his efforts in directions which bring him no nearer to his goal, or even carry him entirely astray. He is like a ship on the open sea, with no one on board who understands the rules of navigation. And in such a case some general study of the guiding principles of reasoning would be sure to be found useful.

The subject could hardly be treated, however, without being first limited; since almost any fact may serve as a guiding principle. But it so happens that there exists a division among facts, such that in one class are all those which are absolutely essential as guiding principles, while in the other are all those which have any other interest as objects of research. This division is between those which are necessarily taken for granted in asking whether a certain conclusion follows from certain premises, and those which are not implied in that question. A moment's thought will show that a variety of facts are already assumed when the logical question is first asked. It is implied, for instance, that there are such states of mind as doubt and belief – that a passage from one to the other is possible, the object of thought remaining the same, and that this transition is subject to some rules which all minds are alike bound by. As these are facts which we must already know before we can have any clear conception of reasoning at all, it cannot be supposed to be any longer of much interest to inquire into their truth or falsity. On the other hand, it is easy to believe that those rules of reasoning which are deduced from the very idea of the process are the ones which are the most essential; and, indeed, that so long as it conforms to these it will, at least, not lead to false conclusions from true premises. In point of fact, the importance of what may be deduced from the assumptions involved in the logical question turns out to be greater than might be supposed, and this for reasons which it is difficult to exhibit at the outset. The only one which I shall here mention is that conceptions which are really products of logical reflections, without being readily seen to be so, mingle with our ordinary thoughts, and are frequently the causes of great confusion. This is the case, for example, with the conception of quality. A quality as such is never an object of observation. We can see that a thing is blue or green, but the quality of being blue and the quality of being green are not things which we see; they are products of logical reflections. The truth is that common sense, or thought as it first emerges above the level of the narrowly practical, is deeply imbued with that bad logical quality to which the epithet *metaphysical* is commonly applied; and nothing can clear it up but a severe course of logic.

III

We generally know when we wish to ask a question and when we wish to pronounce a judgment, for there is a dissimilarity between the sensation of doubting and that of believing.

But this is not all which distinguishes doubt from belief. There is a practical difference. Our beliefs guide our desires and shape our actions. The Assassins, or followers of the Old Man of the Mountain, used to rush into death at his least command, because they believed that obedience to him would insure everlasting felicity. Had they doubted this, they would not have acted as they did. So it is with every belief, according to its degree. The feeling of believing is a more or less sure indication of there being established in our nature some habit which will determine our actions. Doubt never has such an effect.

Nor must we overlook a third point of difference. Doubt is an uneasy and dissatisfied state from which we struggle to free ourselves and pass into the state of belief;[1] while the latter is a calm and satisfactory state which we do not wish to avoid, or to change to a belief in anything else. On the contrary, we cling tenaciously, not merely to believing, but to believing just what we do believe.

Thus, both doubt and belief have positive effects upon us, though very different ones. Belief does not make us act at once, but puts us into such a condition that we shall behave in a certain way, when the occasion arises. Doubt has not the least effect of this sort, but stimulates us to action until it is destroyed. This reminds us of the irritation of a nerve and the reflex action produced thereby; while for the analogue of belief, in the nervous system, we must look to what are called nervous associations – for example, to that habit of the nerves in consequence of which the smell of a peach will make the mouth water.

IV

The irritation of doubt causes a struggle to attain a state of belief. I shall term this struggle *inquiry*, though it must be admitted that this is sometimes not a very apt designation.

The irritation of doubt is the only immediate motive for the struggle to attain belief. It is certainly best for us that our beliefs should be such as may truly guide our actions so as to satisfy our desires; and this reflection will make us reject any belief which does not seem to have been so formed as to insure this result. But it will only do so by creating a doubt in the place of that belief. With the doubt, therefore, the struggle begins, and with the cessation of doubt it ends. Hence, the sole object of inquiry is the settlement of opinion. We may fancy that this is not enough for us, and that we seek not merely an opinion, but a true opinion. But put this fancy to the test, and it proves groundless; for as soon as a firm belief is reached we are entirely satisfied, whether the belief be false or true. And it is clear that nothing out of the sphere of our knowledge can be our object, for nothing which does not affect the mind can be a motive for a mental effort. The most that can be maintained is that we seek for a belief that we shall *think* to be true. But we think each one of our beliefs to be true, and, indeed, it is mere tautology to say so.*

That the settlement of opinion is the sole end of inquiry is a very important proposition. It sweeps away, at once, various vague and erroneous conceptions of proof. A few of these may be noticed here.

1. Some philosophers have imagined that to start an inquiry it was only necessary to utter or question or set it down on paper, and have even recommended us to begin our studies with questioning everything! But the mere putting of a proposition into the interrogative form does not stimulate the mind to any struggle after belief. There must be a real and living doubt, and without all this, discussion is idle.

2. It is a very common idea that a demonstration must rest on some ultimate and absolutely indubitable propositions. These, according to one school, are first principles of a general nature; according to another, are first sensations. But, in point of fact, an inquiry, to have that completely satisfactory result called demonstration, has only to start with propositions perfectly free from all actual doubt. If the premises are not in fact doubted at all, they cannot be more satisfactory than they are.[2]

3. Some people seem to love to argue a point after all the world is fully convinced of it. But no further advance can be made. When doubt ceases, mental action on the subject comes to an end; and, if it did go on, it would be without a purpose, except that of self-criticism.

V

If the settlement of opinion is the sole object of inquiry, and if belief is of the nature of a habit, why should we not attain the desired end, by taking any answer to a question, which we may fancy, and constantly reiterating it to ourselves, dwelling on all which may conduce to that belief, and learning to turn with contempt and hatred from anything which might disturb it? This simple and direct method is really pursued by many men. I remember once being entreated not to read a certain newspaper lest it might change my opinion upon free-trade. "Lest I might be entrapped by its fallacies and misstatements" was the form of expression. "You are not," my friend said, "a special student of political economy. You might,

---

* "For truth is neither more nor less than that character of a proposition which consists in this, that belief in the proposition would, with sufficient experience and reflection, lead us to such conduct as would tend to satisfy the desires we should then have. To say that truth means more than this is to say that it has no meaning at all." Peirce's note of 1903.

therefore, easily be deceived by fallacious arguments upon the subject. You might, then, if you read this paper, be led to believe in protection. But you admit that free-trade is the true doctrine; and you do not wish to believe what is not true." I have often known this system to be deliberately adopted. Still oftener, the instinctive dislike of an undecided state of mind, exaggerated into a vague dread of doubt, makes men cling spasmodically to the views they already take. The man feels that if he only holds to his belief without wavering, it will be entirely satisfactory. Nor can it be denied that a steady and immovable faith yields great peace of mind. It may, indeed, give rise to inconveniences, as if a man should resolutely continue to believe that fire would not burn him, or that he would be eternally damned if he received his *ingesta* otherwise than through a stomach-pump. But then the man who adopts this method will not allow that its inconveniences are greater than its advantages. He will say, "I hold steadfastly to the truth and the truth is always wholesome." And in many cases it may very well be that the pleasure he derives from his calm faith overbalances any inconveniences resulting from its deceptive character. Thus, if it be true that death is annihilation, then the man who believes that he will certainly go straight to heaven when he dies, provided he have fulfilled certain simple observances in this life, has a cheap pleasure which will not be followed by the least disappointment. A similar consideration seems to have weight with many persons in religious topics, for we frequently hear it said, "Oh, I could not believe so-and-so, because I should be wretched if I did." When an ostrich buries its head in the sand as danger approaches, it very likely takes the happiest course. It hides the danger, and then calmly says there is no danger; and, if it feels perfectly sure there is none, why should it raise its head to see? A man may go through life, systematically keeping out of view all that might cause a change in his opinions, and if he only succeeds – basing his method, as he does, on two fundamental psychological laws – I do not see what can be said against his doing so. It would be an egotistical impertinence to object that his procedure is irrational, for that only amounts to saying that his method of settling belief is not ours. He does not propose to himself to be rational, and indeed, will often talk with scorn of man's weak and illusive reason. So let him think as he pleases.

But this method of fixing belief, which may be called the method of tenacity, will be unable to hold its ground in practice. The social impulse is against it. The man who adopts it will find that other men think differently from him, and it will be apt to occur to him in some saner moment that their opinions are quite as good as his own, and this will shake his confidence in his belief. This conception, that another man's thought or sentiment may be equivalent to one's own, is a distinctly new step, and a highly important one. It arises from an impulse too strong in man to be suppressed, without danger of destroying the human species. Unless we make ourselves hermits, we shall necessarily influence each other's opinions; so that the problem becomes how to fix belief, not in the individual merely, but in the community.

Let the will of the state act, then, instead of that of the individual. Let an institution be created which shall have for its object to keep correct doctrines before the attention of the people, to reiterate them perpetually, and to teach them to the young; having at the same time power to prevent contrary doctrines from being taught, advocated, or expressed. Let all possible causes of a change of mind be removed from men's apprehensions. Let them be kept ignorant, lest they should learn of some reason to think otherwise than they do. Let their passions be enlisted, so that they may regard private and unusual opinions with hatred and horror. Then, let all men who reject the established belief be terrified into silence. Let the people turn out and tar-and-feather such men, or let inquisitions be made into the manner of thinking of suspected persons, and, when they are found guilty of forbidden beliefs, let them be subjected to some signal punishment. When complete agreement could not otherwise be reached, a general massacre of all who have not thought in a certain way has proved a very effective means of settling opinion in a country. If the power to do this be wanting, let a list of opinions be drawn up, to which no man of the least independence of thought can assent, and let the faithful be required to accept all these propositions, in order to segregate them as radically as possible from the influence of the rest of the world.

This method has, from the earliest times, been one of the chief means of upholding correct theological and political doctrines, and of preserving their universal or catholic character. In Rome, especially, it has been practiced from the days of Numa Pompilius to those of [Pope] Pius IX. This is the most perfect example in history; but wherever there is a priesthood – and no religion has been without one – this method has been more or less made use of. Wherever there is aristocracy, or a guild, or any association of a class of men whose interests depend or are supposed to depend on certain propositions, there will be inevitably found some traces of this natural product of social feeling. Cruelties always accompany this system; and when it is consistently carried out, they become atrocities of the most horrible kind in the eyes of any rational man. Nor should this occasion surprise, for the officer of a society does not feel justified in surrendering the interests of that society for the sake of mercy, as he might his own private interests. It is natural, therefore, that sympathy and fellowship should thus produce a most ruthless power.

In judging this method of fixing belief, which may be called the method of authority, we must, in the first place, allow its immeasurable mental and moral superiority to the method of tenacity. Its success is proportionally greater; and in fact it has over and over again worked the most majestic results. The mere structures of stone which it has caused to be put together – in Siam, for example, in Egypt, and in Europe – have many of them a sublimity hardly more than rivaled by the greatest works of nature. And, except the geological epochs, there are no periods of time so vast as those which are measured by some of these organized faiths. If we scrutinize the matter closely, we shall find that there has not been one of their creeds which has remained always the same; yet the change is so slow as to be imperceptible during one person's life, so that individual belief remains sensibly fixed. For the mass of mankind, then, there is perhaps no better method than this. If it is their highest impulse to be intellectual slaves, then slaves they ought to remain.

But no institution can undertake to regulate opinions upon every subject. Only the most important ones can be attended to, and on the rest men's minds must be left to the action of natural causes. This imperfection will be no source of weakness so long as men are in such a state of culture that one opinion does not influence another – that is, so long as they cannot put two and two together. But in the most priest-ridden states some individuals will be found who are raised above that condition. These men possess a wider sort of social feeling; they see that men in other countries and in other ages have held to very different doctrines from those which they themselves have been brought up to believe; and they cannot help seeing that it is the mere accident of their having been taught as they have, and of their having been surrounded with the manners and associations they have, that has caused them to believe as they do and not far differently. And their candor cannot resist the reflection that there is no reason to rate their own views at a higher value than those of other nations and other centuries; and this gives rise to doubts in their minds.

They will further perceive that such doubts as these must exist in their minds with reference to every belief which seems to be determined by the caprice either of themselves or of those who originated the popular opinions. The willful adherence to a belief, and the arbitrary forcing of it upon others, must, therefore, both be given up and a new method of settling opinions must be adopted, which shall not only produce an impulse to believe, but shall also decide what proposition it is which is to be believed. Let the action of natural preferences be unimpeded, then, and under their influence let men conversing together and regarding matters in different lights, gradually develop beliefs in harmony with natural causes. This method resembles that by which conceptions of art have been brought to maturity. The most perfect example of it is to be found in the history of metaphysical philosophy. Systems of this sort have not usually rested upon observed facts, at least not in any great degree. They have been chiefly adopted because their fundamental propositions seemed 'agreeable to reason.' This is an apt expression; it does not mean that which agrees with experience, but that which we find ourselves inclined to believe. Plato, for example, finds it agreeable to reason that the distances of the celestial spheres from one another should be proportional to the different lengths of strings which produce harmonious chords. Many philosophers have been led to their main conclusions by considerations like this; but this is the lowest and least developed form which the method takes, for it is clear that another man might find Kepler's [earlier] theory, that the celestial spheres are proportional to the inscribed and circumscribed spheres of the different regular solids, more agreeable to *his* reason. But the shock of opinions will soon lead men to rest on preferences of a far more universal nature. Take, for example, the doctrine that man only acts selfishly – that is, from the consideration that acting in one way will afford him more pleasure than acting in another. This rests on no fact in the world, but it has had a wide acceptance as being the only reasonable theory.

This method is far more intellectual and respectable from the point of view of reason than either of the others which we have noticed. But its failure has been the most manifest. It makes of inquiry something similar to the development of taste; but taste, unfortunately, is always more or less a matter of fashion, and accordingly, metaphysicians have never come to any fixed agreement, but the pendulum has swung backward and forward between a more material and a more spiritual philosophy, from the earliest times to the latest. And so from this, which has been called the *a priori* method, we are driven, in Lord Bacon's phrase, to a true induction. We have examined into this *a priori* method as something which promised to deliver our opinions from their accidental and capricious element. But development, while it is a process which eliminates the effect of some casual circumstances, only magnifies that of others. This method, therefore, does not differ in a very essential way from that of authority. The government may not have lifted its finger to influence my convictions; I may have been left outwardly quite free to choose, we will say, between monogamy and polygamy, and appealing to my conscience only, I may have concluded that the latter practice is in itself licentious. But when I come to see that the chief obstacle to the spread of Christianity among a people of as high culture as the Hindoos has been a conviction of the immorality of our way of treating women, I cannot help seeing that, though governments do not interfere, sentiments in their development will be very greatly determined by accidental causes. Now, there are some people, among whom I must suppose that my reader is to be found, who, when they see that any belief of theirs is determined by any circumstance extraneous to the facts, will from that moment not merely admit in words that that belief is doubtful, but will experience a real doubt of it, so that it ceases in some degree at least to be a belief.

To satisfy our doubts, therefore, it is necessary that a method should be found by which our beliefs may be caused by nothing human, but by some external permanency – by something upon which our thinking has no effect. Some mystics imagine that they have such a method in a private inspiration from on high. But that is only a form of the method of tenacity, in which the conception of truth as something public is not yet developed. Our external permanency would not be external, in our sense, if it was restricted in its influence to one individual. It must be something which affects, or might affect, every man. And, though these affections are necessarily as various as are individual conditions, yet the method must be such that the ultimate conclusion of every man shall be the same, or would be the same if inquiry were sufficiently persisted in. Such is the method of science. Its fundamental hypothesis, restated in more familiar language, is this: There are real things, whose characters are entirely independent of our opinions about them; those realities affect our senses according to regular laws, and, though our sensations are as different as our relations to the objects, yet, by taking advantage of the laws of perception, we can ascertain by reasoning how things really are, and any man, if he have sufficient experience and reason enough about it, will be led to the one true conclusion. The new conception here involved is that of reality. It may be asked how I know that there are any realities. If this hypothesis is the sole support of my method of inquiry, my method of inquiry must not be used to support my hypothesis. The reply is this: (1) If investigation cannot be regarded as proving that there are real things, it at least does not lead to a contrary conclusion; but the method and the conception on which it is based remain ever in harmony. No doubts of the method, therefore, necessarily arise from its practice, as is the case with all the others. (2) The feeling which gives rise to any method of fixing belief is a dissatisfaction at two repugnant [i.e. conflicting] propositions. But here already is a vague concession that there is some *one* thing to which a proposition should conform. Nobody, therefore, can really doubt that there are realities, or, if he did, doubt would not be a source of dissatisfaction. The hypothesis, therefore, is one which every mind admits. So that the social impulse does not cause men to doubt it. (3) Everybody uses the scientific method about a great many things, and only ceases to use it when he does not know how to apply it. (4) Experience of the method has not led us to doubt it, but, on the contrary, scientific investigation has had the most wonderful triumphs in the way of settling opinion. These afford the explanation of my not doubting the method or the hypothesis which it supposes; and not having any doubt, nor believing that anybody else whom I could influence has, it would be the merest babble for me to say more about it. If there be any-body with a living doubt upon the subject, let him consider it.

To describe the method of scientific investigation is the object of this series of papers. At present I have only room to notice some points of contrast between it and other methods of fixing belief.

This is the only one of the four methods which presents any distinction of a right and a wrong way. If I adopt the method of tenacity and shut myself out from all influences, whatever I think necessary to doing this is necessary according to that method. So with the method of authority: the state may try to put down heresy by means which, from a scientific point of view, seems very ill-calculated to accomplish its purposes; but the only test *on that method* is what the state thinks, so that it cannot pursue the method wrongly. So with the *a priori* method. The very essence of it is to think as one is inclined to think. All metaphysicians will be sure to do that, however they may be inclined to judge each other to be perversely wrong. The Hegelian system recognizes every natural tendency of thought as logical, although it is certain to be abolished by countertendencies. Hegel thinks there is a regular system in the succession of these tendencies, in conse-quence of which, after drifting one way and the other for a long time, opinion will at last go right. And it is true that metaphysicians get the right ideas at last; Hegel's system of Nature represents tolerably the science of his day; and one may be sure that whatever scientific investigation has put out of doubt will presently receive *a priori* demonstration on the part of the metaphysicians. But with the scientific method the case is different. I may start with known and observed facts to proceed to the unknown; and yet the rules which I follow in doing so may not be such as investigation would approve. The test of whether I am truly following the method is not an immediate appeal to my feelings and purposes, but, on the contrary, itself involves the application of the method. Hence it is that bad reasoning as well as good reasoning is possible; and this fact is the foundation of the practical side of logic.

It is not to be supposed that the first three methods of settling opinion present no advantage whatever over the scientific method. On the contrary, each has some peculiar convenience of its own. The *a priori* method is distinguished for its comfortable conclusions. It is the nature of the process to adopt whatever belief we are inclined to, and there are certain flatteries to one's vanities which we all believe by nature, until we are awakened from our pleasing dream by rough facts. The method of authority will always govern the mass of mankind; and those who wield the various forms of organized force in the state will never be convinced that dangerous reasoning ought not to be suppressed in some way. If liberty of speech is to be untrammeled from the grosser forms of constraint, then uniformity of opinion will be secured by a moral terrorism to which the respectability of society will give its thorough approval. Following the method of authority is the path of peace. Certain non-conformities are permitted; certain others (considered unsafe) are forbidden. These are different in different countries and in different ages; but, wherever you are let it be known that you seriously hold a tabooed belief, and you may be perfectly sure of being treated with a cruelty no less brutal but more refined than hunting you like a wolf. Thus, the greatest intellectual benefactors of mankind have never dared, and dare not now, to utter the whole of their thought; and thus a shade of *prima facie* doubt is cast upon every proposition which is considered essential to the security of society. Singularly enough, the persecution does not all come from without; but a man torments himself and is oftentimes most distressed at finding himself believing propositions which he has been brought up to regard with aversion. The peaceful and sympathetic man will, therefore, find it hard to resist the temptation to submit his opinions to authority. But most of all I admire the method of tenacity for its strength, simplicity, and directness. Men who pursue it are distinguished for their decision of character, which becomes very easy with such a mental rule. They do not waste time in trying to make up their minds to what they want, but, fastening like lightning upon whatever alternative comes first, they hold to it to the end, whatever happens, without an instant's irresolution. This is one of the splendid qualities which generally accompany brilliant, unlasting success. It is impossible not to envy the man who can dismiss reason, although we know how it must turn out at last.

Such are the advantages which the other methods of settling opinions have over scientific investigation. A man should consider well of them; and then he should consider that, after all, he wishes his opinions to coincide with the fact, and that there is no reason why the results of those first three methods should do so. To bring about this effect is the prerogative of the method of science. Upon such considerations he has to make his choice – a choice which is far more than the adoption of any intellectual opinion, which is one of the ruling decisions of his life, to which when once made he is bound to adhere.

The force of habit will sometimes cause a man to hold on to old beliefs after he is in a condition to see that they have no sound basis. But reflection upon the state of the case will overcome these habits, and he ought to allow reflection full weight. People sometimes shrink from doing this, having an idea that beliefs are wholesome which they cannot help feeling rest on nothing. But let such persons suppose an analogous though different case from their own. Let them ask themselves what they would say to a reformed Mussulman who should hesitate to give up his old notions in regard to the relations of the sexes; or to a reformed Catholic who should still shrink from the Bible. Would they not say that these persons ought to consider the matter fully, and clearly understand the new doctrine, and then ought to embrace it in its entirety? But, above all, let it be considered that what is more wholesome than any particular belief is integrity of belief; and that to avoid looking into the support of any belief from a fear that it may turn out rotten is quite as immoral as it is disadvantageous. The person who confesses that there is such a thing as truth, which is distinguished from falsehood simply by this, that if acted on it should, on full consideration, carry us to the point we aim at and not astray, and then, though convinced of this, dares not know the truth and seeks to avoid it, is in a sorry state of mind, indeed.

Yes, the other methods do have their merits: a clear logical conscience does cost something – just as any virtue, just as all that we cherish, costs us dear. But, we should not desire it to be otherwise. The genius of a man's logical method should be loved and reverenced as his bride, whom he has chosen from all the world. He need not condemn the others; on the contrary, he may honor them deeply, and in doing so he only honors her the more. But she is the one that he has chosen, and he knows that he was right in making that choice. And having made it, he will work and fight for her, and will not complain that there are blows to take, hoping that there may be as many and as hard to give, and will strive to be the worthy knight and champion of her from the blaze of whose splendors he draws his inspiration and his courage.

Notes

1 In a note of 1903, Peirce attempts to rebut a predictable objection based on the existence of enquiring minds which seek out doubts. Admitting such exceptions, Peirce insists that 'doubt essentially involves a struggle to escape it'.
2 Here Peirce is expressing the position which he himself describes as 'fallibilist'. Any belief might conceivably be false, but that is no reason *per se* to doubt that it is actually true.

14 Edmund Husserl, *The Idea of Phenomenology*, Lectures 1–2

From Edmund Husserl, *The Idea of Phenomenology*, tr. W. P. Alston. The Hague: Nijhoff, 1964, pp. 13–32 [some notes omitted; asterisked note is the translator's]; reprinted with kind permission from Kluwer Academic Publishers.

In the four preceding chapters, the authors represented all challenge the epistemological enterprise as conceived and executed by Descartes. Reid, Kant, Nietzsche and Peirce, each in his own way, rejects the idea that the endeavour should or could be one of establishing the domain of knowledge by reflecting on the immediate certainties of subjective experience which remain when everything else has been subjected to methodological doubt. The Cartesian approach, albeit modified, was to make a resounding return, however, in the philosophy of the Moravian-born philosopher, Edmund Husserl (1859–1938).

Husserl refers to his philosophical attitude and method as phenomenology. The aim of phenomenology is to provide 'fundamental' descriptions, free from distortion by theoretical presuppositions and prejudices, of 'things themselves', of 'phenomena'. In the 1907 lectures comprising *The Idea of Phenomenology*, Husserl has a more radical understanding of the execution of this aim than in his earlier *Logical Investigations* and is, in effect, embarking on the course which was to end at the transcendental idealism of *Cartesian Meditations* over two decades later.[1] Phenomenology, he now urges, must begin with a thorough 'critique of cognition', for our ordinary claims to knowledge, reflecting a 'naive' and 'natural attitude' towards the world, turn out to involve a host of prejudices and give rise to 'abysmal difficulties'. None of us really understands how, or even whether, our cognitions 'grasp' or 'reach out to' the transcendent realm of objects we naturally assume they do. Hence we are in no position to refute total scepticism, solipsism and the possibility that our thinking is incoherent (for, so far, the existence of laws of logic remains a mere assumption).

We require, then, a 'new beginning', albeit one reminiscent of Descartes'

---

[1] For a detailed account of the development of Husserl's thinking, see Herbert Spiegelberg, *The Phenomenological Movement*, The Hague: Nijhoff, 1982.

approach. Husserl does not share Descartes' ambition to arrive, after a process of doubting, at the existence of an immaterial 'thinking thing', the cogito, and still less the ambitions of proving the existence of a God and, *via* Him, of the material world. Descartes' achievement, for Husserl, was to have revealed a realm of objects immediately *given* to consciousness and hence indubitable – namely, cognitions or mental acts themselves, abstracted from their possible (and problematic) relation to objects in an actual world.

In his 1907 lectures, Husserl introduces the notion which henceforth plays a central role in his thinking, that of the 'phenomenological reduction' (referred to on p. 231 as the 'epistemological reduction'). The phenomenologist's first task, if he is to expose and describe what is indubitably given to consciousness, is not to *doubt*, but rather simply to 'bracket' or 'abstain from' our 'natural' beliefs. For such purposes, actual objects (if such there be) are 'reduced' to what is immediately given in perception, imagination or whatever. This 'abstention' or *epochē* (the Greek word for 'cessation') is radical. The existence of the external world, and of ourselves as embodied, empirical egos within it, must be 'bracketed'.[2] So, for example, to understand the nature or 'essence' of knowledge or cognition itself, we must ignore our assumed relationship to a material world so as to focus solely on the mental acts of cognition, thereby enabling us to 'intuit' or 'see' wherein their 'essence' consists.

In an important passage (pp. 227f), Husserl is anxious to ward off a misinterpretation of his proposal. It might seem that he intends to confine knowledge to what is 'immanent' in the sense of being 'contained in' our minds, to 'ideas' and 'impressions', in the familiar seventeenth–eighteenth-century manner. He argues, however, that something – an 'essence', say – can be 'immanent' in the sense of being directly given to consciousness without thereby being an ingredient *in* consciousness. It is a mistake, committed by Hume and others, to confuse the two senses of 'immanence', and one which precludes any possible knowledge of the transcendent or extra-mental.

Husserl's epistemology has been extremely influential although, it must be said, primarily by way of serving as a target for later philosophers, including many, like Heidegger and Merleau-Ponty, who belong within a broadly phenomenological tradition. For these writers, we are too much 'beings-in-the-world' for us to 'bracket' that world, and what the attempt at phenomenological reduction ultimately shows is the impossibility of any complete reduction.[3] Certainly Husserl's approach is badly at odds with some currently favoured ones in English-language philosophy. As a champion of 'the given' which

---

[2] For a clear account of the phenomenological reduction and other central notions in Husserl's thought, see Michael Hammond, Jane Howarth and Russell Keat, *Understanding Phenomenology*, Oxford: Blackwell, 1991, chs 1–2.

[3] Maurice Merleau-Ponty, *Phenomenology of Perception*, London: Routledge & Kegan Paul, 1962, p. 85.

constitutes the foundation of all knowledge, Husserl is therefore, for many critics, defending a 'myth'. And his condemnation of the intrusion into the theory of knowledge of scientific, including biological, considerations as 'extremely irrelevant' and 'exceedingly dangerous' puts him at total odds with the programme of 'naturalizing epistemology'.

 Lecture I

[THE NATURAL ATTITUDE IN THINKING AND SCIENCE OF THE NATURAL SORT. THE PHILOSOPHIC (REFLECTIVE) ATTITUDE IN THINKING. THE CONTRADICTIONS OF REFLECTION ON COGNITION, WHEN ONE REFLECTS IN THE NATURAL ATTITUDE, THE DUAL TASK OF TRUE CRITICISM OF COGNITION. TRUE CRITICISM OF COGNITION AS PHENOMENOLOGY OF COGNITION. THE NEW DIMENSION BELONGING TO PHILOSOPHY; ITS PECULIAR METHOD IN CONTRAST TO SCIENCE.]

In earlier lectures I distinguished between *science of the natural sort* and *philosophic science*. The former originates from the natural, the latter from the philosophic attitude of mind.

The *natural attitude of mind* is as yet unconcerned with the critique of cognition. Whether in the act of intuiting or in the act of thinking, in the natural mode of reflection we are turned to *the objects* as they are given to us each time and as a matter of course, even though they are given in different ways and in different modes of being, according to the source and level of our cognition. In perception, for instance, a thing stands before our eyes as a matter of course. It is there, among other things, living or lifeless, animate or inanimate. It is, in short, within a world of which part is perceived, as are the individual things themselves, and of which part is contextually supplied by memory from whence it spreads out into the indeterminate and the unknown.

Our judgments relate to this world. We make (sometimes singular, sometimes universal) judgments about things, their relations, their changes, about the conditions which functionally determine their changes and about the laws of their variations. We find an expression for what immediate experience presents. In line with our experiential motives we draw inferences from the directly experienced (perceived and remembered) to what is not experienced. We generalize, and then apply again general knowledge to particular cases or deduce analytically new generalizations from general knowledge. Isolated cognitions do not simply follow each other in the manner of mere succession. They enter into logical relations with each other, they follow from one another, they "cohere" with one another, they support one another, thereby strengthening their logical power.

On the other hand, they also clash and contradict one another. They do not agree with one another, they are falsified by *assured* cognition, / and their claim to be cognition is discredited. Perhaps the contradictions arise in the sphere that belongs to laws governing the pure predicational form: we have equivocated, we have inferred fallaciously, we have miscounted or miscomputed. In these cases we restore formal consistency. We resolve the equivocation and the like.   <18>

Or the contradictions disturb our expectation of connections based on past experience: empirical evidence conflicts with empirical evidence. Where do we look for help? We now weigh the reasons for different possible ways of deciding or providing an explanation. The weaker must give way to the stronger, and the stronger, in turn, are of value as long as they will stand up, i.e., as long as they in turn do not have to come into a similar logical conflict with new cognitional motives introduced by a broader sphere of cognition.

Thus, natural knowledge makes strides. It progressively takes possession of a reality at first existing for us as a matter of course and as something to be investigated further as regards its extent and content, its elements, its relations and laws. Thus the various sciences of the natural sort (*natürlichen Wissenschaften*) come into being and flourish, the natural sciences (*Naturwissenschaften*) as the sciences of physics and psychology, the sciences of culture (*Geisteswissenschaften*) and, on the other side, the mathematical sciences, the sciences of numbers, classes, relations, etc. The latter sciences deal not with actual but rather with ideal objects; they deal with what is valid *per se*, and for the rest with what are from the first unquestionable possibilities.

In every step of natural cognition pertaining to the sciences of the natural sort, difficulties arise and are resolved, either by *pure logic* or by appeal to *facts*, on the basis of motives or reasons which lie in the things themselves and which, as it were, come from things in the form of *requirements* that they themselves make on our thinking.

Now let, us contrast the natural *mode (or habit)* of *reflection* with the *philosophical*.

With the awakening of reflection about the relation of cognition to its object, abysmal difficulties arise. / Cognition, the thing most taken for granted in natural thinking, suddenly emerges as a mystery. But I must be more exact. What is *taken for granted* in natural thinking is the possibility of cognition. Constantly busy producing results, advancing from discovery to discovery in newer and newer branches of science, natural thinking finds no occasion to raise the question of the possibility of cognition as such. To   <19>

be sure, as with everything else in the world, *cognition*, too, will appear as a problem in a *certain manner*, becoming an object of natural investigation. Cognition is a fact in nature. It is the experience of a cognizing organic being. It is a psychological fact. As any psychological fact, it can be described according to its kinds and internal connections, and its genetic relations can be investigated. On the other hand cognition is essentially *cognition of what objectively is*, and it is cognition through the *meaning* which is intrinsic to it; by virtue of this meaning it is *related* to what objectively is. Natural thinking is also already active in this relating. It investigates in their *formal* generality the *a priori* connections of meanings and postulated meanings and the *a priori* principles which belong to objectivity *as such*; there comes into being a *pure grammar* and at higher stages a pure logic (a whole complex of disciplines owing to its different possible delimitations), and there arises once more a normative and practical logic in the form of an art of thinking, and, especially, of scientific thinking.

So far, we are still in the realm of *natural* thinking.

However, the correlation between cognition as mental process, its referent (*Bedeutung*) and what objectively is, which has just been touched upon in order to contrast the psychology of cognition with pure logic and ontology, is the source of the deepest and most difficult problems. Taken collectively, they are the problem of the possibility of cognition.

<20>   Cognition in all of its manifestations is a psychic act; it is the cognition of a cognizing subject. The objects cognized stand over and against the cognition. But how can we be certain of the correspondence between cognition and the object cognized? How can knowledge transcend itself and reach its object reliably? The unproblematic manner in which the object of cognition is given to natural thought to be cognized now becomes an enigma. In perception the perceived thing is believed to be directly given. Before my perceiving eyes stands the thing. I see it, and I grasp it. Yet the perceiving is simply a mental act of mine, of the perceiving subject. Likewise, memory and expectation are subjective processes; and so are all thought processes built upon them and through which we come to posit that something really is the case and to determine any *truth* about what is. How do I, the cognizing subject, know if I can ever really know, that there exist not only my own mental processes, these acts of cognizing, but also that which they apprehend? How can I ever know that there is anything at all which could be set over against cognition as its object?

Shall I say: only phenomena are truly given to the cognizing subject, he never does and never can break out of the circle of his own mental processes, so that in truth he could only say: I exist, and all that is not-I is mere phenomenon dissolving into phenomenal connections? Am I then to become a solipsist? This is a hard requirement. Shall I, with Hume, reduce all transcendent objectivity to fictions lending themselves to psychological explanation but to no rational justification? But this, too, is a hard requirement. Does not Hume's psychology, along with any psychology, transcend the sphere of immanence? By working with such concepts as habit, human nature, sense-organ, stimulus and the like, is it not working with transcendent existences (and transcendent by its own avowal), while its aim is to degrade to the status of fictions everything that transcends actual "impressions" and "ideas"?

But what is the use of invoking the specter of contradictions when / *logic* <21> *itself* is in question and becomes problematic. *Indeed, the real meaning of logical lawfulness* which natural thinking would not dream of questioning, now becomes *problematic* and *dubious*. Thoughts of a biological order intrude. We are reminded of the modern theory of evolution, according to which man has evolved in the struggle for existence and by natural selection, and with him his intellect too has evolved naturally and along with his intellect all of its characteristic forms, particularly the logical forms. Accordingly, is it not the case that the logical forms and laws express the accidental peculiarity of the human species, which could have been different and which will be different in the course of future evolution? Cognition is, after all, only *human cognition*, bound up with *human intellectual forms*, and unfit to reach the very nature of things, to reach the things in themselves.

But at once another piece of absurdity arises. Can the cognitions by which such a view operates and the possibilities which it ponders make any sense themselves if the laws of logic are given over to such relativism? Does not the truth that there is this and that possibility implicitly presuppose the absolute validity of the principle of non-contradiction, according to which any given truth excludes its contradictory?

These examples should suffice. The possibility of cognition has become enigmatic throughout. If we immerse ourselves in the sciences of the natural sort, we find everything clear and comprehensible, to the extent to which they have developed into exact sciences. We are certain that we are in possession of objective truth, based upon reliable methods of reaching (objective) reality. But whenever we reflect, we fall into errors and confusions. We become entangled in patent difficulties and even self-contradictions. We are in constant danger of becoming sceptics, or still worse, we are in danger of falling into any one of a number of scepticisms all of which have, sad to say, one and the same characteristic: absurdity.

The playground of these unclear and inconsistent theories as well as the endless quarrels associated with them / is the *theory of knowledge*, and <22>

metaphysics which is bound up with it historically and in subject matter. The task of the theory of knowledge or the critique of theoretical reason is, first of all, a critical one. It must brand the well-nigh inevitable mistakes which ordinary reflection makes about the relation of cognition, its meaning and its object, thereby refuting the concealed as well as the unconcealed sceptical theories concerning the essence of cognition by demonstrating their absurdity.

Furthermore, the positive task of the theory of knowledge is to solve the problems of the relations among cognition, its meaning and its object by inquiring into the essence of cognition. Among these, there is the problem of explicating the essential meaning of being a cognizable object or, what comes to the same thing, of being an object at all: of the meaning which is prescribed (for being an object at all) by the correlation *a priori* (or essential correlation) between cognition and being an object of cognition. And this naturally applies also to all basic forms of being an object which are predetermined by the nature of cognition. (To the ontological, the apophantic* as well as the metaphysical forms.)

Precisely by solving these problems the theory of knowledge qualifies as the critique of cognition, more exactly, as *the critique of natural cognition* in all the sciences of a natural sort. It puts us, in other words, in a position to interpret in an accurate and definitive way the teachings of these sciences about what exists. For the confusions of the theory of knowledge into which we are led by natural (pre-epistemological) reflection on the possibility of cognition (on the possibility of cognition's reaching its object) involve not just false views about the essence of cognition, but also self-contradictory, and, therefore, fundamentally misleading *interpretations* of the being that is cognized in the sciences of the natural sort. So, one and the same science is interpreted in materialistic, spiritualistic, dualistic, psychomonistic, positivistic and many other ways, depending upon what interpretation is thought to be the necessary consequence of those pre-epistemological reflections. Only with epistemological reflection do we arrive at the distinction between / the sciences of a natural sort and philosophy. Epistemological reflection first brings to light that the sciences of a natural sort are not yet the ultimate science of being. We need a science of being in the absolute sense. This science, which we call *metaphysics*, grows out of a "critique" of natural cognition in the individual sciences. It is based on what is learned in the general critique of cognition about the essence of cognition and what it is to be an object of cognition of one basic type or

<23>

---

* Tr. note: In Husserl the word "apophantic" refers to predicative judgements or to the theory of such judgements.

other, i.e., in accordance with the different fundamental correlations between cognizing and being an object of cognition.

If then we disregard any metaphysical purpose of the critique of cognition and confine ourselves purely to the task *of clarifying the essence of cognition and of being an object of cognition, then this will be phenomenology of cognition and of being an object of cognition* and will be the first and principal part of phenomenology as a whole.

Phenomenology: this denotes a science, a system of scientific disciplines. But it also and above all denotes a method and an attitude of mind, the specifically *philosophical attitude* of mind, the specifically *philosophical method*.

In contemporary philosophy, insofar as it claims to be a serious science, it has become almost a commonplace that there can be only one method for achieving cognition in all the sciences as well as in philosophy. This conviction accords wholly with the great philosophical traditions of the seventeenth century, which also thought that philosophy's salvation lay wholly in its taking as a model of method the exact sciences, and above all, mathematics and mathematical natural science. This putting philosophy methodologically on a par with the other sciences goes hand in hand with treating them alike with respect to subject matter. It is still the prevailing opinion that philosophy and, more specifically, ontology and the general theory of knowledge not only relate to all the other sciences, but also that they can be grounded upon the conclusions of those other sciences: / in <24> the same way in which sciences are built upon one another, and the conclusions of one of them can serve as premises for the others. I am reminded of the favorite ploy of basing the theory of knowledge on the psychology of cognition and biology. In our day, reactions against these fatal prejudices are multiplying. And prejudices they are.

In the sphere of ordinary inquiry one science can readily build upon another, and the one can serve the other as a model of method even though to a limited extent determined by the nature of the areas of inquiry in question. *But philosophy lies in a wholly new dimension.* It needs an *entirely new point of departure* and an entirely new method distinguishing it in principle from any "natural" science. This is why the logical procedures that give the sciences of a natural sort unity have a unitary character in principle in spite of the special methods which change from one science to another: while the methodological procedures of philosophy have by contrast and in principle a new unity. This is also why *pure* philosophy, within the whole of the critique of cognition and the "critical" disciplines generally, must disregard, and must refrain from using, the intellectual achievements of the sciences of a natural sort and of scientifically undisciplined natural wisdom and knowledge.

To anticipate, this doctrine, the grounds for which will be given in more detail in the sequel, is recommended by the following considerations.

In the sceptical mood which critical reflection about cognition necessarily begets (I mean the reflection that comes first, the one that comes before the scientific critique of cognition and which takes place on the natural level of thought) every science of the natural sort and every method characteristic of such a science ceases to count as something we properly possess. For cognition's reaching its object has become enigmatic and dubious as far as its meaning and possibility are concerned, and exact cognition becomes thereby no less enigmatic than inexact, scientific knowledge no / less than the pre-scientific. The possibility of cognition becomes questionable, more precisely, how it can possibly reach an objectivity which, after all, is in itself whatever it is. Behind this lies the following: What is in question is what cognition can accomplish, the meaning of its claim to validity and correctness, the meaning of the distinction between valid real and merely apparent cognition; on the other hand, also the meaning of being an object which exists and exists as what it is whether it is cognized or not and which as an object is an object of possible cognition, in principle cognizable, even if in fact it has never been and never will be cognized, but is in principle perceptible, imaginable, determinable by predicates in a possible judgment, etc.

However, it is impossible to see how working with presuppositions which are taken from natural cognition, no matter how "exactly founded" they are in it, can help us to resolve the misgivings which arise in the critique of cognition, to find the answers to its problems. If the meaning and value of natural cognition *as such* together with *all* of its methodological presuppositions and all of its exact foundations have become problematic, then this strikes at every proposition which natural cognition presupposes in its starting-point and at every allegedly exact method of giving a foundation. Neither the most exact mathematics nor mathematical natural science has here the slightest advantage over any actual or alleged cognition through ordinary experience. It is then clear that there can be no such talk as that philosophy (which begins in the critique of cognition and which, whatever else it is, is rooted in the critique of cognition) has to model itself after the exact sciences methodologically (or even as regards subject matter!), or that it has to adopt as a standard their methodology, or that it is philosophy's task to implement and to complete the work done in the exact sciences according to a single method, in principle the same for all the sciences. In contradistinction to all natural cognition, philosophy lies, I repeat, within a new dimension; and what corresponds to this new dimension, even if, as the phrase suggests, it is essentially connected with the old dimensions, is a

<25>

new and *radically new method* which / is set over against the "natural" <26> method. He who denies this has failed to understand entirely the whole of the level at which the characteristic problem of the critique of cognition lies, and with this he has failed to understand what philosophy really wants to do and should do, and what gives it its own character and authority *vis-à-vis* the whole of natural cognition and science of the natural sort.

Lecture II

[THE BEGINNING OF THE CRITIQUE OF COGNITION; TREATING AS QUESTIONABLE EVERY (CLAIM TO) KNOWING. REACHING THE GROUND OF ABSOLUTE CERTAINTY IN PURSUANCE OF DESCARTES'S METHOD OF DOUBT. THE SPHERE OF THE THINGS THAT ARE ABSOLUTELY GIVEN. REVIEW AND AMPLIFICATION: REFUTATION OF THE ARGUMENT AGAINST THE POSSIBILITY OF A CRITIQUE OF COGNITION. THE RIDDLE OF NATURAL COGNITION: TRANSCENDENCE. DISTINCTION BETWEEN THE TWO CONCEPTS OF IMMANENCE AND TRANSCENDENCE. THE INITIAL PROBLEM OF THE CRITIQUE OF COGNITION THE POSSIBILITY OF TRANSCENDENT COGNITION. THE PRINCIPLE OF EPISTEMOLOGICAL REDUCTION.]

At the outset of the critique of cognition the entire world of nature, physi- <29> cal and psychological, as well as one's own human self together with all the sciences which have to do with these objective matters, are *put in question*. Their being, their validity are left up in the air.

Now the question is: How can *the critique of cognition get under way?* The critique of cognition is the attempt of cognition to find a scientific understanding of itself and to establish objectively what cognition is in its essence, what is the meaning of the relation to an object which is implicit in the claim to cognition and what its objective validity or the reaching of its object comes to if it is to be cognition in the true sense. Although the ἐποχή [*epoche*], which the critique of cognition must employ, begins with the doubt of all cognition, its own included, it cannot remain in such doubt nor can it refuse to take as valid everything given, including that which it brings to light itself. If it must presuppose nothing as *already given*, then it must begin with some cognition which it does not take unexamined from elsewhere but rather gives to itself, which it itself posits as primal.

This primal cognition must contain nothing of the unclarity and the doubt which otherwise give to cognition the character of the enigmatic and problematic so that we are finally in the embarrassing position of having to say that cognition as such is a problem, something incomprehensible, in need of elucidation and dubious in its claims. Or, to speak differently:

If we are not allowed to take anything as already given because our lack of clarity about cognition implies that we cannot understand what it could mean for something *to be known in itself* yet *in the context of cognition*, then it must after all be possible to make evident something which we have to acknowledge as absolutely given and indubitable; / insofar, that is,   <
as it is given with such complete clarity that every question about it will and must find an immediate answer.

And now we recall the Cartesian doubt. Reflecting on the multifarious possibilities of error and deception, I might reach such a degree of sceptical despair that I finally say: Nothing is certain, everything is doubtful. But it is at once evident that not everything is doubtful, for while I am judging that everything is doubtful, it is indubitable that I am so judging; and it would be absurd to want to persist in a universal doubt. And in every case of a definite doubt, it is indubitably certain that I have this doubt. And likewise with every *cogitatio*. Howsoever I perceive, imagine, judge, infer, howsoever these acts may be certain or uncertain, whether or not they have objects that exist as far as the perceiving itself is concerned, it is absolutely clear and certain that I am perceiving this or that, and as far as the judgment is concerned that I am judging of this or that, etc.

Descartes introduced these considerations for other purposes.[1] But with suitable modifications, we can use them here.

If we inquire into the essence of cognition, then whatever status it and our doubts about its reaching the object may have one thing is clear: that cognition itself is a name for a manifold sphere of being which can be given to us absolutely, and which can be given absolutely each time in the particular case. The thought processes which I really perform are given to me insofar as I *reflect* upon them, receive them and set them up in a *pure "seeing."* I can speak vaguely about cognition, perception, imagination, experience, judgment, inference, etc.; but then, when I reflect, all that is given, and absolutely given at that, is this phenomenon of vaguely "talking about and intending cognition, experience, judgment, etc." Even this phenomenon of vagueness is one of those that comes under the heading of cognition in the broadest sense. I can, however, have an actual perception and inspect it. I can, moreover, represent to myself in imagination or memory a perception and survey it as so given to imagination. In that case I am no longer / vacuously talking about perception or having a vague intension or   <
idea of it. Instead, perception itself stands open to my inspection as actually or imaginatively given to me. And the same is true of every intellectual process, of every form of thinking and cognizing.

I have here put on the same level the "seeing" [act of] reflective perception and [the "seeing" act of reflective] imagination. If one followed the

Cartesian view, one would have to emphasize perception first; it would in some measure correspond to the so-called inner perception of traditional epistemology, though this is an ambivalent concept.

Every intellectual process and indeed every mental process whatever, while being enacted, *can be made the object of a pure "seeing" and understanding, and is something absolutely given in this "seeing."* It is given as something that is, that is here and now, and whose being cannot be sensibly *doubted*. To be sure, I can wonder what sort of being this is and how this mode of being is related to other modes. It is true I can wonder what givenness means *here*, and reflecting further I can "see" the "seeing" itself in which this givenness, or this mode of being, is constituted. But all the same I am now working on an absolute foundation: namely, this perception is, and remains as long as it lasts, something absolute, something here and now, something that in itself is what it is, something by which I can measure as by an ultimate standard what being and being given can mean and here must mean, at least, obviously, as far as the sort of being and being given is concerned which a "here and now" exemplifies. And that goes for all specific ways of thinking, whenever they are given. All of these, however, can also be data in imagination; they can "as it were" stand before our eyes and yet not stand before them as actualities, as actually accomplished perceptions, judgments, etc.; even then, they are, in a certain sense, data. They are there *open to intuition*. We talk about them not in just vague hints and empty intention. We inspect them, and while inspecting them we can observe their essence, their constitution, their intrinsic character, and we can make our speech conform in a pure measure to what is "seen" in its full clarity. But this requires to be supplemented / by a discussion of the concept and cognition of essences.

For the moment we keep it firmly in mind that a sphere of the absolutely given can be indicated at the outset; and this is just the sphere we need if it is to be possible to aim at a theory of knowledge. Indeed, lack of clarity with regard to the meaning or essence of cognition requires a science of cognition, a science whose sole end is to clarify the essential nature of cognition. It is not to explain cognition as a psychological fact; it is not to inquire into the natural causes and laws of the development and occurrence of cognitions. Such inquiry is the task of a science of the natural sort, of a psychology which deals with the mental processes of persons who are undergoing them. Rather, the task of the critique of cognition is to clarify, to cast light upon, the essence of cognition and the legitimacy of its claim to validity that belongs to its essence; and what else can this mean but to make the essence of cognition directly self-given.

Recapitulation and Amplification. In its constantly successful progress

<32>

in the various sciences, cognition of the natural sort is altogether self-assured that it reaches the object and has no cause to worry about the possibility of cognition and about the meaning of cognized objectivity. But as soon as we begin to reflect on the correlation between cognition and reality (and eventually also on the ideal meanings on the one hand and, on the other, on the objects of cognition) there arise difficulties, absurdities, inconsistent yet seemingly well-founded theories which drive one to the admission that the possibility of cognition as far as its reaching the object is concerned is an enigma.

A new science, the critique of cognition, is called for. Its job is to resolve confusions and to clarify the essence of cognition. Upon the success of this science depends the possibility of a metaphysics, a science of being in the absolute and fundamental sense. But how / can such a science of cognition   <⁀
in general get started? That which a science questions it cannot use as a presupposition. But what is in question is the possibility of all cognition in that the critique of cognition regards as problematic the possibility of cognition in general and its capacity to reach the object. Once it is launched, the critique of cognition cannot take any cognition for granted. Nor can it take over anything whatever from pre-scientific cognition. All cognition bears the mark of being questionable.

Without some cognition given at the outset, there is also no advancement of cognition. The critique of cognition cannot, therefore, begin. There can be no such science at all.

I already suggested that in all this there is an element of truth. In the beginning no cognition can be assumed *without examination*. However, even if the critique of cognition must not take over any antecedent cognition it still can begin by *giving* itself cognition, and naturally cognition which it does not base on, or logically derive from, anything else as this would presuppose some other immediate cognition already given. It must rather base itself on the cognition which is immediately evident and of such a kind that, as absolutely clear and indubitable, it excludes every doubt of its possibility and contains none of the puzzles which had led to all the sceptical confusions. I then pointed to the *Cartesian method of doubt* and to the domain of the absolutely given, viz., of absolute cognition which comes under the heading of evidence (*Evidenz*) of the *cogitatio*. It remained to be shown that the *immanence* of this cognition makes it an appropriate point of departure for the theory of cognition; that, furthermore, *because of this immanence*, it is free of the puzzlement which is the source of all sceptical embarrassment. Finally, it remained to be shown *that immanence is the generally necessary characteristic of all epistemological cognition*, and that it is nonsensical not only at the start but also in general to borrow from the sphere of transcendence, in other words, to try to found the theory of cognition on psychology or on any science whatever of the natural sort.

<34>   I may add the following: there is a plausible argument / to the effect that the theory of knowledge cannot get started because it questions cognition as such and hence regards as questionable every cognition with which we might begin. Moreover, it is alleged that if all cognition must be a riddle to the epistemologist, so must any initial cognition with which epistemology itself begins be a riddle. I repeat that this plausible argument is a deception. The deception is due to the vague generality of the wording. Cognition in general "is questioned." Surely, however, it is not denied that there is cognition in general (such denial would lead to contradiction); rather, cognition presents a certain problem, namely, of how it can accomplish a certain task attributed to it, namely, the task of reaching the object: I may even doubt whether this task can be accomplished at all. But doubt as I may, this doubt is a first step toward canceling itself out because some cognitions can be brought to light which render such doubt groundless. Moreover, if I begin by not understanding cognition at all, then this incomprehension with its indeterminate universality admittedly encompasses every cognition. But that is not to say that every cognition I might run up against in the future has to remain forever incomprehensible. It may be that there is a big puzzle to begin with connected with a particular class of cognitions, those that thrust themselves most immediately to the fore, and that I now reach a general embarrassment and say: cognition as such is a riddle, even though it soon appears that the riddle does not belong to certain other kinds of cognition. And, as we shall see presently, this is indeed the case.

    I said that the cognitions with which the critique of cognition must begin must contain nothing doubtful or questionable. They must contain none of that which precipitates epistemological confusion and gives impetus to the critique of cognition. We have to show that this holds true of the sphere of the *cogitatio*. For this we need a more deeply probing reflection, one that will bring us substantial advantages.

    If we look closer at what is so enigmatic and what, in the course of subsequent reflection on the possibility of cognition, causes embarrassment, we will find it to be the transcendence of cognition. All cognition of the natural sort, and especially the prescientific, is cognition which makes
<35> its object transcendent. / It posits objects as existent, claims to reach matters of fact which are not "strictly given to it," are not "immanent" to it.

    But on closer view, this *transcendence* is admittedly *ambiguous*. One thing one can mean by transcendence is that the object of cognition is not genuinely (*reell*) contained in the cognitive act so that one would be meaning by "being truly given" or "immanently given" that the object of the cognitive act is genuinely contained in the act: the cognitive act, the *cogitatio*, has genuine abstract parts genuinely constituting it: but the physical thing which it intends or supposedly perceives or remembers, etc., is not to be found in the *cogitatio* itself, as a mental process; the physical thing is not to be found as a genuine (*reell*) concrete part (*Stück*), not as something which really exists within the *cogitatio*. So the question is: how can the mental process so to speak transcend itself? *Immanent here means then genuinely (reell) immanent in the cognitive mental process.*

But there is still *another transcendence* whose opposite is an altogether different immanence, namely, *absolute* and *clear givenness, self-givenness in the absolute sense*. This givenness, which rules out any meaningful doubt, consists of a simply immediate "seeing" and apprehending of the intended object itself as it is, and it constitutes the precise concept of evidence (*Evidenz*) understood as immediate evidence. All cognition which is not evident, which though it intends or posits something objective yet *does not see it itself*, is transcendent in this second sense. In such cognition we go beyond what at any time *is truly given*, beyond what can be *directly "seen"* and *apprehended*. At this point we may ask: How can cognition posit something as existing that is not directly and truly given in it?

At first, before we come to a deeper level of critical epistemological reflection, these two kinds of immanence and transcendence run confusedly into each other. It is indeed clear that whoever raises the first question about the possibility of genuine (*reell*) transcendence is at the same time really also raising the second question: namely, how can there be transcendence beyond the realm of evident givenness? In this there is the unspoken supposition that the only actually understandable, unquestionable, absolutely evident givenness is the givenness of *the abstract part genuinely (reell) contained* within the cognitive act, / and this is why anything in the   <3‹ way of a cognized objectivity that is not genuinely (*reell*) contained within that act is regarded as a puzzle and as problematic. We shall soon hear that this is a fatal mistake.

One may now construe transcendence in one sense or the other, or, at first even ambiguously, but transcendence is both the initial and the central problem of the critique of cognition. It is the riddle that stands in the path of cognition of the natural sort and is the incentive for new investigations. One could at the outset designate the solution to this problem as being the task of the critique of cognition. One would thereby delimit the new discipline in a preliminary fashion, instead of generally designating as its theme the problem of the essence of any cognition whatever.

If then the riddle connected with the initial establishment of the discipline lies *here*, it becomes more definitely clear what must not be claimed as presupposed. *Nothing transcendent must be used as a presupposition.* If I do not understand *how* it is possible that cognition reach something transcendent, then I also do not know *whether* it is possible. The scientific warrant for believing in a transcendent existence is of no help. For every mediated warrant goes back to something immediate; and it is the unmediated which contains the riddle.

Still someone might say: "It is certain that mediated no less than immediate cognition contains the riddle. But it is only the *how* that is puzzling, whereas the *that* is absolutely certain. No sensible man will doubt the existence of the world, and the sceptic in action belies his own creed." Very well. Then let us answer him with a more powerful and far-reaching argument. For it proves that the theory of cognition has, *neither at the outset nor throughout its course*, any license to fall back upon the content of the sciences of a natural sort which treat their object as transcendent. What is proved is the fundamental thesis *that the theory of knowledge can never be based upon any science of the natural sort, no matter what the more specific nature of that science may be.* Hence we ask: What will our opponent do with his transcendent knowledge? We put freely at his disposal the entire stock of transcendent truths contained in the objective / sciences, and we   <37> take it that those truths are not altered by the emergence of the puzzle of how a science of the transcendent is possible. What will he now do with his all-embracing knowledge? How does he think he can go from the "that" to the "how"? That he knows for a fact that cognition of the transcendent is actual guarantees as logically obvious that cognition of the transcendent is possible. But the riddle is, *how* is it possible? Can he solve it even if he presupposes all the sciences, all or any cognition of the transcendent? Consider: What more does he really need? That cognition of the transcendent is possible he takes for granted, even as analytically certain in saying to himself, there is in my case knowledge of the transcendent. What he lacks is obvious. He is unclear about the relation to transcendence. He is unclear about the "reaching the transcendent" which is ascribed to cognition, to knowledge. Where and how can he achieve clarity? He could do so if the essences of this relation were somehow *given* to him, so that he could "see" it and could directly inspect the unity of cognition and its object, a unity denoted by the locution "reaching the object." He would thereby not only know this unity to be possible, but he would have this possibility clearly before him. The possibility itself counts for him as something transcendent, as a possibility which is known but not of itself given, "seen." He obviously thinks: cognition is a thing apart from its object; cognition is given but the object of cognition is not given; and yet cognition is supposed to relate to the object, to cognize it. How can I understand this possibility? Naturally the reply is: I could understand it only if the relation itself were given as something to be "seen." As long as the object is, and remains, something transcendent, and cognition and its objects are actually separate, then indeed he can see nothing here, and his hopes for reaching a solution, perhaps even by way of falling back on transcendent presuppositions, are patent folly.

<38>   However, if he is to be consistent with these views, he should give up his starting point: he should acknowledge that in this case cognition of the transcendent is impossible, and that his pretence to know is mere prejudice. Then the problem is no longer: How is cognition of the transcendent possible? But rather, How do we account for the prejudice which ascribes a transcendent feat to cognition? And this exactly was the path Hume took.

Let us emphatically reject that approach and let us go on to illustrate the basic idea that the problem of the "how" (how cognition of the transcendent is possible and even more generally, how cognition is possible at all) can never be answered on the basis of a prior knowledge of the transcendent, of prior judgments about it, no matter whence the knowledge or the judgments are borrowed, not even if they are taken from the exact sciences. Here is an illustration: A man born deaf knows that there are sounds, that sounds produce harmonies and that a splendid art depends upon them. But he cannot understand *how* sounds do this, how musical compositions are possible. Such things he cannot *imagine*, i.e., he cannot "see" and in "seeing" grasp the "how" of such things. His knowledge about what exists helps him in no way, and it would be absurd if he were to try to deduce the *how* of music from his knowledge, thinking that thereby he could achieve clarity about the possibility of music through conclusions drawn from things of which he is cognizant. It will not do to draw conclusions from existences of which one knows but which one cannot "see." "Seeing" does not lend itself to demonstration or deduction. It is patently absurd to try to explain possibilities (and unmediated possibilities at that) by drawing logical conclusions from non-intuitive knowledge. Even if I could be wholly certain that there are transcendent worlds, even if I accept the whole content of the sciences of a natural sort, even then I cannot borrow from them. I must never fancy that by relying on transcendent presuppositions and scientific inferences I can arrive where I want to go in the critique of cognition – namely, to assess the possibility of a transcendent objectivity of cognition. And that goes not just for the beginning but for the whole course of the critique of cognition, so long as there still remains the problem of *how*

<39> *cognition is possible.* / And, evidently, that goes not just for the problem of transcendent objectivity but also for the elucidation of every possibility.

If we combine this with the extraordinarily strong inclination to make a transcendently oriented judgment and thus to fall into a μετάβασις εἰς ἀλλο γενος [a change into some other kind] in every case where a thought process involves transcendence and a judgment has to be based upon it, then we arrive at a sufficient and complete deduction of the *epistemological principle* that an epistemological *reduction* has to be accomplished in the case of every epistemological inquiry of whatever sort of cognition. That is to say, everything transcendent that is involved must be bracketed, or be assigned the index of indifference, of epistemological nullity, an index which indicates: the existence of all these transcendencies, whether I believe in them or not, is not here my concern; this is not the place to make judgments about them; they are entirely irrelevant.

All the basic errors of the theory of knowledge go hand in hand with the above mentioned μετάβασις, on the one hand the basic error of psychologism, on the other that of anthropologism and biologism. The μετάβασις is so exceedingly dangerous, partly because the proper sense of the problem is never made clear and remains totally lost in it, and partly because even those who have become clear about it find it hard to remain clear and slip easily, as their thinking proceeds, back into the temptations of the natural modes of thought and judgment as well as into the false and seductive conceptions of the problems which grow on their basis.

Note

1 Husserl's 'purpose' differs from Descartes' in the following general way. He was not concerned initially to doubt nearly all our beliefs in order, later, to reinstate them on a firm basis. The purpose of the Husserlian *epochē* is to 'purify' consciousness and its immediate objects by ignoring everything extraneous. This abstention is not something the phenomenologist can ever abandon, since it is the standing prerequisite of that focusing on 'things themselves' or phenomena which is his job.

Bertrand Russell, 'Knowledge by Acquaintance and Knowledge by Description'

From Bertrand Russell, *The Problems of Philosophy*. Oxford: Oxford University Press, 1959, pp. 46–59; reprinted by permission of Oxford University Press.

The English language is sometimes faulted for more than niggardliness in employing the single word 'know' where other languages have two – '*connâitre*' and '*savoir*' in French, '*kennen*' and '*wissen*' in German, for example. Whereas the English both know London and *that* London is foggy, Germans *kennen* Berlin but *wissen* that Berlin is damp. Failure to heed this distinction between knowing things (places, people, etc.) and knowing *about* them or *that* they are such-and-such has, at any rate, been held responsible for misguided assumptions in epistemology – for instance, for the view that all knowledge is a matter of the presence to the mind of certain items, such as 'ideas', which we know (*kennen*).[1]

The English logician and philosopher Bertrand Russell (1872–1970) was not the first to call attention to the importance of the distinction and to label the former kind of knowledge 'knowledge by acquaintance'.[2] But he was perhaps the first to attempt a precise account of it and a demonstration of its centrality for the theory of knowledge. The distinction's importance, for Russell, is due to his conviction that all other knowledge is 'ultimately reducible to knowledge concerning what is known by acquaintance' – a principle which he takes to be equivalent to the truism that we cannot make judgements about things 'without knowing what it is that we are judging about' (p. 241 below).

Two questions are raised by this conviction. First, what are the things we can know by acquaintance? Second, how is it that we may have knowledge about

---

[1] See Jonathan Bennett, *Locke, Berkeley and Hume: Central Themes*, Oxford: Clarendon Press, 1971.

[2] See David B. Martens, 'Knowledge by acquaintance/by description', in *A Companion to Epistemology*, ed. J. Dancy and E. Sosa, Oxford: Blackwell, 1992. Russell's first discussion of the distinction was in a 1911 article bearing the same name as the somewhat amended and simplified Chapter V in *The Problems of Philosophy* of 1912.

things when we are not acquainted with them? That second question may not seem a daunting one given our everyday, liberal understanding of acquaintance, on which someone may be acquainted with people, places, periods of history, philosophical movements and so on. So massive, on this understanding, is the domain of people's acquaintance that it hardly seems puzzling how, on such a basis, knowledge about things outside that domain could be built up.

Russell, however, writes in the tradition of British empiricism and takes a much narrower view of what, strictly, we can be acquainted with.[3] Somewhat in the manner of Husserl (see chapter 14 above), it is only 'subjective things' – sense-data, concepts (or 'universals') and possibly one's own self – which, for Russell, are objects of acquaintance. The second question therefore becomes urgent: for without an answer to it, we do not understand, says Russell, 'what enables us to pass beyond the limits of our private experience' to knowledge of, say, tables and people.

Russell's answer is that knowledge *of, about* or *that* is 'knowledge by description'. The answer is reached by reflecting on an apparent implication of his narrow construal of acquaintance. If we cannot be acquainted with the actual table, then the expression 'this table' cannot, as we naively imagine, really 'stand for' or 'mean' the table. Now in earlier writings on logic, notably 'On denoting' (1905), Russell had developed his 'theory of descriptions' to resolve paradoxes which arise when expressions that only *apparently* 'stand for' objects are construed as *really* doing so. For example, if 'The Golden Mountain does not exist' is construed as being about something referred to by the noun-phrase, it would, in effect, require the existence of the very thing whose existence it denies. Russell's proposal was that such expressions are not names or denoting terms but concealed descriptions, so that statements containing them are to the effect that something does (or does not) fit a certain description.

Russell exploits this proposal when explaining the nature of our knowledge of things with which we cannot be aquainted. To know, say, that the table is brown is to know that there is something of which a certain description is true, where all the terms in the description genuinely stand for items of acquaintance, notably sense-data and concepts. It is Russell's view, argued for in an earlier chapter of *The Problems of Philosophy*, that we have at least very strong reasons to believe that there exist actual tables *causing* our sense-data, and so that there are objects fitting such descriptions as 'cause such-and-such sense-data'.

It is not only Russell's empiricist restriction of items of acquaintance to 'private experience' which has attracted later criticism. His distinction between

---

[3] For an excellent account of Russell's relation to the empiricist tradition, see David Pears, *Bertrand Russell and the British Tradition in Philosophy*, London: Fontana, 1967.

knowledge by acquaintance and by description remains contentious even when a more generous list of items is allowed. By opposing the two kinds of knowledge, Russell is in effect holding that there can, indeed must, be direct knowledge which is non-propositional in form, unmediated by conceptual judgement. For many critics, the mere presence to perceptual awareness of a colour or whatever cannot, in the absence of judgement, constitute a case of knowledge at all. If they are right then, perhaps, there is only knowledge by description, important as acquaintance might be in the aetiology of knowledge-claims. The English language, arguably, is not after all to be faulted for failing to mark two supposedly distinct kinds of knowledge.

Knowledge by Acquaintance and Knowledge by Description

In the preceding chapter we saw that there are two sorts of knowledge: knowledge of things, and knowledge of truths. In this chapter we shall be concerned exclusively with knowledge of things, of which in turn we shall have to distinguish two kinds. Knowledge of things, when it is of the kind we call knowledge by *acquaintance*, is essentially simpler than any knowledge of truths, and logically independent of knowledge of truths, though it would be rash to assume that human beings ever, in fact, have acquaintance with things without at the same time knowing some truth about them. Knowledge of things by *description*, on the contrary, always involves, as we shall find in the course of the present chapter, some knowledge of truths as its source and ground. But first of all we must make clear what we mean by 'acquaintance' and what we mean by 'description'.

We shall say that we have *acquaintance* with anything of which we are directly aware, without the intermediary of any process of inference or any knowledge of truths. Thus in the presence of my table I am acquainted with the sense-data that make up the appearance of my table – its colour, shape, hardness, smoothness, etc.; all these are things of which I am immediately conscious when I am seeing and touching my table. The particular shade of colour that I am seeing may have many things said about it – I may say that it is brown, that it is rather dark, and so on. But such statements, though they make me know truths *about* the colour, do not make me know the colour itself any better than I did before: so far as concerns knowledge of the colour itself, as opposed to knowledge of truths about it, I know the colour perfectly and completely when I see it, and no further knowledge of it itself is even theoretically possible. Thus the sense-data which make up the appearance of my table are things with which I have acquaintance, things immediately known to me just as they are.

My knowledge of the table as a physical object, on the contrary, is not direct knowledge. Such as it is, it is obtained through acquaintance with the sense-data that make up the appearance of the table. We have seen that it is possible, without absurdity, to doubt whether there is a table at all, whereas it is not possible to doubt the sense-data. My knowledge of the table is of the kind which we shall call 'knowledge by description'. The table is 'the physical object which causes such-and-such sense-data'. This *describes* the table by means of the sense-data. In order to know anything at all about the table, we must know truths connecting it with things with which we have acquaintance: we must know that 'such-and-such sense-data are caused by a physical object'. There is no state of mind in which we are directly aware of the table; all our knowledge of the table is really knowledge of *truths*, and the actual thing which is the table is not, strictly speaking, known to us at all. We know a description, and we know that there is just one object to which this description applies, though the object itself is not directly known to us. In such a case, we say that our knowledge of the object is knowledge by description.

All our knowledge, both knowledge of things and knowledge of truths, rests upon acquaintance as its foundation. It is therefore important to consider what kinds of things there are with which we have acquaintance.

Sense-data, as we have already seen, are among the things with which we are acquainted; in fact, they supply the most obvious and striking example of knowledge by acquaintance. But if they were the sole example, our knowledge would be very much more restricted than it is. We should only know what is now present to our senses: we could not know anything about the past – not even that there was a past – nor could we know any truths about our sense-data, for all knowledge of truths, as we shall show, demands acquaintance with things which are of an essentially different character from sense-data, the things which are sometimes called 'abstract ideas', but which we shall call 'universals'. We have therefore to consider acquaintance with other things besides sense-data if we are to obtain any tolerably adequate analysis of our knowledge.

The first extension beyond sense-data to be considered is acquaintance by *memory*. It is obvious that we often remember what we have seen or heard or had otherwise present to our senses, and that in such cases we are still immediately aware of what we remember, in spite of the fact that it appears as past and not as present. This immediate knowledge by memory is the source of all our knowledge concerning the past: without it, there could be no knowledge of the past by inference, since we should never know that there was anything past to be inferred.

The next extension to be considered is acquaintance by *introspection*.

We are not only aware of things, but we are often aware of being aware of them. When I see the sun, I am often aware of my seeing the sun; thus 'my seeing the sun' is an object with which I have acquaintance. When I desire food, I may be aware of my desire for food; thus 'my desiring food' is an object with which I am acquainted. Similarly we may be aware of our feeling pleasure or pain, and generally of the events which happen in our minds. This kind of acquaintance, which may be called self-consciousness, is the source of all our knowledge of mental things. It is obvious that it is only what goes on in our own minds that can be thus known immediately. What goes on in the minds of others is known to us through our perception of their bodies, that is, through the sense-data in us which are associated with their bodies. But for our acquaintance with the contents of our own minds, we should be unable to imagine the minds of others, and therefore we could never arrive at the knowledge that they have minds. It seems natural to suppose that self-consciousness is one of the things that distinguish men from animals; animals, we may suppose, though they have acquaintance with sense-data, never become aware of this acquaintance. I do not mean that they *doubt* whether they exist, but that they have never become conscious of the fact that they have sensations and feelings, nor therefore of the fact that they, the subjects of their sensations and feelings, exist.

We have spoken of acquaintance with the contents of our minds as *self-consciousness*, but it is not, of course, consciousness of our *self*: it is consciousness of particular thoughts and feelings. The question whether we are also acquainted with our bare selves, as opposed to particular thoughts and feelings, is a very difficult one, upon which it would be rash to speak positively. When we try to look into ourselves we always seem to come upon some particular thought or feeling, and not upon the 'I' which has the thought or feeling. Nevertheless there are some reasons for thinking that we are acquainted with the 'I', though the acquaintance is hard to disentangle from other things. To make clear what sort of reason there is, let us consider for a moment what our acquaintance with particular thoughts really involves.

When I am acquainted with 'my seeing the sun', it seems plain that I am acquainted with two different things in relation to each other. On the one hand there is the sense-datum which represents the sun to me, on the other hand there is that which sees this sense-datum. All acquaintance, such as my acquaintance with the sense-datum which represents the sun, seems obviously a relation between the person acquainted and the object with which the person is acquainted. When a case of acquaintance is one with which I can be acquainted (as I am acquainted with my acquaintance with the sense-datum representing the sun), it is plain that the person acquainted is myself. Thus, when I am acquainted with my seeing the sun, the whole fact with which I am acquainted is 'Self-acquainted-with-sense-datum'.

Further, we know the truth 'I am acquainted with this sense-datum'. It is hard to see how we could know this truth, or even understand what is meant by it, unless we were acquainted with something which we call 'I'. It does not seem necessary to suppose that we are acquainted with a more or less permanent person, the same to-day as yesterday, but it does seem as though we must be acquainted with that thing, whatever its nature, which sees the sun and has acquaintance with sense-data. Thus, in some sense it would seem we must be acquainted with our Selves as opposed to our particular experiences. But the question is difficult, and complicated arguments can be adduced on either side. Hence, although acquaintance with ourselves seems *probably* to occur, it is not wise to assert that it undoubtedly does occur.

We may therefore sum up as follows what has been said concerning acquaintance with things that exist. We have acquaintance in sensation with the data of the outer senses, and in introspection with the data of what may be called the inner sense – thoughts, feelings, desires, etc.; we have acquaintance in memory with things which have been data either of the outer senses or of the inner sense. Further, it is probable, though not certain, that we have acquaintance with Self, as that which is aware of things or has desires towards things.

In addition to our acquaintance with particular existing things, we also have acquaintance with what we shall call *universals*, that is to say, general ideas, such as *whiteness, diversity, brotherhood*, and so on. Every complete sentence must contain at least one word which stands for a universal, since all verbs have a meaning which is universal. We shall return to universals later on, in Chapter IX; for the present, it is only necessary to guard against the supposition that whatever we can be acquainted with must be something particular and existent. Awareness of universals is called *conceiving*, and a universal of which we are aware is called a *concept*.

It will be seen that among the objects with which we are acquainted are not included physical objects (as opposed to sense-data), nor other people's minds. These things are known to us by what I call 'knowledge by description', which we must now consider.

By a 'description' I mean any phrase of the form 'a so-and-so' or 'the so-and-so'. A phrase of the form 'a so-and-so' I shall call an 'ambiguous' description; a phrase of the form 'the so-and-so' (in the singular) I shall call a 'definite' description. Thus 'a man' is an ambiguous description, and 'the man with the iron mask' is a definite description. There are various problems connected with ambiguous descriptions, but I pass them by, since they do not directly concern the matter we are discussing, which is the nature of our knowledge concerning objects in cases where we know that there is an object answering to a definite description, though we are not *acquainted* with any such object. This is a matter which is concerned exclusively with *definite* descriptions. I shall therefore, in the sequel, speak simply of 'descriptions' when I mean 'definite descriptions'. Thus a description will mean any phrase of the form 'the so-and-so' in the singular.

We shall say that an object is 'known by description' when we know that it is 'the so-and-so', i.e. when we know that there is one object, and no more, having a certain property; and it will generally be implied that we do not have knowledge of the same object by acquaintance. We know that the man with the iron mask existed, and many propositions are known about him; but we do not know who he was. We know that the candidate who gets the most votes will be elected, and in this case we are very likely also acquainted (in the only sense in which one can be acquainted with some one else) with the man who is, in fact, the candidate who will get most votes; but we do not know which of the candidates he is, i.e. we do not know any proposition of the form 'A is the candidate who will get most votes' where A is one of the candidates by name. We shall say that we have 'merely descriptive knowledge' of the so-and-so when, although we know that the so-and-so exists, and although we may possibly be acquainted with the object which is, in fact, the so-and-so, yet we do not know any proposition '*a* is the so-and-so', where *a* is something with which we are acquainted.

When we say 'the so-and-so exists', we mean that there is just one object which is the so-and-so. The proposition '*a* is the so-and-so' means that *a* has the property so-and-so, and nothing else has. 'Mr. A. is the Unionist candidate for this constituency' means 'Mr. A. is a Unionist candidate for this constituency, and no one else is'. 'The Unionist candidate for this constituency exists' means 'some one is a Unionist candidate for this constituency, and no one else is'. Thus, when we are acquainted with an object which is the so-and-so, we know that the so-and-so exists; but we may know that the so-and-so exists when we are not acquainted with any object which we know to be the so-and-so, and even when we are not acquainted with any object which, in fact, is the so-and-so.

Common words, even proper names, are usually really descriptions. That is to say, the thought in the mind of a person using a proper name correctly can generally only be expressed explicitly if we replace the proper name by a description. Moreover, the description required to express the thought will vary for different people, or for the same person at different times. The only thing constant (so long as the name is rightly used) is the object to which the name applies. But so long as this remains constant, the particular description involved usually makes no difference to the truth or falsehood of the proposition in which the name appears.

Let us take some illustrations. Suppose some statement made about Bismarck. Assuming that there is such a thing as direct acquaintance with oneself, Bismarck himself might have used his name directly to designate the particular person with whom he was acquainted. In this case, if he made a judgement about himself, he himself might be a constituent of the judgement. Here the proper name has the direct use which it always wishes to have, as simply standing for a certain object, and not for a description of the object. But if a person who knew Bismarck made a judgement about him, the case is different. What this person was acquainted with were certain sense-data which he connected (rightly, we will suppose) with Bismarck's body. His body, as a physical object, and still more his mind, were only known as the body and the mind connected with these sense-data. That is, they were known by description. It is, of course, very much a matter of chance which characteristics of a man's appearance will come into a friend's mind when he thinks of him; thus the description actually in the friend's mind is accidental. The essential point is that he knows that the various descriptions all apply to the same entity, in spite of not being acquainted with the entity in question.

When we, who did not know Bismarck, make a judgement about him, the description in our minds will probably be some more or less vague mass of historical knowledge – far more, in most cases, than is required to identify him. But, for the sake of illustration, let us assume that we think of him as 'the first Chancellor of the German Empire'. Here all the words are abstract except 'German'. The word 'German' will, again, have different meanings for different people. To some it will recall travels in Germany, to some the look of Germany on the map, and so on. But if we are to obtain a description which we know to be applicable, we shall be compelled, at some point, to bring in a reference to a particular with which we are acquainted. Such reference is involved in any mention of past, present, and future (as opposed to definite dates), or of here and there, or of what others have told us. Thus it would seem that, in some way or other, a description known to be applicable to a particular must involve some reference to a particular with which we are acquainted, if our knowledge about the thing described is not to be merely what follows *logically* from the description. For example, 'the most long-lived of men' is a description involving only universals, which must apply to some man, but we can make no judgements concerning this man which involve knowledge about him beyond what the description gives. If, however, we say, 'The first Chancellor of the German Empire was an astute diplomatist', we can only be assured of the truth of our judgement in virtue of something with which we are acquainted – usually a testimony heard or read. Apart from the information we convey to others, apart from the fact about the actual Bismarck, which gives importance to our judgement, the thought we really have contains the one or more particulars involved, and otherwise consists wholly of concepts.

All names of places – London, England, Europe, the Earth, the Solar System – similarly involve, when used, descriptions which start from some one or more particulars with which we are acquainted. I suspect that even the Universe, as considered by metaphysics, involves such a connexion with particulars. In logic, on the contrary, where we are concerned not merely with what does exist, but with whatever might or could exist or be, no reference to actual particulars is involved.

It would seem that, when we make a statement about something only known by description, we often *intend* to make our statement, not in the form involving the description, but about the actual thing described. That is to say, when we say anything about Bismarck, we should like, if we could, to make the judgement which Bismarck alone can make, namely, the judgement of which he himself is a constituent. In this we are necessarily defeated, since the actual Bismarck is unknown to us. But we know that there is an object B, called Bismarck, and that B was an astute diplomatist. We can thus *describe* the proposition we should like to affirm, namely, 'B was an astute diplomatist', where B is the object which was Bismarck. If we are describing Bismarck as 'the first Chancellor of the German Empire', the proposition we should like to affirm may be described as 'the proposition asserting, concerning the actual object which was the first Chancellor of the German Empire, that this object was an astute diplomatist'. What enables us to communicate in spite of the varying descriptions we employ is that we know there is a true proposition concerning the actual Bismarck, and that however we may vary the description (so long as the description is correct) the proposition described is still the same. This proposition, which is described and is known to be true, is what interests us; but we are not acquainted with the proposition itself, and do not know *it*, though we know it is true.

It will be seen that there are various stages in the removal from acquaintance with particulars: there is Bismarck to people who knew him; Bismarck to those who only know of him through history; the man with the iron mask; the longest-lived of men. These are progressively further removed from acquaintance with particulars; the first comes as near to acquaintance as is possible in regard to another person; in the second, we shall still be said to know 'who Bismarck was'; in the third, we do not know who was the man with the iron mask, though we can know many propositions about him which are not logically deducible from the fact that he wore an iron mask; in the fourth, finally, we know nothing beyond what is logically deducible from the definition of the man. There is a similar hierarchy in the region of universals. Many universals, like many particulars, are only known to us by description. But here, as in the case of particulars, knowledge concerning what is known by description is ultimately reducible to knowledge concerning what is known by acquaintance.

The fundamental principle in the analysis of propositions containing descriptions is this: *Every proposition which we can understand must be composed wholly of constituents with which we are acquainted.*

We shall not at this stage attempt to answer all the objections which may be urged against this fundamental principle. For the present, we shall merely point out that, in some way or other, it must be possible to meet these objections, for it is scarcely conceivable that we can make a judgement or entertain a supposition without knowing what it is that we are judging or supposing about. We must attach *some* meaning to the words we use, if we are to speak significantly and not utter mere noise; and the meaning we attach to our words must be something with which we are acquainted. Thus when, for example, we make a statement about Julius Caesar, it is plain that Julius Caesar himself is not before our minds, since we are not acquainted with him. We have in mind some *description* of Julius Caesar: 'the man who was assassinated on the Ides of March', 'the founder of the Roman Empire', or, perhaps, merely 'the man whose name was *Julius Caesar*'. (In this last description, *Julius Caesar* is a noise or shape with which we are acquainted.) Thus our statement does not mean quite what it seems to mean, but means something involving, instead of Julius Caesar, some description of him which is composed wholly of particulars and universals with which we are acquainted.

The chief importance of knowledge by description is that it enables us to pass beyond the limits of our private experience. In spite of the fact that we can only know truths which are wholly composed of terms which we have experienced in acquaintance, we can yet have knowledge by description of things which we have never experienced. In view of the very narrow range of our immediate experience, this result is vital, and until it is understood, much of our knowledge must remain mysterious and therefore doubtful.

16

Moritz Schlick, 'On the Foundation of Knowledge'

From Oswald Hanfling (ed.), *Essential Readings in Logical Positivism*. Oxford: Blackwell, 1981, pp. 178–96 [notes omitted]; originally in *Philosophical Papers*, Volume II (1925–1936), ed. H. L. Mulder and B. van de Velde-Schlick (D. Reidel, 1979), © 1980 by Albert M. Schlick and Barbara F. B. van de Velde-Schlick. Reprinted with kind permission from Kluwer Academic Publishers.

Moritz Schlick (1882–1936) was the founder and main organizer of the famous Vienna Circle in the 1920–30s, a group of scientists and philosophers who formed the epicentre of the Logical Positivist movement. That movement is best known for the theory of meaning to which it subscribed, according to which propositions (other than 'trivial', analytic ones) are meaningful only if, in some (disputed) sense, they are verifiable. On such a theory, meaning is understood in epistemic terms, and anyway the theory of knowledge was bound to be of central concern to the Positivists given their shared ambition to establish the credentials of scientific enquiry at the same time as dismissing those of 'metaphysics'.

For at least two reasons, many in the Vienna Circle were dissatisfied with the foundationalist approach, still apparent in Russell (see chapter 15 above), of a more traditional empiricism. On that approach, typically, the basic propositions on which the edifice of knowledge rests are regarded as 'subjective' ones corresponding to indubitable mental data or experiences. For many Positivists, this approach not only creates the dilemma of how so public and communicable an enterprise as science could rest upon purely 'private' foundations, but it also falls foul of Wittgenstein's strictures, in his *Tractatus Logico-Philosophicus*, against talking *about* the relation between language and reality. As they construed this work, which had strongly influenced them, it condemned any such talk as 'metaphysical' and hence 'non-sense'.

Much of the interest of Schlick's 1933 paper 'On the foundation of knowledge' resides in his critical exposure of some of the more radical attempts, by fellow-members of the Circle, to identify and define a set of fundamental (or 'protocol') propositions in a manner which avoided the alleged pitfalls of more traditional foundationalist approaches. For example, he describes and rejects the proposals of Rudolf Carnap, Otto Neurath and others to define these protocol propositions in terms of their coherence within a body of scientific statements, or of the structural role (as axioms, say) conferred on them by scientists.[1]

It is Schlick's view that all such proposals make it impossible properly to respond to scepticism and relativism. Any adequate response must, he insists, share the traditional insight that fundamental propositions are those which record personal experiences of pain, colour or whatever. In this respect, Schlick belonged to the more conservative wing of the Logical Positivist movement. Indeed, in a later article he wrily notes his reputation, within the Vienna Circle, as a 'metaphysician and poet'.[2]

But in at least two other respects, Schlick's foundationalism differs from that of the older empiricist tradition. First he rejects, or at any rate downplays, the *genetic* role traditionally attributed to basic observations, their role as building-blocks on which we then erect a body of scientific knowledge. The real role of basic propositions ('affirmations', as Schlick calls them) is that of verifying or falsifying scientific hypotheses, whatever the source of these latter might be. Paradoxically, as it were, 'affirmations' serve to 'found' other propositions by 'coming at the end', for they are the indubitable truths which scientific hypotheses must entail or at least lead us towards if these hypotheses are to be accepted.

Second, and rather puzzlingly, Schlick's 'affirmations' turn out not really to be propositions at all, for a proposition, as something articulated and spoken or written down, is not something indubitable. And whereas propositions refer to or are about perceptions, the 'affirmations' themselves mention no perceptions and so are not really *about* them. 'Affirmations' are, rather, the 'occasions' for the most basic propositions we can articulate, as if through a process of 'combustion'.

Schlick, it seems, is open to the kind of criticism that could be levelled against Russell as well (see p. 234 above). The allegedly foundational items in the edifice of knowledge do not, in Schlick's account, look like structured, cognitive claims at all, in which case their role in supporting or verifying the claims of science is obscure. If, for example, Schlick's 'affirmation' of pain amounts to no more than simply having the pain, then it is hard to see that such 'affirmations' can be entailed by hypotheses and so serve to verify them.[3] Perhaps Schlick recognizes this, for at the end of the paper he switches to a rhetorical mode of indicating his view – talking, for example, of scientific knowledge not as

[1] Much of Schlick's criticism is directed against Carnap's paper '*Über Protokollsätze*', in *Erkenntnis*, 3, 1932.
[2] 'Facts and propositions', also in *Essential Readings in Logical Positivism*, ed. Hanfling, p. 196.
[3] On this issue, see John McDowell, *Mind and World*, Cambridge, MA: Harvard University Press, 1995.

entailing 'affirmations', but as 'flickering out' towards them.[4] It is not perhaps surprising, given the difficulties Schlick runs into, that some of the views he criticizes in the first half of his paper currently enjoy rather more favour than his own.

 ## On the Foundation of Knowledge

I

All great attempts at establishing a theory of knowing arise from the problem of the reliability of human cognition, and this question again arises from the wish for absolute certainty of knowledge.

That the statements of everyday life and of science can ultimately lay claim only to probable status, and that even the most universal findings of inquiry, confirmed in all experience, can only have the character of hypotheses – this is an insight that has repeatedly spurred philosophers from the time of Descartes, and less clearly, indeed, from antiquity onwards, to seek for an unshakeable foundation, immune from all doubt and forming the firm basis on which the tottering edifice of our knowledge is reared. The unsafeness of the structure has mostly been put down to the fact that it was impossible – perhaps in principle – to build anything more solid by the power of human thought; but this did not prevent a search for the natural bedrock which is there *before* building commences, and does not itself sway.

This search is a praiseworthy honest endeavour, and also exerts an influence among 'relativists' and 'skeptics' who would dearly like to be ashamed of it. It makes its appearance in various forms and leads to strange differences of opinion. The question of 'protocol propositions', their function and structure, is the latest form in which philosophy, or rather the radical empiricism of our day, invests the problem of the ultimate ground of knowledge.

As the name implies, 'protocol propositions' originally meant those propositions which in absolute simplicity, without any forming, change or addition, set forth the *facts*, whose elaboration constitutes the substance of all science, and which are prior to all knowledge, to every claim about the world. It makes no sense to speak of uncertain facts – it is only statements, only our knowledge that can be uncertain; and if it is therefore possible to reproduce the raw facts quite purely in 'protocol propositions', the latter

---

[4] For a useful discussion of Schlick's epistemology, see B. S. Gower, 'Realism and empiricism in Schlick's philosophy', in *Science and Subjectivity*, ed. D. Bell and W. Vossenkuhl, Berlin: Akademie Verlag, 1993.

seem to be the absolute indubitable starting-points of all knowledge. They are indeed again left behind, the moment we go over to propositions which are really useable in life or science (such a transition appears to be that from 'singular' to 'general' statements), but they constitute, for all that, the firm basis to which all our knowledge owes the whole of whatever validity it may still possess.

It makes no difference here whether these so-called protocol propositions are ever indeed formulated, i.e., actually uttered, written or even merely explicitly 'thought'; it is important only to know what propositions the designations actually made are based on, and to be able at any time to reconstruct them. If a research worker, for example, records that 'under such and such circumstances the pointer stands at 10.5', he knows that this means 'two black lines coincide', and that the words 'under such and such circumstances' (which we here suppose to be enumerated), are likewise to be resolved into particular protocol propositions, which he could also state exactly in principle if he wanted to, though it might be a trouble to do so.

The fact is clear, and to my knowledge has not been contested by anyone, that knowledge in life and in the research situation *begins* in *some* sense with the establishing of facts, and that 'protocol propositions', in which this establishment takes place, stand in a like sense at the *beginning* of science. What is this sense? Is the 'beginning' to be understood in a temporal sense or a logical one?

Here already we find a great deal of wavering and unclarity. When I said above that it did not matter whether the crucial propositions were also uttered or enunciated as protocols, this obviously implies that they do not have to stand at the beginning *in time*, but can equally well be brought in afterwards, if this should be required. And required it will be, whenever we wish to make clear the real meaning of the sentence actually written down. So is the talk about protocol propositions to be understood in a *logical* sense? In that case they would be marked out by specific logical properties, by their structure, their position in the system of science, and the task would arise of actually specifying these properties. In fact, this is the form in which [Rudolf] Carnap, for example, expressly posed the problem of protocol propositions at an earlier stage, whereas later he declared it a question to be settled by arbitrary decision.

On the other side we find numerous arguments apparently presupposing that we are to count as 'protocol propositions' only such statements as also take precedence in time over the other assertions of science. And is this not correct? For we have to remember that we are dealing here with the ultimate foundation of our knowledge of *reality*, and that it cannot suffice for this purpose to treat the propositions merely as if they were 'ideal structures' (as in Platonizing fashion it was earlier the custom to say). On the contrary, we have to concern ourselves with real happenings, with the temporally occurring events in which the passing of judgement consists, and hence with mental acts of 'thinking' or physical acts of 'speaking' or 'writing'. Since the mental acts of judgement appear fitted to serve as a basis for intersubjectively valid knowledge only after having been translated into oral or written expression (i.e., into a physical sign-system), it was proposed to regard as 'protocol propositions' certain spoken, written or printed sentences, i.e., certain sign-complexes consisting of sounds, writing fluid or printer's ink, which if rendered out of the customary abbreviations into a fully articulate language would signify somewhat as follows: 'Mr So-and-so, at such-and-such a time and place, is observing this or that'. (This view was particularly upheld by Otto Neurath.) And in fact, if we retrace the road whereby we have actually arrived at all our knowledge, we undoubtedly always come upon these same sources: printed sentences in books, words from the mouth of the teacher, and our own observations (in the latter case we are ourselves Mr So-and-so).

According to this view, protocol propositions would be real occurrences in the world, and would have to be prior in time to the other real processes constituting the 'construction of science', or even the production of knowledge in an individual.

I don't know how far the distinction here drawn between the logical and temporal priority of protocol propositions may correspond to differences in the view actually taken by particular authors – but that is no part of our present concern. For our purpose is not to determine who has said the right thing, but what the right thing *is*. And in this our distinction of the two standpoints will serve us well.

De facto, both views might be compatible, for the propositions recording simple data of observation and standing at the beginning in time could at the same time be those which, in virtue of their structure, must constitute the logical starting-point of science.

II

The question which ought first to interest us is this: what progress is attained by formulating the problem of the ultimate foundation of knowledge with the aid of the concept of 'protocol proposition'? The answering of this question should prepare us for the solution of the problem itself.

It seems to me to signify a great improvement in method, to try to arrive at the foundation of knowledge by searching, not for the primary *facts*, but for the primary *propositions*. But it seems to me also that there has been no understanding of how to make proper use of this advantage, and this perhaps because there has been no real awareness that at bottom the issue was none other than this old problem of the foundation of knowledge. I believe, in fact, that the view arrived at by these considerations about protocol propositions is untenable. They lead towards a peculiar relativism, which seems to be a necessary consequence of the view that regards protocol propositions as empirical facts, on which, as time goes on, the edifice of knowledge is raised.

For as soon as one asks about the certainty with which one may maintain the truth of protocol propositions regarded in this fashion, one has to admit that it is exposed to all manner of doubt.

There is a sentence in a book which says, for example, that So-and-so made such-and-such an observation with such-and-such an instrument. Although, given certain assumptions, one may have the utmost confidence in this statement, it, and hence the observation, can never be regarded as *absolutely* assured. For the possibilities of error are innumerable. So-and-so can inadvertently or deliberately have noted down something which fails to give a correct report of the fact observed; in writing or printing an error may have crept in – indeed the very assumption that the letters in a book preserve their shape even for a minute and do not rearrange themselves 'on their own' into new sentences, is an empirical hypothesis, which as such can never be strictly verified, since every verification would depend on similar assumptions, on the presupposition that our memory does not deceive us at least over short periods, and so forth.

This means of course – and some of our authors have been almost triumphant in pointing it out – that protocol propositions so conceived are in principle exactly the same in character as all other statements of science: they are hypotheses and nothing else. They are anything but irrefutable and can be employed in the construction of the knowledge-system only so long as they are supported, or at least not contradicted, by other hypotheses. We therefore reserve the right to make corrections at any time even to protocol propositions, and such corrections are often enough made, indeed, whenever we eliminate certain protocol data and maintain afterwards that they must have been due to some kind of error.

Even in propositions asserted by ourselves, we never in principle exclude the possibility of error. We admit that at the moment of passing judgement our mind was perhaps utterly confused, and that an experience we now claim to have had two seconds ago might be declared on subsequent examination to have been a hallucination, or even to have never happened at all.

It is clear, then, that for anyone in search of a firm foundation for knowledge the view outlined provides, in its 'protocol propositions', *nothing* of the kind. On the contrary, its only real outcome is that the distinction at first introduced between protocol and other propositions is subsequently done away with again as meaningless. We may therefore understand how the view was arrived at that any propositions we please may be picked out from science and designated as 'protocol propositions', and that it is merely a matter of expediency which ones we care to choose for the purpose.

But can we agree to this? Are there really only grounds of expediency? Is it not rather a question of where the particular propositions come from, of what their origin and history may be? What meaning, in any case, does expediency have here? What is the purpose pursued in setting up and se-lecting the propositions?

The purpose can only be that of science itself, namely to provide a *true* account of the facts. We think it self-evident that the problem of the founda-tion of all knowledge is nothing else but the question of the criterion of truth. The term 'protocol propositions' was undoubtedly first introduced so that by means of it certain propositions might be singled out, by whose truth it should then be possible to measure, as if by a yardstick, the truth of all other statements. According to the view described, this yardstick has now turned out to be just as relative as, say, all the standards of measurement in physics. And that view with its consequences has been commended [by Carnap], also, as an eviction of the last remnant of 'absolutism' from philosophy.

But then what do we have left as a criterion of truth? Since we are not to have it that all statements of science are to accord with a specific set of protocol propositions, but rather that all propositions are to accord with all others, where each is regarded as in principle corrigible, truth can consist only in the *mutual agreement of the propositions with one another*.

III

This doctrine (expressly stated and defended in the above context by Otto Neurath, for example) is well known in the history of modern philosophy. In England it is commonly referred to as the 'coherence theory of truth' and contrasted with the older 'correspondence theory' (on which it should be noted that the term 'theory' is by no means appropriate here, since remarks about the nature of truth are quite different in character from scientific theories, which always consist of a system of hypotheses).

The two views are usually contrasted by saying that on the first or tradi-tional theory the truth of a proposition consists in its agreement with the facts, whereas on the second or 'coherence' theory it consists in its agree-ment with the system of all other propositions.

I shall not here investigate in general whether the formulation of the latter doctrine cannot also be so interpreted as to draw attention to something perfectly correct (namely that there is a quite specific sense in which, as Wittgenstein puts it, we 'cannot get out of language'); my business here is to show, rather, that in the interpretation that must be given to it in our present context, the doctrine is wholly untenable.

If the truth of a proposition is to consist in its coherence or agreement with other propositions, we have to be clear about what is meant by 'agreement', and *which* propositions the 'others' are supposed to be.

The first point should be easy enough to dispose of. Since it cannot be intended that the statement under examination says the *same* as the others, the only alternative is that it merely has to be *consistent* with them, and hence that no contradiction shall obtain between them and it. Truth would thus consist simply in absence of contradiction. But now the question of whether truth can be straightforwardly identified with freedom from contradiction, ought no longer to be a matter of discussion. It should long since have been generally recognized that non-contradiction and truth (if one wishes to employ this word at all) can be equated only in propositions of a tautological character, e.g., in those of pure geometry. But in propositions of that kind all connection with reality is deliberately severed; they are merely formulae within an established calculus. Of the statements of *pure* geometry it makes no sense to ask whether they agree with the facts of the world or not; in order to be called true or correct, they merely have to be consistent with the axioms arbitrarily laid down at the outset (though it is customarily also required that they should *follow* from these). Here we are confronted with precisely what in earlier days was designated *formal* truth and distinguished from *material* truth.

The latter is the truth of synthetic propositions or factual statements, and if it is desired to describe them by means of the concept of non-contradiction or consistency with other propositions, this can be done only by saying that they may not stand in contradiction to certain *quite specific* statements, namely those very statements which record 'facts of immediate observation'. It is not consistency with *any* sort of propositions you please that can serve as the criterion of truth; what is required, rather, is conformity with certain very particular statements which can by no means be chosen at will. In other words, the criterion of non-contradiction alone is utterly inadequate for material truth; it is wholly a matter, rather, of consistency with very special statements of a peculiar kind; and for *this* consistency there is nothing to prevent – indeed everything, in my view, to justify – our employment of the good old phrase 'agreement with reality'.

The astonishing error of the 'coherence theory' can only be explained by the fact that, in setting up and elaborating this theory, attention was invariably paid only to propositions actually occurring in science, and that these alone were employed as examples. The non-contradictory connection between them was then in fact sufficient, but only because these propositions are already of a quite definite kind. For in a certain sense (yet to be described) they have their 'origin' in observational propositions, and derive, as one may confidently say in the traditional terms, 'from experience'.

Anyone who takes coherence seriously as the sole criterion of truth must consider any fabricated tale to be no less true than a historical report or the pro-positions in a chemistry text-book, so long as the tale is well enough fashioned to harbour no contradictions anywhere. With the aid of fantasy I can portray a grotesque world of adventure; the coherence philosopher has to believe in the truth of my account, provided only that I have a care for the mutual consistency of my claims and discreetly avoid any collision with the customary description of the world, by laying the sense of my recital on a distant star, where observation is no longer possible. Indeed, strictly speaking, I have no need at all of such discretion; I can equally well insist that others have to adjust themselves to my story, and not the other way round. The others cannot even object, in that case, that this procedure conflicts with observation, for according to the coherence theory no 'observations' of any kind are involved here, but only the consistency of the statements in question.

Since it does not occur to anybody to suppose the propositions in a storybook true, and those in a physics book false, the coherence view is a total failure. Something else must be added to coherence, namely a principle whereby consistency is to be established, and this alone would then be the actual criterion.

If I am given a set of statements, some of which are also contradictory, I can indeed achieve consistency in various ways, in that on one occasion, for example, I pick out certain statements and abandon or correct them, while on another I do the same with those which contradict the first.

This brings out the logical impossibility of the coherence view; it provides absolutely no unambiguous criterion of truth, for by means of it I can arrive at as many internally non-contradictory proposition-systems as I like, although they are not consistent with each other.

The absurdity is avoided only by not permitting the abandonment or correction of any statements you please, but rather by specifying those which are to be upheld, and to which the remainder have to conform.

IV

The coherence theory is now disposed of, and we have long ago arrived in the meantime at the second point of our critical deliberations, namely the question whether *all* propositions are corrigible, or whether there are also some which cannot be shaken. The latter would in fact form the 'foundation' of all knowledge that we were in search of, and towards which we have so far advanced not a single step.

By what rule, then are we to seek out those propositions which themselves remain unaltered, and with which all others must be brought into agreement? In what follows we shall speak of them not as 'protocol propositions', but as 'fundamental propositions', since it is in fact doubtful whether they occur at all in the protocols of science.

The first thing, no doubt, would be to look for the desired rule in a sort of economy-principle, and to say, in other words, that those propositions are to be chosen as fundamental whose adoption requires a *minimum* of changes in the entire system of statements, in order to free it from all contradiction.

It deserves to be noted that such a rule of economy would not establish some particular set of statements once and for all as fundamental propositions; it might happen, rather, that with the progress of knowledge the fundamental propositions that had hitherto served as such were again downgraded, since it had turned out more economical to drop them in favour of newly discovered propositions which from then on – until further notice – would play the part of a foundation. So while the standpoint would indeed be no longer that of pure coherence, but rather one of economy, it would be equally prone to 'relativism'.

It seems to me beyond question that the supporters of the view just criticized were in fact taking the economy principle as their true guideline, whether they stated this or left it unsaid; I have therefore already assumed above that in the relativistic theory it is grounds of expediency that determine the choice of 'protocol propositions', and I asked: 'Can we agree to this?'

To this question I now give the answer 'No!'. It is not in fact economic expediency, but properties of a wholly different kind, which mark out the truly fundamental propositions.

The process of choosing these propositions could be called economic if it consisted, say, in an accommodation to the opinions (or 'protocol propositions') of the majority of inquirers. Now it is indeed the case that we accept a fact, e.g., of geography or history, or even a natural law, as indubitably established, if we very often find its existence mentioned in the places appropriate to such reports. It then simply does not occur to us to want to check it again for ourselves. We therefore concur with what is universally acknowledged. But the reason for this is that we know precisely in what way such factual statements ordinarily come to be made, and this way inspires our confidence; it is not because it corresponds to the majority view.

On the contrary, it could only attain to universal acknowledgement because each individual feels the same confidence. Whether and to what extent we declare a statement to be corrigible or capable of annulment depends entirely *on its origin*, and (apart from quite special cases) in no way on whether its retention requires the correcting of very many other statements, and perhaps a rearrangement of the whole system of knowledge.

Before the economy-principle can be applied, we have to know: *which* propositions is it to apply to? And if the principle were to be the *only* decisive rule, the answer could only be: well, to *all* propositions that are advanced, or ever have been advanced, with the claim to validity. In point of fact, the clause 'with the claim to validity' should be left out, for how are we to distinguish such propositions from those advanced purely arbitrarily, having been thought up as a joke, or in order to mislead? This distinction simply cannot be formulated, without taking the *origin* of the statements into account. So we find ourselves repeatedly referred back to the question of their source. Without having classified the statements according to their origin, any application of the economic principle of compatibility would be utterly absurd. But once we have investigated the propositions in respect of their origin, we notice right away that in so doing we have already at the same time ranged them in an order of validity, that – apart from certain special cases in still uncompleted areas of science – there is simply no room for any application of the economy-principle, and that the order in question simultaneously points the way to the foundations we are seeking.

V

At this point, indeed, the most extreme caution is called for. For here we hit upon the very path which has been followed from time immemorial, by all who have embarked on the journey to the ultimate grounds of truth. And the goal has always failed of achievement. For in this ordering of propositions according to their origin, which I attempt in order to judge their certainty, an exceptional position is immediately taken by those which I advance *myself*. And of these, a secondary position is again occupied by those lying in the past, since we believe that their certainty can be impaired by 'deceptions of memory' – and the more so, in general, the further back in time they lie. At the forefront, however, as immune from all doubt, stand those propositions which give expression to a matter of personal 'perception' or 'experience' (or whatever the term may be) that lies *in the present*. And however clear and simple this may appear to be, the philosophers have fallen into a hopeless labyrinth as soon as they have actually tried to employ propositions of the last-mentioned kind as the foundation of all knowledge. Some puzzling alleys in this labyrinth include, for example, those formulae and arguments which, under such names as 'evidence of inner perception', 'solipsism', 'solipsism of the moment', 'self-certainty of consciousness', and so on, have been at the heart of so many philosophical disputes. The most famous destination to which pursuit of this path has led is the Cartesian *cogito ergo sum*, already reached beforehand, as it happens, by St. Augustine. And as to the *cogito ergo sum*, our eyes have nowadays been sufficiently opened by logic: we know that it is simply a pseudo-proposition, which again does not become a genuine statement through being expressed in the form: *cogitatio est* – 'contents of consciousness exist'. Such a proposition, which itself says nothing, can in no sense serve as the foundation of anything; it is not itself a piece of knowledge, and none is based upon it; it can lend no assurance to anything we know.

There is therefore the utmost danger that in pursuing the path recommended we may arrive at nothing but empty word-patterns, instead of the foundation we seek. It was, indeed, from the wish to obviate this danger that the critical theory of protocol propositions arose. But its chosen way out was unable to satisfy us; its *essential* defect consists in failing to recognize the differing status of propositions, most clearly revealed in the fact that for the system of knowledge which anyone accepts as the 'correct' one, his *own* propositions still ultimately play the only decisive role.

It is theoretically conceivable that the statements made by everyone else about the world should be in no way confirmed by my own observations. It might be the case that all the books I read and all the pronouncements I hear are in perfect agreement among themselves and never contradict one another, but that they are utterly irreconcilable with a large part of my own observation propositions. (In this case, the problem of language-learning and its use for communication would create certain difficulties, but they are soluble by means of certain assumptions as to whereabouts alone the contradictions are to appear.) According to the theory under criticism, in such a case I would simply have to sacrifice my own 'protocol propositions', since they are certainly at odds with the overwhelming mass of the others, which do harmonize together, and which there can be no possible expectation of correcting by reference to my own limited and fragmentary experience.

But what would really happen in the case supposed? Well, I would not give up my own observation propositions under any circumstances, for I find, rather, that I can only adopt a system of knowledge which they fit into without mutilation. And such a system I should always be able to construct. I need only regard other people as dreaming fools, whose madness has uncommon method in it – or to put it more concretely – I would say that the others are actually living in a different world from mine, which has only just so much in common with the latter as to permit communication in the same language. In any event, and whatever the world-picture I construct, I would always test its truth only by my own experience; this support I would never allow to be taken from me, my own observation propositions would always be the final criterion. I would proclaim, as it were: 'What I see, I see!'.

VI

In the light of these critical preliminaries, it is clear in what direction we have to seek for the solution of the difficulties that bewilder us; we must utilize stretches of the Cartesian road, so far as they are sound and passable, but then must beware of losing ourselves in the *cogito ergo sum* and similar absurdities. This we may do by attaining clarity as to the meaning and role which are in fact possessed by propositions stating what is 'immediately observed'.

What actually lies behind the statement that they are 'absolutely certain'? And in what sense can they be designated as the ultimate ground of all knowledge?

Let us first consider the second question. If we suppose that I at once take note of every observation – it makes no difference in principle whether I do so on paper or in memory – and now start out from thence to construct science, I would have before me genuine 'protocol propositions', standing temporally at the outset of knowledge. From them the remaining propositions of science would gradually be evolved through the process which we call 'induction', and which consists simply in the fact that, stimulated or incited by the protocol propositions, I tentatively set up general propositions ('hypotheses'), from which these first propositions, along with innumerable others, logically follow. Now if these others say the *same* as later observation statements, obtained under quite specific circumstances that have to be exactly stated in advance, then the hypotheses continue to rank as confirmed so long as observation statements do not crop up which are in contradiction to the propositions derived from the hypotheses, and hence to the hypotheses themselves. So long as this does not happen, we believe ourselves to have guessed correctly at a law of nature. Induction is therefore nothing else but a methodically guided guessing, a psychological, biological process whose execution has certainly nothing to do with 'logic'.

Here we have a schematic description of the actual procedure of science. It is clear what role is played in it by assertions about the 'immediately perceived'. They are not identical with statements written or remembered, i.e., with what could properly be called 'protocol propositions', but are the *occasion* for framing them. As we have long since conceded, the protocol propositions preserved in a book or in memory are doubtless to be compared in their validity with *hypotheses*, for if we have such a proposition before us, it is a mere assumption that it is true, that it accords with the observation statement which gave rise to it. (Perhaps, indeed, it was not occasioned by any observation statement, but arose out of some game or other.) What I call an observation-statement cannot be identical with a real protocol proposition, if only because in a certain sense it cannot be noted down at all – a point to be dealt with shortly.

In the schema of knowledge-construction that I have described, therefore, the role of the observation statements is firstly that of standing in time at the outset of the whole process, occasioning it and setting it to work. How much of their content enters into knowledge, remains as first essentially undecided. With some justice the observation statements can therefore be regarded as the ultimate origin of all knowledge, but ought they to be designated as its foundation, its ultimate certain ground? This is scarcely advisable, for this 'origin' is still connected in too questionable a manner with the edifice of knowledge. Moreover, we have certainly conceived the true process in a schematically simplified fashion. In reality, what is actually stated in a protocol is less closely connected with the observed as such, and in general we should not even assume that pure observation statements are interpolated at all between the observation and the 'protocol'.

But now it seems that these propositions, the statements about the immediately perceived, or 'affirmations' [*Konstatierungen*], as we might also call them, have yet another function to perform, namely in confirming hypotheses, or in *verification*.

Science makes prophecies that are tested by 'experience'. It is in making predictions that its essential function lies. It says, for example: 'If, at such and such a time, you look through a telescope focussed in such and such a manner, you will see a speck of light (a star) coinciding with a black line (cross-wires).' Let us assume that on following these instructions the event prophesied actually occurs; this means, of course, that we make an affirmation for which we are prepared; we pass an observational judgement that we *expected*, and have in doing so a sense of *fulfilment*, a wholly characteristic satisfaction; we are *content*. It is quite proper to say that the affirmations or observation statements have fulfilled their true mission, as soon as this peculiar satisfaction is obtained.

And we obtain it at the very moment in which the affirmation occurs, the observation statement is made. This is of the utmost importance, for it means that the function of propositions about the *presently* experienced itself lies in the present. We saw, indeed, that they have, as it were, no duration, that as soon as they are over we have available in their stead only designations or memory traces, which can play only the role of hypotheses and are thereby lacking in ultimate certainty. Upon affirmations no logically tenable structure can be erected, for they are already gone at the moment building begins. If they stand in time at the outset of the process of knowledge, they are logically of no use. It is quite otherwise, however, when they come at the end; they complete the act of verification (or falsification), and at the moment of their appearance have already performed their duty. Nothing else is logically deduced from them, no conclusions are drawn from them, they are an absolute end.

Psychologically and biologically, of course, the satisfaction they produce is the beginning of a new process of knowledge: the hypotheses whose verification concludes in them are regarded as confirmed, the framing of more extensive hypotheses is attempted, and the seeking and guessing after universal laws resumes its progress. For these temporally subsequent processes the observation statements therefore form the origin and incentive, in the sense already described.

By means of these considerations it seems to me that a new and vivid light is thrown upon the question of the ultimate foundation of knowledge; we get a clear picture of how the system of our knowledge is built up, and of the role that 'affirmations' play in it.

Knowledge is originally a means in the service of life. In order to fit into his environment and to accommodate his actions to events, man must in some degree be able to foresee these events. For this he needs universal propositions, findings of knowledge, and these he can make use of only insofar as the prophecies really come to pass. Now in science this character of knowledge remains completely intact; the only difference is that it no longer serves the purposes of life, and is not pursued for the sake of utility. Once the prediction comes to pass, the aim of science is achieved: the joy in knowledge is joy in verification, the exaltation of having guessed correctly. And this it is that the observation statements convey to us; in them science, as it were, attains its goal, and for their sake it exists. The question concealed behind the problem of the absolutely certain foundation of knowledge is, so to speak, that of the legitimacy of the satisfaction which verification fills us with. Are our predictions actually realized? In every single case of verification or falsification an 'affirmation' answers unambiguously with yes or no, with joy of fulfilment or disillusion. The affirmations are final.

Finality is a very suitable word to describe the significance of observation statements. They are an absolute end, and in them the current task of knowledge is fulfilled. That the joy in which they culminate, and the hypotheses they leave behind, are then the beginning of a new task, is no longer their affair. Science does not rest on them, but leads to them, and they show that it has led aright. They are really the absolutely fixed points; we are glad to reach them, even if we cannot rest there.

VII

What does this fixity consist in? We come here to the question earlier postponed for the time being: In what sense can we speak of the 'absolute certainty' of observation statements?

I should like to elucidate this by first saying something about a quite different kind of proposition, namely *analytic propositions*, and then comparing these with 'affirmations'. In analytic judgements the question of their validity notoriously poses no problem. They are valid *a priori*, we must not and cannot be convinced of their correctness by experience, because they say nothing whatever about the objects of experience. Hence, too, they possess only 'formal truth' i.e., they are not 'true' because they correctly express any facts; their truth, rather, consists solely in the fact that they are framed with formal correctness, i.e., conform to our arbitrarily established definitions.

But now some philosophical authors have felt obliged to ask: 'Well, how do I know in the given case whether a proposition is really in accordance with the definitions, and so is really analytic and therefore indubitable? Must I not bear in mind the proposed definitions, the meaning of all the words employed, while I utter, hear or read the proposition? But can I be sure that my mental capacities are equal to this? Is it not possible, for example, that by the end of the proposition, were it to last only for a second, I might have forgotten the beginning or wrongly remembered it? Must I not therefore admit that for psychological reasons I am never sure of the validity even of an analytic judgement?'

To this it must be replied that the possibility of malfunction in the mental mechanism must naturally always be conceded, but that the consequences that follow from it are not correctly described in the skeptical questions just propounded.

It can happen that through weakness of memory, and a thousand other causes, we fail to understand a proposition, or understand it wrongly (i.e., otherwise than it was intended) – but what is the significance of that? Well, so long as I have not understood a proposition, it is for me no statement at all, but a mere string of words, sounds or characters. In this case there is no problem, for only of a proposition can one ask if it is analytic or synthetic, not of an uncomprehended string of words. If, however, I have interpreted a series of words wrongly, but at all events as some sort of proposition – then I know of *this* particular proposition whether it is analytic, and so valid *a priori*, or not. It should not be thought that I could have grasped a proposition as such and then still be in doubt about its analytic character, for if it is analytic, I have only just then understood it, when I have understood it as analytic, For to understand means in fact nothing else but to be clear about the rules for employment of the words involved; but it is precisely such rules which make the proposition analytic.[1] If I do not know whether a word-complex constitutes an analytic proposition or not, this means simply that at this moment I am without rules for employment of the words, and thus have failed entirely to understand the proposition. The situation is, therefore, that either I have understood nothing whatever, and then there is no more to be said, or else I know whether the proposition that I *have* understood is analytic or synthetic (which is not to assume, of course, that in so doing these words hover before me, or are even known to me). In the case of an analytic proposition, I then know at the same time that it is valid and possesses formal truth.

The foregoing doubts about the validity of analytic propositions were thus misplaced. I can indeed doubt whether I have correctly grasped the meaning of some sign-complex, and even whether I shall ever understand the meaning of a given word-series at all; but I cannot ask whether I am also really able to discern the correctness of an analytic proposition. For in an analytic judgement, to understand its meaning and to discern its *a priori* validity, are *one and the same process*. A synthetic statement, by contrast, is characterized by the fact that if I have merely discerned its meaning, I have no notion whether it is true or false; its truth is established only by a comparison with experience. The process of discerning the meaning is here entirely different from that of verification.

There is only one exception to this. And here we return to our 'affirmations'. For these are always of the form 'Here now so-and-so', e.g., 'Here now two black spots coincide', or 'Here now blue is bounded by yellow', or even 'Here now pain . . .', etc. What is common to all these statements is that they contain *demonstrative* terms having the meaning of a present gesture, i.e., their rules of use stipulate that in making the statement in which they occur, an experience occurs, attention is directed to something observed. The meaning of the words 'here', 'now', 'this here', etc. cannot be stated by means of general definitions in words, but only through such words assisted by pointings and gesticulations. 'This here' makes sense only in combination with a gesture. In order, therefore, to understand the significance of such an observation statement, one must simultaneously make the gesture, one must in some way point to reality.

In other words, I can understand the meaning of an 'affirmation' only on and by way of a comparison with the facts, i.e., a carrying-out of the process required for the verification of all synthetic propositions. But whereas in all other synthetic statements, establishing the meaning and establishing the truth are separate, clearly distinguishable processes, in observation statements they coincide, just as they do in analytic judgements. However different the 'affirmations' may be from analytic propositions, they have this in common, that in both the process of understanding is at the same time the process of verification. Along with their meaning I simultaneously grasp their truth. To ask of an affirmation whether I might perhaps be mistaken about its truth, makes no more sense than with a tautology. Both have absolute validity. The analytical or tautological proposition, however, is at the same time devoid of content, whereas the observation statement gives us the satisfaction of a genuine acquaintance with reality.

It has now become clear, let us hope, that everything here turns upon the character of immediacy which is peculiar to observation statements, and to which they owe their value both positive and negative; the positive value of absolute validity, and the negative value of being useless as an enduring foundation.

The misunderstanding of this character is in large part responsible for the unfortunate issue concerning protocol propositions which formed the starting-point of our inquiry. When I make the affirmation 'Here now blue', that is *not* the same as the protocol proposition 'On such-and-such a date in April 1934, at such-and-such a time and place, Schlick perceived blue'. For the latter proposition is a hypothesis, and as such is always fraught with uncertainty. It is equivalent to the statement '(at the given time and place) . . . Schlick made the affirmation "Here now blue" '. And clearly this statement is not identical with the affirmation occurring in it. In protocol propositions the reference is *always* to perceptions (or they are to be supplied mentally; the personal identity of the perceiving observer is important for a scientific protocol), while in affirmations they are *never* mentioned. A genuine affirmation cannot be written down, for as soon as I put down the demonstrative terms 'here' and 'now', they lose their meaning. Nor can they be replaced by an indication of time and place, for as soon as this is attempted, the observation statement is unavoidably replaced, as we have seen, by a protocol proposition, which as such has an altogether different nature.

VIII

The problem of the foundation of knowledge has now, I believe, been elucidated.

If we look on science as a system of propositions, whose logical interconnection is the only feature of interest to us as logicians, then the question of their foundation, which in that case would be a 'logical' one, can be answered as we please, for we are free to define the foundation at will. In an abstract proposition-system, after all, there is intrinsically no priority and no posteriority. The most general propositions of science, i.e., those which are most commonly selected as 'axioms', could be designated, for example, as its ultimate foundation; but the name could equally well be reserved for the most specific propositions of all, which would then in fact actually correspond to the protocols written down; or some other choice would be possible. But the propositions of science are one and all *hypotheses*, the moment they are seen from the standpoint of their truth-value, or validity.

If we turn our attention to the connection of science with reality, and see in the system of its propositions what it really is, namely a means of orienting oneself among the facts, of attaining to the joy of confirmation, the feeling of finality, then the problem of the 'foundation' will automatically transform itself into that of the unshakeable points of contact between knowledge and reality. These absolutely fixed points, the affirmations, we have come to know in their particularity; they are the only synthetic propositions *which are not hypotheses*. In no sense do they lie at the basis of science, but knowledge, as it were, flickers out to them, reaching each one for a moment only, and at once consuming it. And newly fed and strengthened, it then flares on toward the next.

These moments of fulfilment and combustion are of the essence. From them comes all the light of knowledge. And it is this light for whose source the philosopher is actually asking, when he seeks the foundation of all knowledge.

Note

1 The idea that *a priori* propositions are all analytic, and that analytic truths are determined simply by rules for the employment of their component terms, was popular among the Logical Positivists, and an important aspect of their overall epistemology.

17

Ludwig Wittgenstein, *On Certainty*, Sections 1–42, 91–105, 192–284

From Ludwig Wittgenstein, *On Certainty*, tr. D. Paul and G. E. M. Anscombe, ed. G. E. M. Anscombe and G. H. von Wright. Oxford: Blackwell, 1969, pp. 2–8, 14–16, 27–37 [some notes and passages omitted; asterisked note is the editors']. Reprinted by permission of the publisher.

Like the Logical Positivists, whom his early work *Tractatus Logico-Philosophicus* had so influenced, the primary interest of the Austrian-born philosopher Ludwig Wittgenstein (1889–1951) was in the theory of meaning. Throughout his writings, the aim was to explore the limits of what can be significantly said, but since these will also be the limits of what can be sensibly thought and believed, the bearing of Wittgenstein's work on epistemological issues is apparent. Even in the *Tractatus*, where such issues are generally not to the fore, important contributions are to be found – for example, the criticism of Bertrand Russell's analysis of belief (5.542ff).

By the 1930s, Wittgenstein had abandoned the attempt to provide a general criterion of meaningfulness in terms of the formal features of propositions. Attention had instead shifted to the many "language-games" – commanding, telling jokes, forming and testing hypotheses, praying and so on – which speakers "play" and in relation to which our utterances, like the moves in a real game, have their place and sense. Although, in his *Philosophical Investigations*, epistemology is still not the main focus, the notion of language-games is invoked by Wittgenstein when reaching some conclusions of the first importance in that area. He argues, for example, that utterances like "I am in pain", far from describing indubitable mental states, do not describe or state anything at all, but are, rather, *expressions* of pain, replacements as it were for wincing and screaming (Part I, §244). In treating them as reports of sensations, philosophers have allocated them to the wrong language-game.

An important theme in these later writings is that many of the questions raised and the answers offered by philosophers are without any clear sense. This is because philosophers are prone to consider concepts dislocated from the contexts, or language-games, within which they perform their roles.

Language, in the mouths of philosophers, "goes on holiday", their pronouncements akin to moves outside any game that could lend them significance.

This is a theme which is salient in Wittgenstein's reflections of his final years, posthumously published as *On Certainty*, when, for the only time, epistemological issues became the main object of his attention. These reflections were prompted by his reading of two articles by G. E. Moore which attempted to rebut scepticism and idealism.[1] Moore's argument, highly reminiscent of Thomas Reid's defence of commonsense (see chapter 10 above), was simplicity itself. There are some things a person surely *knows*, such as that he has two hands or has never strayed far from the earth's surface – things whose truth is not only more certain than any considerations which could be marshalled against them, but which entails that sceptical or idealist denials of the external world's existence must be mistaken.

Much of the discussion in *On Certainty* consists in remarks on such concepts as doubt, mistake and knowledge itself, which aim to show that both Moore and his sceptical opponents are guilty of abstracting these concepts from the real-life contexts in which they have a significant use. Doubting, making mistakes and knowing must, if they are to deserve their names, engage with our behaviour and lives in ways that they do *not* in the writings of Moore and his opponents.[2]

Concentration on just these rather piecemeal remarks would, however, blind one to the radical character of Wittgenstein's attitude towards epistemology. For good reason, he gets numbered among those philosophers announcing the so-called "death of epistemology". If epistemology is understood as the endeavour to identify a set of propositions or beliefs which are absolutely certain and serve as the foundation for all other beliefs, then, for Wittgenstein, it is indeed a dead-end. Precisely because knowledge-claims are highly context-bound – significant in some contexts, not in others – it is absurd to attempt, as does Moore, to enumerate a set of propositions which *per se* register certain knowledge (see §6).

Like Moore, however, Wittgenstein does think that some of our convictions have a privileged status. This is not, though, because their truth is established beyond doubt: indeed, they should hardly be called "true" at all – not because they are false, but because they shape the framework within which all attributions of truth and falsity, all verification and falsification, all giving of reasons, take place. Such convictions as that everyone has parents, that cats don't grow on trees, and that the world didn't begin 100 years ago, are ones which we cannot do without, for without them the whole network or system of our

---

[1] 'Proof of an external world' and 'A defence of commonsense', both in Moore's *Philosophical Papers*, London: Allen & Unwin, 1959.
[2] A clear and crisp discussion of these remarks is to be found in Anthony Kenny, *Wittgenstein*, Harmondsworth: Penguin, 1975, ch. 11.

beliefs would collapse.[3] These convictions cannot be justified, for they belong to our "picture of the world", something we inherit and cannot establish as correct (§94). Converting aliens to such a picture is just that – conversion or "persuasion", not a process of rational argument from true premises (§§609ff).

Readers may be reminded by this of Hume's way of responding to scepticism (see chapter 9 above). But whereas the natural convictions which Hume thinks could never be abandoned are "natural" in the sense of belonging to our abiding human make-up, Wittgenstein allows that over time the "river-bed" of our thinking may change. What was once central to our picture of the world may shift to the periphery, while other convictions move centre-stage. What belongs in the river-bed reflects a "form of life", and however deeply rooted in our "natural history" these forms of life may be, they have a history. And that is another reason why, for Wittgenstein, it is hopeless to seek out a set of propositions which, timelessly, constitute the indubitable foundations of knowledge.

1. If you do know that *here is one hand*, we'll grant you all the rest.

When one says that such and such a proposition can't be proved, of course that does not mean that it can't be derived from other propositions; any proposition can be derived from other ones. But they may be no more certain than it is itself. . . .

2. From its *seeming* to me – or to everyone – to be so, it doesn't follow that it *is* so.

What we can ask is whether it can make sense to doubt it.

3. If e.g. someone says "I don't know if there's a hand here" he might be told "Look closer". – This possibility of satisfying oneself is part of the language-game. Is one of its essential features.

4. "I know that I am a human being." In order to see how unclear the sense of this proposition is, consider its negation. At most it might be taken to mean "I know I have the organs of a human". (E.g. a brain which, after all, no one has ever yet seen.) But what about such a proposition as "I know I have a brain"? Can I doubt it? Grounds for *doubt* are lacking! Everything speaks in its favour, nothing against it. Nevertheless it is imaginable that my skull should turn out empty when it was operated on.

[3] Wittgenstein's stress on, and imagery of, our beliefs constituting a system which threatens to collapse when some of them are removed are similar to those in W. V. O. Quine's 'Two dogmas of empiricism', in his *From a Logical Point of View*, Cambridge, MA: Harvard University Press, 1953.

5.   Whether a proposition can turn out false after all depends on what I make count as determinants for that proposition.

6.   Now, can one enumerate what one knows (like Moore)? Straight off like that, I believe not. – For otherwise the expression "I know" gets misused. And through this misuse a queer and extremely important mental state seems to be revealed.

7.   My life shews that I know or am certain that there is a chair over there, or a door, and so on. – I tell a friend e.g. "Take that chair over there", "Shut the door", etc. etc.

8.   The difference between the concept of "knowing" and the concept of "being certain" isn't of any great importance at all, except where "I know" is meant to mean: I *can't* be wrong. In a law-court, for example, "I am certain" could replace "I know" in every piece of testimony. We might even imagine its being forbidden to say "I know" there. . . .

9.   Now do I, in the course of my life, make sure I know that here is a hand – my own hand, that is?

10.   I know that a sick man is lying here? Nonsense! I am sitting at his bedside, I am looking attentively into his face. – So I don't know, then, that there is a sick man lying here? Neither the question nor the assertion makes sense. Any more than the assertion "I am here", which I might yet use at any moment, if suitable occasion presented itself. – Then is "2 × 2 = 4" nonsense in the same way, and not a proposition of arithmetic, apart from particular occasions? "2 × 2 = 4" is a true proposition of arithmetic – not "on particular occasions" nor "always" – but the spoken or written sentence "2 × 2 = 4" in Chinese might have a different meaning or be out and out nonsense, and from this is seen that it is only in use that the proposition has its sense. And "I know that there's a sick man lying here", used in an *unsuitable* situation, seems not to be nonsense but rather seems matter-of-course, only because one can fairly easily imagine a situation to fit it, and one thinks that the words "I know that . . ." are always in place where there is no doubt, and hence even where the expression of doubt would be unintelligible.

11.   We just do not see how very specialized the use of "I know" is.

12.   – For "I know" seems to describe a state of affairs which guarantees

what is known, guarantees it as a fact. One always forgets the expression "I thought I knew".

13. For it is not as though the proposition "It is so" could be inferred from someone else's utterance: "I know it is so". Nor from the utterance together with its not being a lie. – But can't I infer "It is so" from my own utterance "I know etc."? Yes; and also "There is a hand there" follows from the proposition "He knows that there's a hand there". But from his utterance "I know . . ." it does not follow that he does know it.

14. That he does know takes some shewing.

15. It needs to be *shewn* that no mistake was possible. Giving the assurance "I know" doesn't suffice. For it is after all only an assurance that I can't be making a mistake, and it needs to be *objectively* established that I am not making a mistake about *that*.

16. "If I know something, then I also know that I know it, etc." amounts to: "I know that" means "I am incapable of being wrong about that". But whether I am so needs to be established objectively.

17. Suppose now I say "I'm incapable of being wrong about this: that is a book" while I point to an object. What would a mistake here be like? And have I any *clear* idea of it?

18. "I know" often means: I have the proper grounds for my statement. So if the other person is acquainted with the language-game, he would admit that I know. The other, if he is acquainted with the language-game, must be able to imagine *how* one may know something of the kind.

19. The statement "I know that here is a hand" may then be continued: "for it's *my* hand that I'm looking at". Then a reasonable man will not doubt that I know. – Nor will the idealist; rather he will say that he was not dealing with the practical doubt which is being dismissed, but there is a further doubt *behind* that one. – That this is an *illusion* has to be shewn in a different way.

20. "Doubting the existence of the external world" does not mean for example doubting the existence of a planet, which later observations proved to exist. – Or does Moore want to say that knowing that here is his hand is different in kind from knowing the existence of the planet Saturn?

Otherwise it would be possible to point out the discovery of the planet Saturn to the doubters and say that its existence has been proved, and hence the existence of the external world as well.

21.   Moore's view really comes down to this: the concept "know" is analogous to the concepts "believe", "surmise", "doubt", "be convinced" in that the statement "I know . . ." can't be a mistake. And if that *is* so, then there can be an inference from such an utterance to the truth of an assertion. And here the form "I thought I knew" is being overlooked. – But if this latter is inadmissible, then a mistake in the *assertion* must be logically impossible too. And anyone who is acquainted with the language-game must realize this – an assurance from a reliable man that he *knows* cannot contribute anything.

22.   It would surely be remarkable if we had to believe the reliable person who says "I can't be wrong"; or who says "I am not wrong".

23.   If I don't know whether someone has two hands (say, whether they have been amputated or not) I shall believe his assurance that he has two hands, if he is trustworthy. And if he says he *knows* it, that can only signify to me that he has been able to make sure, and hence that his arms are e.g. not still concealed by coverings and bandages, etc. etc. My believing the trustworthy man stems from my admitting that it is possible for him to make sure. But someone who says that perhaps there are no physical objects makes no such admission.

24.   The idealist's question would be something like: "What right have I not to doubt the existence of my hands?" (And to that the answer can't be: I *know* that they exist.) But someone who asks such a question is overlooking the fact that a doubt about existence only works in a language-game. Hence, that we should first have to ask: what would such a doubt be like?; and don't understand this straight off.

25.   One may be wrong even about "there being a hand here". Only in particular circumstances is it impossible. – "Even in a calculation one can be wrong – only in certain circumstances one can't."

26.   But can it be seen from a *rule* what circumstances logically exclude a mistake in the employment of rules of calculation?
      What use is a rule to us here? Mightn't we (in turn) go wrong in applying it?

27.   If, however, one wanted to give something like a rule here, then it would contain the expression "in normal circumstances". And we recognize normal circumstances but cannot precisely describe them. At most, we can describe a range of abnormal ones.

28.   What is "learning a rule"? – *This.*
     What is "making a mistake in applying it"? – *This.* And what is pointed to here is something indeterminate.

29.   Practice in the use of the rule also shews what is a mistake in its employment.

30.   When someone has made sure of something, he says: "Yes, the calculation is right", but he did not infer that from his condition of certainty. One does not infer how things are from one's own certainty.
     Certainty is *as it were* a tone of voice in which one declares how things are, but one does not infer from the tone of voice that one is justified.

31.   The propositions which one comes back to again and again as if bewitched – these I should like to expunge from philosophical language.

32.   It's not a matter of *Moore's* knowing that there's a hand there, but rather we should not understand him if he were to say "Of course I may be wrong about this". We should ask "What is it like to make such a mistake as that?" – e.g. what's it like to discover that it was a mistake?

33.   Thus we expunge the sentences that don't get us any further.

34.   If someone is taught to calculate, is he also taught that he can rely on a calculation of his teacher's? But these explanations must after all sometime come to an end. Will he also be taught that he can trust his senses – since he is indeed told in many cases that in such and such a special case you *cannot* trust them? –
     Rule and exception.

35.   But can't it be imagined that there should be no physical objects? I don't know. And yet "There are physical objects" is nonsense. Is it supposed to be an empirical proposition? –
     And is *this* an empirical proposition: "There seem to be physical objects"?

36.   "A is a physical object" is a piece of instruction which we give only to

someone who doesn't yet understand either what "A" means, or what "physical object" means. Thus it is instruction about the use of words, and "physical object" is a logical concept. (Like colour, quantity, . . .) And that is why no such proposition as: "There are physical objects" can be formulated. Yet we encounter such unsuccessful shots at every turn.

37.   But is it an adequate answer to the scepticism of the idealist, or the assurances of the realist, to say that "There are physical objects" is nonsense? For them after all it is not nonsense. It would, however, be an answer to say: this assertion, or its opposite is a misfiring attempt to express what can't be expressed like that. And that it does misfire can be shewn; but that isn't the end of the matter. We need to realize that what presents itself to us as the first expression of a difficulty, or of its solution, may as yet not be correctly expressed at all. Just as one who has a just censure of a picture to make will often at first offer the censure where it does not belong, and an *investigation* is needed in order to find the right point of attack for the critic.

38.   Knowledge in mathematics: Here one has to keep on reminding oneself of the unimportance of the "inner process" or "state" and ask "Why should it be important? What does it matter to me?" What is interesting is how we *use* mathematical propositions.

39.   *This* is how calculation is done, in such circumstances a calculation is *treated* as absolutely reliable, as certainly correct.

40.   Upon "I know that here is my hand" there may follow the question "How do you know?" and the answer to that presupposes that *this* can be known in *that* way. So, instead of "I know that here is my hand", one might say "Here is my hand", and then add *how* one knows.

41.   "I know where I am feeling pain", "I know that I feel it *here*" is as wrong as "I know that I am in pain". But "I know where you touched my arm" is right.

42.   One can say "He believes it, but it isn't so", but not "He knows it, but it isn't so". Does this stem from the difference between the mental states of belief and of knowledge? No. – One may for example call "mental state" what is expressed by tone of voice in speaking, by gestures etc. It would thus be *possible* to speak of a mental state of conviction, and that may be the same whether it is knowledge or false belief. To think that

different states must correspond to the words "believe" and "know" would be as if one believed that different people had to correspond to the word "I" and the name "Ludwig", because the concepts are different.

. . .

91.   If Moore says he knows the earth existed etc., most of us will grant him that it has existed all that time, and also believe him when he says he is convinced of it. But has he also got the right *ground* for his conviction? For if not, then after all he doesn't *know* (Russell).

92.   However, we can ask: May someone have telling grounds for believing that the earth has only existed for a short time, say since his own birth? – Suppose he had always been told that, – would he have any good reason to doubt it? Men have believed that they could make rain; why should not a king be brought up in the belief that the world began with him? And if Moore and this king were to meet and discuss, could Moore really prove his belief to be the right one? I do not say that Moore could not convert the king to his view, but it would be a conversion of a special kind; the king would be brought to look at the world in a different way. Remember that one is sometimes convinced of the *correctness* of a view by its *simplicity* or *symmetry*, i.e, these are what induce one to go over to this point of view. One then simply says something like: "*That's* how it must be."

93.   The propositions presenting what Moore "*knows*" are all of such a kind that it is difficult to imagine *why* anyone should believe the contrary. E.g. the proposition that Moore has spent his whole life in close proximity to the earth. – Once more I can speak of myself here instead of speaking of Moore. What could induce me to believe the opposite? Either a memory, or having been told.– Everything that I have seen or heard gives me the conviction that no man has ever been far from the earth. Nothing in my picture of the world speaks in favour of the opposite.

94.   But I did not get my picture of the world by satisfying myself of its correctness; nor do I have it because I am satisfied of its correctness. No: it is the inherited background against which I distinguish between true and false.

95.   The propositions describing this world-picture might be part of a kind of mythology. And their role is like that of rules of a game; and the game can be learned purely practically, without learning any explicit rules.

96. It might be imagined that some propositions, of the form of empirical propositions, were hardened and functioned as channels for such empirical propositions as were not hardened but fluid; and that this relation altered with time, in that fluid propositions hardened, and hard ones became fluid.

97. The mythology may change back into a state of flux, the river-bed of thoughts may shift. But I distinguish between the movement of the waters on the river-bed and the shift of the bed itself; though there is not a sharp division of the one from the other.

98. But if someone were to say "So logic too is an empirical science" he would be wrong. Yet this is right: the same proposition may get treated at one time as something to test by experience, at another as a rule of testing.

99. And the bank of that river consists partly of hard rock, subject to no alteration or only to an imperceptible one, partly of sand, which now in one place now in another gets washed away, or deposited.

100. The truths which Moore says he knows, are such as, roughly speaking, all of us know, if he knows them.

101. Such a proposition might be e.g. "My body has never disappeared and reappeared again after an interval".

102. Might I not believe that once, without knowing it, perhaps in a state of unconsciousness, I was taken far away from the earth – that other people even know this, but do not mention it to me? But this would not fit into the rest of my convictions at all. Not that I could describe the system of these convictions. Yet my convictions do form a system, a structure.

103. And now if I were to say "It is my unshakeable conviction that etc.", this means in the present case too that I have not consciously arrived at the conviction by following a particular line of thought, but that it is anchored in all my *questions and answers*, so anchored that I cannot touch it.

104. I am for example also convinced that the sun is not a hole in the vault of heaven.

105. All testing, all confirmation and disconfirmation of a hypothesis takes place already within a system. And this system is not a more or less arbitrary

and doubtful point of departure for all our arguments: no, it belongs to the essence of what we call an argument. The system is not so much the point of departure, as the element in which arguments have their life.

. . .

192.   To be sure there is justification; but justification comes to an end.

193.   What does this mean: the truth of a proposition is *certain?*

194.   With the word "certain" we express complete conviction, the total absence of doubt, and thereby we seek to convince other people. That is *subjective* certainty.
      But when is something objectively certain? When a mistake is not possible. But what kind of possibility is that? Mustn't mistake be *logically* excluded?

195.   If I believe that I am sitting in my room when I am not, then I shall not be said to have *made a mistake*. But what is the essential difference between this case and a mistake?

196.   Sure evidence is what we *accept* as sure, it is evidence that we go by in *acting* surely, acting without any doubt.
      What we call "a mistake" plays a quite special part in our language-games, and so too does what we regard as certain evidence.

197.   It would be nonsense to say that we regard something as sure evidence because it is certainly true.

198.   Rather, we must first determine the role of deciding for or against a proposition.

199.   The reason why the use of the expression "true or false" has something misleading about it is that it is like saying "it tallies with the facts or it doesn't", and the very thing that is in question is what "tallying" is here.

200.   Really "The proposition is either true or false" only means that it must be possible to decide for or against it. But this does not say what the ground for such a decision is like.

201.   Suppose someone were to ask: "Is it really right for us to rely on the evidence of our memory (or our senses) as we do?"

202. Moore's certain propositions almost declare that we have a right to rely upon this evidence.

203. [Everything that we regard as evidence indicates that the earth already existed long before my birth. The contrary hypothesis has *nothing* to confirm it at all.

If everything speaks *for* an hypothesis and nothing against it, is it objectively *certain?* One can *call* it that. But does it *necessarily* agree with the world of facts? At the very best it shows us what "agreement" means. We find it difficult to imagine it to be false, but also difficult to make use of it.]*

What does this agreement consist in, if not in the fact that what is evidence in these language-games speaks for our proposition? (*Tractatus Logico-Philosophicus*)

204. Giving grounds, however, justifying the evidence, comes to an end; – but the end is not certain propositions' striking us immediately as true, i.e. it is not a kind of *seeing* on our part; it is our *acting*, which lies at the bottom of the language-game.

205. If the true is what is grounded, then the ground is not *true*, nor yet false.

206. If someone asked us "but is that *true?*" we might say "yes" to him; and if he demanded grounds we might say "I can't give you any grounds, but if you learn more you too will think the same".

If this didn't come about, that would mean that he couldn't for example learn history.

207. "Strange coincidence, that every man whose skull has been opened had a brain!"

208. I have a telephone conversation with New York. My friend tells me that his young trees have buds of such and such a kind. I am now convinced that his tree is. . . . Am I also convinced that the earth exists?

209. The existence of the earth is rather part of the whole *picture* which forms the starting-point of belief for me.

---

* Passage crossed out in MS. (*Editors*)

210. Does my telephone call to New York strengthen my conviction that the earth exists?

Much seems to be fixed, and it is removed from the traffic. It is so to speak shunted onto an unused siding.

211. Now it gives our way of looking at things, and our researches, their form. Perhaps it was once disputed. But perhaps, for unthinkable ages, it has belonged to the *scaffolding* of our thoughts. (Every human being has parents.)

212. In certain circumstances, for example, we regard a calculation as sufficiently checked. What gives us a right to do so? Experience? May that not have deceived us? Somewhere we must be finished with justification, and then there remains the proposition that *this* is how we calculate.

213. Our "empirical propositions" do not form a homogeneous mass.

214. What prevents me from supposing that this table either vanishes or alters its shape and colour when no one is observing it, and then when someone looks at it again changes back to its old condition? – "But who is going to suppose such a thing!" – one would feel like saying.

215. Here we see that the idea of "agreement with reality" does not have any clear application.

216. The proposition "It is written".

217. If someone supposed that *all* our calculations were uncertain and that we could rely on none of them (justifying himself by saying that mistakes are always possible) perhaps we would say he was crazy. But can we say he is in error? Does he not just react differently? We rely on calculations, he doesn't; we are sure, he isn't.

218. Can I believe for one moment that I have ever been in the stratosphere? No. So do I *know* the contrary, like Moore?

219. There cannot be any doubt about it for me as a reasonable person. – That's it.–

220. The reasonable man does *not have* certain doubts.

221. Can I be in doubt at *will*?

222. I cannot possibly doubt that I was never in the stratosphere. Does that make me know it? Does it make it true?

223. For mightn't I be crazy and not doubting what I absolutely ought to doubt?

224. "I *know* that it never happened, for if it had happened I could not possibly have forgotten it."
     But, supposing it *did* happen, then it just would have been the case that you had forgotten it. And how do you know that you could not possibly have forgotten it? Isn't that just from earlier experience?

225. What I hold fast to is not *one* proposition but a nest of propositions.

226. Can I give the supposition that I have ever been on the moon any serious consideration at all?

227. "*Is* that something that one can forget?!"

228. "In such circumstances, people do not say "Perhaps we've all forgotten", and the like, but rather they assume that. . . ."

229. Our talk gets its meaning from the rest of our proceedings.

230. We are asking ourselves: what do we do with a statement "I *know* . . ."? For it is not a question of mental processes or mental states.
     And *that* is how one must decide whether something is knowledge or not.

231. If someone doubted whether the earth had existed a hundred years ago, I should not understand, for *this* reason: I would not know what such a person would still allow to be counted as evidence and what not.

232. "We could doubt every single one of these facts, but we could not doubt them *all*."
     Wouldn't it be more correct to say: "we do not doubt them *all*".
     Our not doubting them all is simply our manner of judging, and therefore of acting.

233.   If a child asked me whether the earth was already there before my birth, I should answer him that the earth did not begin only with my birth, but that it existed long, long before. And I should have the feeling of saying something funny. Rather as if the child had asked if such and such a mountain were higher than a tall house that it had seen. In answering the question I should have to be imparting a picture of the world to the person who asked it.

   If I do answer the question with certainty, what gives me this certainty?

234.   I believe that I have forebears, and that every human being has them. I believe that there are various cities, and, quite generally, in the main facts of geography and history. I believe that the earth is a body on whose surface we move and that it no more suddenly disappears or the like than any other solid body: this table, this house, this tree, etc. If I wanted to doubt the existence of the earth long before my birth, I should have to doubt all sorts of things that stand fast for me.

235.   And that something stands fast for me is not grounded in my stupidity or credulity.

236.   If someone said "The earth has not long been . . ." what would he be impugning? Do I know?

   Would it have to be what is called a scientific belief? Might it not be a mystical one? Is there any absolute necessity for him to be contradicting historical facts? or even geographical ones?

237.   If I say "an hour ago this table didn't exist" I probably mean that it was only made later on.

   If I say "this mountain didn't exist then", I presumably mean that it was only formed later on – perhaps by a volcano.

   If I say "this mountain didn't exist half an hour ago", that is such a strange statement that it is not clear what I mean. Whether for example I mean something untrue but scientific. Perhaps you think that the statement that the mountain didn't exist then is quite clear, however one conceives the context. But suppose someone said "This mountain didn't exist a minute ago, but an exactly similar one did instead". Only the accustomed context allows what is meant to come through clearly.

238.   I might therefore interrogate someone who said that the earth did not exist before his birth, in order to find out which of my convictions he was at odds with. And then it *might* be that he was contradicting my funda-

mental attitudes, and if that were how it was, I should have to put up with it. Similarly if he said he had at some time been on the moon.

239.   I believe that every human being has two human parents; but Catholics believe that Jesus only had a human mother. And other people might believe that there are human beings with no parents, and give no credence to all the contrary evidence. Catholics believe as well that in certain circumstances a wafer completely changes its nature, and at the same time that all evidence proves the contrary. And so if Moore said "I know that this is wine and not blood", Catholics would contradict him.

240.   What is the belief that all human beings have parents based on? On experience. And how can I base this sure belief on my experience? Well, I base it not only on the fact that I have known the parents of certain people but on everything that I have learnt about the sexual life of human beings and their anatomy and physiology: also on what I have heard and seen of animals. But then is that really a proof?

241.   Isn't this an hypothesis, which, as I *believe*, is again and again completely confirmed?

242.   Mustn't we say at every turn: "I *believe* this with certainty"?

243.   One says "I know" when one is ready to give compelling grounds. "I know" relates to a possibility of demonstrating the truth. Whether someone knows something can come to light, assuming that he is convinced of it.

But if what he believes is of such a kind that the grounds that he can give are no surer than his assertion, then he cannot say that he knows what he believes.

244.   If someone says "I have a body", he can be asked "Who is speaking here with this mouth?"

245.   To whom does anyone say that he knows something? To himself, or to someone else. If he says it to himself, how is it distinguished from the assertion that he is *sure* that things are like that? There is no subjective sureness that I know something. The certainty is subjective, but not the knowledge. So if I say "I know that I have two hands", and that is not supposed to express just my subjective certainty, I must be able to satisfy myself that I am right. But I can't do that, for my having two hands is not less certain before I have looked at them than afterwards. But I could say:

"That I have two hands is an irreversible belief." That would express the fact that I am not ready to let anything count as a disproof of this proposition.

246. "Here I have arrived at a foundation of all my beliefs." "This position I will *hold*!" But isn't that, precisely, only because I am completely *convinced* of it? – What is "being completely convinced" like?

247. What would it be like to doubt now whether I have two hands? Why can't I imagine it at all? What would I believe if I didn't believe that? So far I have no system at all within which this doubt might exist.

248. I have arrived at the rock bottom of my convictions.
And one might almost say that these foundation-walls are carried by the whole house.

249. One gives oneself a false picture of *doubt*.

250. My having two hands is, in normal circumstances, as certain as anything that I could produce in evidence for it.
    That is why I am not in a position to take the sight of my hand as evidence for it.

251. Doesn't this mean: I shall proceed according to this belief unconditionally, and not let anything confuse me?

252. But it isn't just that *I* believe in this way that I have two hands, but that every reasonable person does.

253. At the foundation of well-founded belief lies belief that is not founded.

254. Any "reasonable" person behaves like *this*.

255. Doubting has certain characteristic manifestations, but they are only characteristic of it in particular circumstances. If someone said that he doubted the existence of his hands, kept looking at them from all sides, tried to make sure it wasn't "all done by mirrors", etc., we should not be sure whether we ought to call that doubting. We might describe his way of behaving as like the behaviour of doubt, but his game would not be ours.

256. On the other hand a language-game does change with time.

257.   If someone said to me that he doubted whether he had a body I should take him to be a half-wit. But I shouldn't know what it would mean to try to convince him that he had one. And if I had said something, and that had removed his doubt, I should not know how or why.

258.   I do not know how the sentence "I have a body" is to be used.
   That doesn't unconditionally apply to the proposition that I have always been on or near the surface of the earth.

259.   Someone who doubted whether the earth had existed for 100 years might have a scientific, or on the other hand a philosophical, doubt.

260.   I would like to reserve the expression "I know" for the cases in which it is used in normal linguistic exchange.

261.   I cannot at present imagine a reasonable doubt as to the existence of the earth during the last 100 years.

262.   I can imagine a man who had grown up in quite special circumstances and been taught that the earth came into being 50 years ago, and therefore believed this. We might instruct him: the earth has long . . . etc. – We should be trying to give him our picture of the world.
   This would happen through a kind of *persuasion*.

263.   The schoolboy *believes* his teachers and his schoolbooks.

264.   I could imagine Moore being captured by a wild tribe, and their expressing the suspicion that he has come from somewhere between the earth and the moon. Moore tells them that he knows etc. but he can't give them the grounds for his certainty, because they have fantastic ideas of human ability to fly and know nothing about physics. This would be an occasion for making that statement.

265.   But what does it say, beyond "I have never been to such and such a place, and have compelling grounds for believing that"?

266.   And here one would still have to say what are compelling grounds.

267.   "I don't merely have the visual impression of a tree: I *know* that it is a tree."

268. "I know that this is a hand." – And what is a hand? – "Well, *this*, for example."

269. Am I more certain that I have never been on the moon than that I have never been in Bulgaria? Why am I so sure? Well, I know that I have never been anywhere in the neighbourhood – for example I have never been in the Balkans.

270. "I have compelling grounds for my certitude." These grounds make the certitude objective.

271. What is a telling ground for something is not anything *I* decide.

272. I know = I am familiar with it as a certainty.

273. But when does one say of something that it is certain?
For there can be dispute whether something *is* certain; I mean, when something is *objectively* certain.
There are countless general empirical propositions that count as certain for us.

274. One such is that if someone's arm is cut off it will not grow again. Another, if someone's head is cut off he is dead and will never live again.
Experience can be said to teach us these propositions. However, it does not teach us them in isolation: rather, it teaches us a host of interdependent propositions. If they were isolated I might perhaps doubt them, for I have no experience relating to them.

275. If experience is the ground of our certainty, then naturally it is past experience.
And it isn't for example just *my* experience, but other people's, that I get knowledge from.
Now one might say that it is experience again that leads us to give credence to others. But what experience makes me believe that the anatomy and physiology books don't contain what is false? Though it is true that this trust is *backed up* by my own experience.

276. We believe, so to speak, that this great building exists, and then we see, now here, now there, one or another small corner of it.

277. "I can't help believing. . . ."

278. "I am comfortable that that is how things are."

279. It is quite sure that motor cars don't grow out of the earth. We feel that if someone could believe the contrary he could believe *everything* that we say is untrue, and could question everything that we hold to be sure. But how does this *one* belief hang together with all the rest? We should like to say that someone who could believe that does not accept our whole system of verification.

 This system is something that a human being acquires by means of observation and instruction. I intentionally do not say "learns".

280. After he has seen this and this and heard that and that, he is not in a position to doubt whether. . . .

281. *I*, L. W., believe, am sure, that my friend hasn't sawdust in his body or in his head, even though I have no direct evidence of my senses to the contrary. I am sure, by reason of what has been said to me, of what I have read, and of my experience. To have doubts about it would seem to me madness – of course, this is also in agreement with other people; but *I* agree with them.

282. I cannot say that I have good grounds for the opinion that cats do not grow on trees or that I had a father and a mother.

 If someone has doubts about it – how is that supposed to have come about? By his never, from the beginning, having believed that he had parents? But then, is that conceivable, unless he has been taught it?

283. For how can a child immediately doubt what it is taught? That could mean only that he was incapable of learning certain language-games.

284. People have killed animals since the earliest times, used the fur, bones etc. etc. for various purposes; they have counted definitely on finding similar parts in any similar beast.

 They have always learnt from experience; and we can see from their actions that they believe certain things definitely, whether they express this belief or not. By this I naturally do not want to say that men *should* behave like this, but only that they do behave like this.

Index